Pronunciation Practice Activities

Cambridge Handbooks for Language Teachers

This is a series of practical guides for teachers of English and other languages. Illustrative examples are usually drawn from the field of English as a foreign or second language, but the ideas and techniques described can equally well be used in the teaching of any language.

Recent titles in this series:

Lessons from Nothing
Activities for language teaching with limited time and resources
BRUCE MARSLAND

Beginning to Write
Writing activities for elementary and intermediate learners
ARTHUR BROOKES *and* PETER GRUNDY

Ways of Doing
Students explore their everyday and classroom processes
PAUL DAVIS, BARBARA GARSIDE *and*
MARIO RINVOLUCRI

Using Newspapers in the Classroom
PAUL SANDERSON

Teaching Adult Second Language Learners
HEATHER MCKAY *and* ABIGAIL TOM

Teaching English Spelling
A practical guide
RUTH SHEMESH *and* SHEILA WALLER

Using Folktales
ERIC TAYLOR

Personalizing Language Learning
Personalized language learning activities
GRIFF GRIFFITHS *and* KATHRYN KEOHANE

Teach Business English
A comprehensive introduction to business English
SYLVIE DONNA

Learner Autonomy
A guide to activities which encourage learner responsibility
ÁGOTA SCHARLE *and* ANITA SZABÓ

The Internet and the Language Classroom
Practical classroom activities and projects
GAVIN DUDENEY

Planning Lessons and Courses
Designing sequences of work for the language classroom
TESSA WOODWARD

Using the Board in the Language Classroom
JEANNINE DOBBS

Learner English (second edition)
MICHAEL SWAN *and* BERNARD SMITH

Teaching Large Multilevel Classes
NATALIE HESS

Writing Simple Poems
Pattern poetry for language acquisition
VICKI L. HOLMES *and* MARGARET R. MOULTON

Laughing Matters
Humour in the language classroom
PÉTER MEDGYES

Using Authentic Video in the Language Classroom
JANE SHERMAN

Stories
Narrative activities for the language classroom
RUTH WAJNRYB

Language Activities for Teenagers
edited by SETH LINDSTROMBERG

Pronunciation Practice Activities

A resource book for teaching English pronunciation

Martin Hewings

CAMBRIDGE
UNIVERSITY PRESS

PUBLISHED BY THE PRESS SYNDICATE OF THE UNIVERSITY OF CAMBRIDGE
The Pitt Building, Trumpington Street, Cambridge, United Kingdom

CAMBRIDGE UNIVERSITY PRESS
The Edinburgh Building, Cambridge CB2 2RU, UK
40 West 20th Street, New York, NY 10011–4211, USA
477 Williamstown Road, Port Melbourne, VIC 3207, Australia
Ruiz de Alarcón 13, 28014 Madrid, Spain
Dock House, The Waterfront, Cape Town 8001, South Africa

www.cambridge.org

First published 2004
Reprinted 2005

Printed in the United Kingdom at the University Press, Cambridge

Typeface: Adobe Sabon 10/13 pt   *System:* QuarkXPress™   [SE]

A catalogue record for this book is available from the British Library

Library of Congress Cataloguing in Publication data applied for

ISBN 0 521 75457 7 pack

Contents

Contents

Acknowledgements

I have had considerable help from a number of people while I have been preparing this book, and I would like to thank them here. At Cambridge University Press, my thanks to Alison Sharpe for suggesting the project in the first place, to Frances Amrani for efficiently steering the work through its various stages, and to Yvonne Harmer for her care and attention to detail. My thanks to James Richardson and Studio AVP for the CD recording. A number of people have commented on drafts of the material, and I wish particularly to thank Richard Cauldwell, and my colleagues at the English for International Students Unit of the University of Birmingham. Special thanks to my colleague Philip King for his voice. The series editor, Penny Ur, has been an excellent source of advice and guidance through her detailed comments on versions of the manuscript. At home, my thanks as always to Suzanne, David and Ann for their interest, support and good humour.

The authors and publishers are grateful to the authors, publishers and others who have given permission for the use of copyright material identified in the text. It has not been possible to identify the sources of all the material used and in such cases the publishers would welcome information from copyright owners.

pp. 40–41: extract from 'The Way up to Heaven', a short story by Roald Dahl, published by Penguin. With kind permission of David Higham Associates; p. 214: extracts from entries in The Cambridge Learner's Dictionary (2001), edited by Elizabeth Walter, published by Cambridge University Press; p. 219: 'Knock, knock' jokes extracted from The Funniest Joke Book in the World Ever, published by Red Fox. Used by permission of The Random House Group Limited; p. 225: reproduced from Funny Poems by permission of Usborne Publishing, 83–85 Saffron Hill, London EC1N 8RT. Copyright © 1990 Usborne Publishing Ltd.; p. 227: for the poem, 'Parents' Evening' from Heard it in the playground (Viking, 1989), Copyright © Allan Ahlberg, 1989. Reproduced by permission of Penguin Books Ltd.; p. 228: © 2003 Kellogg Company. The words 'Be awake, Be very awake' are reproduced by kind permission of Kellogg Company; p. 230: for the cartoon 'I think you misunderstood what I said', by Dan Wasserman (1990). Reproduced with kind permission of TMS Reprints.

Audio material: for the extract from the Radio 4 programme, Back Row, broadcast 10 May 2003, with kind permission of Sir Michael Caine and Jim White. By licence of BBC Worldwide Limited; for the following extracts from Pronunciation for Advanced Learners of English: Part A: 1 from p. 57, Example 5.2, 2a; 2 from p. 78, Example 7.4, 1; 3 from p. 13, Example 1.10, 1; 4 from p. 35, Example 3.6, 5. Part B: 1 from p. 45, Example 4.7, 3; 2 from p. 89, Example 8.6, 2; 3 from p. 23, Example 2.6 (part); 4 from p. 31, Example 3.1, 1, written by D. Brazil, published by Cambridge University Press (1994); for the extract (from Streaming Speech) on pp. 30–31 with kind permission of Richard Cauldwell.

Introduction

Aims

In writing this book, I had three aims in mind. First, I wanted to report some of the pronunciation teaching activities I have used in over 25 years of English language teaching with students of many different nationalities and levels of ability, in the hope that other teachers might find some of them interesting and useful. Most of the activities presented have been used in one form or another in the classroom with, I have judged, some success, although many have been considerably revised for publication.

No single book of this type, which provides example teaching activities, can be a comprehensive source for teaching all students all of the time. The best it can hope to do is provide activities which are immediately usable, but also (and just as importantly) give suggestions and principles for teachers to go further. My second aim, then, was to offer a collection of pronunciation teaching materials that would provide ideas – and, I hope, inspiration – for teachers to go on to devise their own. Consequently, I have tried to write the activities in such a way that teachers can develop them and devise related ones for subsequent use with students. Suggestions are frequently given on how this might be done.

As a preface to a set of teaching materials like this, it is useful to provide some background to show the general thinking behind them and to give enough technical knowledge to make them comprehensible to the teacher. There are a number of books already available that do a very good job of presenting phonetics and phonology to English language teachers. My third aim, then, was to write a book which provides a minimum of information about the details of English pronunciation (on the basis that interested teachers can refer to other more detailed sources for further information) but sufficient to make the activities comprehensible. In addition, I wanted to outline some of the current areas of debate on pronunciation teaching (issues such as what models to teach, priorities for pronunciation teaching, and so on), to give a broader context for the activities.

Organisation

The Introduction provides a brief description of the elements that together make up English pronunciation. Key terms are highlighted, and these are used in the activities later in the book. There is also a discussion of a number of important key issues. The aim is both to provide tentative answers to the questions posed and also to encourage readers to consider the relevance of these questions to their own teaching contexts.

Chapters 1–8 present a series of teaching activities that are intended to be immediately usable by the teacher. For each, an indication is given of the general level of ability the activity is aimed at. Those marked 'Elementary+' will be of use to students at all levels. (However, you obviously will be the best judge of which are appropriate to the level of ability of your own students.) Many activities include material in Boxes that you can photocopy for use in the classroom. The Extension section gives suggestions on how the activity might be further developed, either immediately after using it or at a later stage in the course.

Phonetic symbols are used to represent pronunciation throughout the book, and there is a full list of these in Appendix 1. However, I realise that not all teachers will feel confident in recognising these, and where they are used, if it is not obvious what is represented, a supporting example (a word or letter[s]) is included. So it is not necessary to be familiar with phonetic symbols to work with the activities.

The recording (on CD) includes much of the text provided in the Boxes, and the symbol ⊙ is given when there is a relevant section on the recording. It is important to note that the recording is not essential for any of the activities in the book; the activities can all be based on your own reading aloud of the texts. The recording is intended to be used on those occasions when you perhaps lack confidence that you are pronouncing something in the way required in the exercise, or simply to provide a different accent or voice for your students to listen to. The people on the recording are all speakers of southern British English, but it is not the intention that this variety should necessarily be the 'target model' for your students. (See the discussion of models on pp. 11–13.)

The appendices provide reference material that you might find useful, and these are referred to at various places in the activities. The Bibliography contains references from the text and suggests books for further reading which include additional pronunciation teaching activities and background on phonetics, phonology, and pronunciation teaching.

Many of the activities included in the book have been inspired by exercises I have seen demonstrated, used in classrooms, or have read in other sources. Where I have been able to trace the originator of an idea developed in activities, I have acknowledged this. Where the original source is lost from my memory or my notes, I have not been able to give explicit acknowledgement. I apologise in advance for the resulting omissions.

What is pronunciation?

This section introduces some of the main components of speech which together combine to form the pronunciation of a language. These components range from the individual sounds that make up speech, to the way in which pitch – the rise and fall of the voice – is used to convey meaning. The particular characteristics of English pronunciation are highlighted, together with important differences between English and other languages. It is these differences which often result in difficulties for learners. Key terms, which are explained in this section and used in the activities in Chapters 1–8, are set in bold the first time they appear, and displayed in boxes.

Sounds

The building blocks of pronunciation are the individual sounds, the **vowels** and **consonants** that go together to make words. We think of consonants such as /b/ and /p/ as separate in English because if we interchange them we can make new words; for example, in *bit* and *pit*. Similarly, the vowels /ɪ/ (as in *it*) and /ʌ/ (as in *up*) are separate because to interchange them gives us *bit* and *but*. These separate sounds are often referred to as **phonemes**, and pairs of words which differ by only one vowel or consonant sound (*bit/pit*, *bit/but*) are referred to as **minimal pairs**. In British English, around 44 phonemes (20 vowels and 24 consonants) are generally recognised, but different languages use different ones, with around 70 per cent of languages having between 20 and 37. Undoubtedly, many of the pronunciation problems faced by any learner of a new language relate to differences in the phonemes used in the first and the target language. For example, we can gather some idea of the challenge facing Swahili speakers learning English when we note that Swahili has only 5 vowels, none of which is identical to any of the 20 vowels in British English!

Key terms

vowel   consonant   phoneme   minimal pair

It is important to remember that there is a difference between vowel and consonant *letters* and vowel and consonant *sounds*. The five letter vowels in the alphabet are *A, E, I, O, U*, and sometimes *Y*, and the remainder are consonants. These figures are rather different from the 20 vowel sounds and

24 consonant sounds in British English noted above, and there are many cases where two or more letters represent just one sound. For example, *ea* in *head* is pronounced /e/, *ch* in *chemist* is pronounced /k/, and *augh* in *daughter* is pronounced /ɔ:/.

Syllables

Vowel and consonant sounds combine into **syllables**. It can be helpful to think of the structure of English syllables as:

[consonant(s)] + vowel + [consonant(s)]

This means that various combinations of vowels and consonants are possible:

- vowel only (e.g. in *a*)
- consonant + vowel (e.g. in *me*)
- vowel + consonant (e.g. in *eat*)
- consonant + vowel + consonant (e.g. in *bag*).

In some languages, not all of these combinations are possible or common. In Japanese, for example, only syllables with vowel only and consonant + vowel are commonly used. Perhaps more problematic for language learners is the issue of what is possible in English in the 'consonant' elements of syllables. At the beginning of syllables, up to three consonant sounds are possible, as in *string* or *split*; while at the end, up to four consonants are possible, as in *glimpsed* (/-mpst/) and *texts* (/-ksts/). These combinations of consonants are often referred to as **consonant clusters**. It is not very common in other major languages to have consonant clusters at the beginning of syllables and very rare to have more than two, as occurs in English.

Key terms

syllable   consonant cluster

Words

A word can be either a single syllable (e.g. *cat*, *own*) or a sequence of two or more syllables (e.g. *window*, *about* [two syllables]; *lemonade* [three], *electricity* [five]). When a word has more than one syllable, one of these syllables is **stressed** in relation to the other syllables in the word – that is, it is said with relatively more force or heard as being more emphatic – while other syllables are said to be **unstressed**. For example, in *window* the first syllable is stressed and the second unstressed, while in *about* the first syllable is unstressed and the second stressed. Dictionaries often show stress patterns in words. For example, the *Cambridge Advanced Learner's Dictionary* (CALD) represents these words as /ˈwɪn.dəʊ/ and /əˈbaʊt/ using the symbol ˈ before the syllable with primary stress[1] (see Activity 8.1 for an illustration). Some words, particularly those with three or more syllables, have an intermediate level of stress so that a distinction is made between **primary stress, secondary stress** (on the syllable with the second most important emphasis) and **unstressed syllables**. If a word has primary and secondary stress, most dictionaries will indicate both. For example, CALD represents the words *electricity* and *lemonade* respectively as /ˌɪl.ekˈtrɪs.ɪ.ti/ and /ˌlem.əˈneɪd/ using the symbol ˌ to indicate secondary stress. One interesting feature of stress in English words is that in certain contexts when some words with both primary and secondary stress are actually spoken it is the secondary stressed syllable that takes the **main stress**. For example, a dictionary entry for the word *Chinese* will indicate primary stress on -ese and secondary stress on *Chi-* (/ˌtʃaɪˈniːz/). However, in the phrase *a Chinese company*, main stress is likely to shift back to the first syllable in the word (/ˈtʃaɪˌniːz /). This is sometimes referred to as **stress shift**. A wide variety of patterns of stress in words exists in English, although with the exception of stress shift, each word has a fixed pattern of stress. In other languages, one pattern predominates. For example, in Finnish most words are stressed on the first syllable, while in Turkish most words are stressed on the last.

Compounds are combinations of words which function mainly as a single noun or adjective. Examples of compounds are *bookcase, tape measure, chocolate biscuit* and *easy-going*. Although it is most common for compounds to have main stress in their first part (e.g. ˈ*bookcase*, ˈ*tape measure*) some have primary stress in their second part and secondary stress in their first (e.g. ˌ*chocolate* ˈ*biscuit*, ˌ*easy-*ˈ*going*). In other languages, different patterns of stress in compounds are found. For example, in Farsi (spoken in Iran and surrounding regions), compound nouns usually have stress on their final syllable. Swedish follows a similar pattern to English in that the majority of compound nouns are stressed in their first part. However, the compounds which are exceptions to this general rule are different in Swedish and English.

---

[1] CALD also uses the symbol . to mark the boundary between syllables.

> **Key terms**
>
> stress   stressed syllable   unstressed syllable   primary stress
> secondary stress   main stress   stress shift   compound

Words in connected speech

A dictionary gives the pronunciation of a word when it is said in isolation: as if in response to the word being written down and the question asked 'How is this word pronounced?'. This is often referred to as its **citation form**. However, when words come into contact in **connected speech**, certain common changes take place, mainly as a consequence of the speed of speaking and in order to make the production of sequences of sounds easier. First, when certain sounds come into contact at word boundaries, one or both of the sounds may change. In its citation form, the word *ten* is pronounced /ten/, but in *It's ten past*, influenced by the following /p/ sound, it will be pronounced closer to /tem/. Second, sounds may be missed out. The citation form of *looked* is pronounced /lʊkt/ but in *It looked bad* the /t/ sound may be omitted completely, simplifying the consonant cluster /-ktb-/ and pronounced closer to /ɪt lʊkbæd/. Third, in other cases, extra sounds are inserted. For example, the citation form of *for* in accents where /r/ is not normally pronounced at the end of a word (such as in south-east England) is /fɔː/. However, in *for example* a /r/ sound is inserted between the words. Changes such as these probably occur in some form in all languages and to some extent learners will make them automatically when they are speaking fluently. However, we have seen that different languages have different combinations of sounds in syllables and words and, consequently, the kinds of sounds that come into contact at word boundaries will differ from language to language. This may mean that some of the changes that are made automatically by native English speakers are problematic for learners. For example, most native speakers would run two consecutive /t/ sounds together as a single, longer /t/ sound so that *I met Tom* is pronounced something like /metɒm/. Russian speakers, however, tend to pronounce the two /t/ sounds separately, producing /met tɒm/.

> **Key terms**
>
> citation form   connected speech

Strong and weak forms

In English many grammatical words have two forms: one its citation form, used when the word is said in isolation and when it is highlighted or stressed in connected speech; the other when it is unstressed or used with no special emphasis. These two forms are sometimes called the **strong** and **weak** forms of a word.

> ## Key terms
>
> strong form   weak form

Here are some examples:

word	strong form	weak form(s)	word	strong form	weak form(s)
and	/ænd/	/ənd/, /ən/, /n/	from	/frɒm/	/frəm/
but	/bʌt/	/bət/	of	/ɒv/	/əv/, /ə/
not	/nɒt/	/nt/	to	/tu:/	/tə/
could	/kʊd/	/kəd/, /kd/	him	/hɪm/	/ɪm/

Many other languages either have fewer words that have a weak and strong form or do not have this kind of distinction at all, and there is a tendency for learners to produce strong forms in contexts where there is no reason for highlighting these words and weak forms would therefore be appropriate. This may be a particular problem where the learning experience of students focuses on written text; strong forms often seem closer to their written form and there may be a temptation to produce these when reading aloud.

Intonation

Essentially, intonation refers to the way the pitch of the voice falls or rises. For example, in a telephone conversation we might hear:

(Phone rings)

A: Hello?

B: Hi, Tom, it's Sue.

A: Hello! Nice to hear from you.

with the voice rising on the first *hello* and falling on the second. In addition to choosing whether to make the pitch of our voice fall or rise, the *place* at which we begin to fall or rise is also important. For example, in the following conversation the first of the two responses is more likely:

    A: I thought I left my bag on the table.

    B: It's UNDer the table.   B: It's under the TABle.

with the fall beginning on the stressed syllable of the word *under* rather than *table*. If you listen to English speech, you can often hear that it is divided into a sequence of units (referred to as **tone units**), each of which has one main fall or rise in pitch (a **tone**) beginning on a word that is then heard as highlighted (the **tonic word**). Other words may also be highlighted (**prominent words**).

Key terms

intonation   tone unit   tone   tonic word   prominent word

Here is an extract[2] from authentic speech marked with tone units (//), tones (↗ ↘), and tonic and other prominent words (both in capitals):

    //now you KNOW where the OFFice is//WHAT i want you to DO//

    //is to GO to the OFFice//and FIND SUSan//and ASK SUSan//

    //for the KEY//to my ROOM//

A number of kinds of meaning are conveyed by intonation in English. One of these is to indicate how information is structured; that is, whether something is 'new' or whether it is part of what is already known in the discourse. For example, what B says in the following conversation consists of something that is 'new' (*but engineers*) followed by something that is already being talked about (*build bridges*):

    A: My brother is an accountant. He builds bridges.

    B: //but engiNEERS// build BRIDGes//

---

2 From Brazil, D. (1994, p. 125).

and this is indicated in the choice of falling tone (for 'new' material) and rising tone (for material already known). Intonation is also used to show how discourse is divided up into sections. For example, if we listen to a monologue such as a lecture or a radio news report, the speaker will often begin new sections with a step up in pitch and end sections with a falling tone to a relatively low pitch. Intonation also contributes to the expression of a wide range of attitudes. This is clear if you think about how *hello* might be said in the 'Tom and Sue' example above, and how we might change the intonation of the second *hello* to express attitudes other than pleasure. However, it is important to remember that intonation works together with a wide range of other features of communication, including loudness, pitch range (wide or narrow), gesture and facial expression, to convey attitude.

Many other languages use intonation in very different ways from English. For example, some languages, such as Chinese and Vietnamese, use tones to distinguish between word meaning, so that a syllable will change in meaning depending on the pattern of pitch that is used with it. Even those languages which use intonation in broadly similar ways to English differ in the details of use. For example, in British English a falling-rising tone is very common and in conversations is often associated with politeness. Where we politely disagree with someone a falling-rising tone may well be used:

A: Clarke's a great goalkeeper, isn't he?

B: Well in MY opinion, he needs to get a lot fitter.

In many other languages, this tone is less common and when speakers of these languages use English they may use a rising tone where a British speaker uses a falling-rising tone.

Pronunciation and spelling

Although pronunciation is a feature of speech and spelling a feature of writing, spelling will often have an influence on the learning of pronunciation as the majority of learners use written texts in their studies. The relationship between them in English is often thought to be complex and chaotic. A single written letter might have a number of different pronunciations in different words, a single sound might be represented by a number of letters or letter combinations in different words, and written letters may not have a directly corresponding pronunciation. For example, the letter *f* can be pronounced /v/ in *of* but /f/ in *roof*; the sound /ʃ/ can be represented by a variety of letters and letter combinations including *s* (*sure*), *sh* (*shop*), *ch* (*machine*) and *sch* (in the usual British pronunciation of *schedule*); and the letter *e* is not sounded in the word *showed*. However, David Crystal (1987, p. 214) reports the widely cited figure that around 75 per cent of English words are spelt according to a regular pattern. But he also notes that, unfortunately, of the 400 or so words with irregular spellings, most are among the most frequently used in the language! In many other languages, such as Italian and Portuguese, there is a much closer connection between spelling and pronunciation with a near one-to-one correspondence between letters and sounds, and with fewer letters unsounded.

It is important to help students develop their awareness of the relationships between spelling and pronunciation so that when they come across a written word that is new to them they can attempt to pronounce it correctly and, conversely, when they hear a new word they can make an attempt to write it with its correct spelling. For most students, awareness undoubtedly increases with exposure to the language. However, we can also highlight certain regularities in spelling to sound correspondences that are reasonably easy to remember and have few exceptions. For example:

- the addition of the letter *e* after a consonant lengthens the preceding vowel, so that it 'says its alphabet name', in pairs such as *at/ate*, *rid/ride*, *not/note* and *cut/cute* (see Activity 6.2)
- the letters *c* and *g* are pronounced /s/ and /dʒ/ respectively before *e*, *i* and *y* (e.g. *gem*, *city*, *cycle*), and elsewhere they are pronounced /k/ and /g/ respectively (e.g. *cold*, *gap*) (see Activity 6.5)
- certain suffixes control where stress is placed in a word; for example, the suffixes *-ic* and *-ity* cause the stress to be placed on the syllable before the suffix (compare *athlete/able* [ˈæθliːt/ ˈeɪbl] with stress on the first syllable, and *athletic/ability* [æθˈletɪk/əˈbɪlɪti] with stress on the second) (see Activity 4.13).

Key issues in pronunciation teaching and learning

Why is it important to teach pronunciation?

It can be frustrating and demotivating for students if they have repeated experiences where communication breaks down because of problems with their English pronunciation. This is perhaps especially true for those who have a good command of other aspects of language such as vocabulary and grammar. At the University of Birmingham, I recently worked with a research student from Hong Kong who was coming to the end of his PhD studies. His first language was Cantonese and his second language English. Although his written English was of a very high standard, features of his English pronunciation made his speech sometimes difficult to understand. When he was speaking to individuals, he was usually able to make himself understood. However, his research work was highly regarded and he was being encouraged, and was keen, to share his findings through seminar and conference presentations. It soon became clear, however, that in this formal setting, audiences (usually a mix of native and non-native English speakers) were having considerable difficulties understanding him. Naturally, he found this experience demoralising and he was concerned that it would have a major impact on his academic career.

This example is perhaps an extreme case demonstrating the importance of pronunciation in effective communication. Difficulties with pronunciation might mean that students fail to get their message across, even when the correct words are being used, or they might fail to understand what is said to them. Potentially even more confusing is the possibility that what students say might be understood to mean something they didn't intend.

A further consideration is that pronunciation is something that students often feel is important to them in their language learning. Most want their pronunciation to be easily understandable and are often prepared to work hard to achieve this. Sometimes, however, teaching doesn't always reflect this wish, and pronunciation is treated as a low priority area of study. But if students give pronunciation a high priority in their learning, then we should recognise and respond to this in our teaching.

Incidentally, the research student from Hong Kong worked hard on his pronunciation and, although his English is still heavily accented, he now has a successful academic career and is a regular presenter at international conferences.

What model of pronunciation should I teach my students?

As is true of any language, there are almost as many ways of pronouncing English as there are English speakers. Not only do we find different accents in regions within a country, but no two individuals within a region will have exactly the same pronunciation. English is perhaps particularly variable because of its use around the world as a first or second language; so we label varieties 'British', 'American', 'Australian', 'Indian', 'Malaysian' English, and so on, partly based on their differences in pronunciation. The growing use of English as an international language, as a means of communication between non-native speakers with different first languages, is likely to lead to the development of further varieties.

This, of course, makes a decision on what model of English pronunciation to teach students a complex one, with a number of questions you might consider. These include:

- *In what contexts will your students mainly be using English after the course?*
  For example, if students are going on to study in the United States, then it may be most appropriate to use a model of North American English. If students are business people in Thailand, who will mainly be using English to communicate with other business people in East Asia, then the model provided by a Thai national who speaks English fluently and in an easily intelligible way may be best.
- *Are there varieties that have a particularly high or low status in your teaching context?*
  In some countries native-speaker varieties of English have a higher status than non-native varieties. Whether you feel this is right, or that all varieties should have equal status, this factor might influence your decision on what model to use.
- *Is there a variety that your students have particular exposure to outside the classroom?*
  For example, a student learning English in Australia will naturally be exposed to Australian accents outside the classroom. Using the same model inside the classroom is likely to produce the most efficient pronunciation improvement.
- *Do your students show an inclination to speak English with a particular pronunciation?*
  For example, young students who enjoy pop music and TV programmes from North America might be motivated more by having North American models of pronunciation in the classroom.
- *Does one variety of pronunciation predominate in the teaching materials available to you?*
  Published coursebooks and supplementary textbooks will often have accompanying recordings. Some will use speakers sharing one variety of English. When these are used for listening activities or when students repeat after recordings these speakers are providing a model of pronunciation for students.

- *What accent of English do you have?*
  In most classrooms the English pronunciation that students will hear most, and will probably be asked to imitate most frequently, is that of the teacher. Few teachers have the ability to change their usual English accent consistently so as to provide a model of another variety.

Finally, it is important to distinguish between a model as a 'target' and as a 'point of reference'. A target is some standard of pronunciation to which the students aspire or which the teacher selects as a goal for students; for example, it might be a native-speaker variety, such as 'general American' or a second-language variety such as 'Singaporean English'. As a point of reference, a model is presented as a guide to English pronunciation with the understanding that variation from this model is acceptable provided it does not get in the way of effective communication.

Whether you use a model as a target or as a point of reference can have a significant impact on how you teach pronunciation. For example, there may well be differences between the English pronunciation found on published recordings (often southern British English or general American) and your own pronunciation. How you treat these differences depends on your view of models of pronunciation. If you see a model as a target then you will need to say that one or other accent (your own, or that found on recordings) has a greater value and should be the goal of your students (but see the discussion in the next section). If, however, you see a model as a point of reference then these differences can be treated simply as part of the natural variation found in pronunciation.

How good does my students' pronunciation need to be?

It is now generally accepted that the target of a 'native-speaker pronunciation' is unachievable for the vast majority of learners of a second or foreign language, even if a native-speaker variety is the target model chosen. It is rare for a non-native to acquire a pronunciation of English that would be taken to be that of a native speaker unless they are brought up in an English-speaking environment.

However, for the vast majority of learners, a native-speaker pronunciation is neither necessary nor even desirable. The aim of most is to achieve an easily understandable pronunciation in most situations with most people, with both native and non-native English speakers. It is also important to remember that a person's pronunciation (of both their first and other languages) contributes significantly to the impression of their identity

13

that is conveyed to others. It is probably the case that most people would wish to retain identifiable traces of their national or first language identity when they speak English. So, for example, an Italian would prefer to be identified as 'an Italian who speaks English very well' rather than simply 'a non-native speaker of English' or even be taken for a native English speaker.

For most learners, then, a more appropriate and reasonable goal is to achieve an English pronunciation which is usually understandable in international communication, but retains unobtrusive features of a non-English accent.

Of course, what is in fact achievable depends not only on these broad considerations, but also on a number of more specific factors. It is often said that people who begin to learn a second language when they are young have an advantage when it comes to pronunciation, so if you are teaching young children, the ultimate goals you set may be different from those you have for adult beginners. However, this is complicated by evidence to suggest that older learners may be able to compensate with a clearer wish to sound like others from a particular speech group. Another factor to be considered is the likely tolerance and experience of those people the students are going to communicate with. A lot of international business and administration is conducted in contexts where English is the medium of communication, but where the various people involved have different first languages. Business people who often work in such contexts may well be used to hearing and understanding a wide variety of non-native pronunciations of English. In other contexts, people may be less experienced. Hospital staff recruited from overseas to British hospitals, for example, have sometimes found it difficult to make themselves understood, even when their English is very proficient, by patients and other staff who are unused to having to understand non-native-speaker accents.

Perhaps the most important outcome of recognising the complexity in the setting of goals is that learners should think about what they would like to achieve in their English pronunciation, recognising that a native-speaker pronunciation is probably an unrealistic and not particularly desirable target. They can be encouraged to consider who they want to sound like when they speak English; and perhaps the ideal 'target' in this respect is someone who shares their first language. Suggested activities for this are given in Chapter 1 (Developing awareness).

What are the most important features of pronunciation to teach?

When we are deciding on our priorities for pronunciation teaching, it is useful to know in general what kinds of errors are most likely to interfere with communication, and what special problems particular first-language speakers will have with English pronunciation.

Here is a suggested 'top five' of things it is important for students to get right in order to avoid being misunderstood:

1 *Consonants*

In most circumstances, substituting one consonant with another is more likely to lead to communication breakdown than when a wrong vowel is used. To give a clear example: in a fast-food restaurant in Britain, one of my Japanese students asked for a *banilla milkshake* (intending *vanilla*) and was given a banana milkshake.

2 *Consonant clusters*

Perhaps the biggest problems here are caused by missing out consonants from a cluster at the beginning of a word and adding unnecessary vowels. For example, *pice* (/paɪs/) for *price* or *sipot* (/sɪpɒt/) for *spot*.

3 *Vowel length*

Some vowels are, on average, longer than others; for example, compare the vowels in the words *tins* (short) and *teens* (long). Producing short vowels where long vowels are needed, and vice versa, can seriously interfere with understanding; for example, *this* might be heard as *these* if a long vowel is used.

4 *Word stress*

When primary stress in a word or compound is misplaced – for example, when 'eVENT' is said 'Event' or 'BABy-sit' said 'baby-SIT' – it can be difficult for a listener to understand what is intended.

5 *Tonic words*

In the exchange A: 'Was it expensive?' B: 'Quite expensive', we would expect B to say 'QUITE expensive' (with *quite* as the tonic word) rather than 'quite exPENsive' (with *expensive* as the tonic word). Misplacing the tonic word has the potential to cause difficulties in effective communication.

Getting other aspects of pronunciation wrong is less likely to cause a communication breakdown. These lower priority features include:

• the exact shape of vowels (for example, saying the vowel in *c<u>au</u>ght* like the vowel in *c<u>ar</u>t*)

- weak and strong forms (for example, saying /frɒm/ rather than /frəm/)
- using features of connected speech (for example, linking words with a *r* sound: saying *far away* as /fɑː əweɪ/ rather than /fɑːrəweɪ/)
- tones (for example, using a falling-rising tone rather than a rising tone)
- the overall pitch range of the voice (for example, using a narrower pitch range than would a native English speaker).

However, deciding the order of importance for pronunciation teaching is a matter of balancing general considerations and the particular difficulties of a group of students.

For example, though we might generally give work on consonants a high priority, it is also useful to know which consonants are problematic and which are not for the particular first-language groups we are teaching, so that we can focus work accordingly. It may also be appropriate for certain groups of learners that some of the generally lower priority features listed above should be given a higher priority. For example, for students who tend to 'clip' the ends of words by leaving out final consonants or shortening final long vowels, work on features of connected speech, such as linking the sounds at the end of a word and the beginning of the next, may help to make their speech more intelligible. A further consideration is the emphasis we give to developing listening and speaking skills, and this is discussed in the next section.

Appendix 2 gives a list of common English pronunciation difficulties for speakers of some major languages. (For more information, see *Learner English*, 2001.)

What is the connection between listening and pronunciation?
Pronunciation is an important aspect of both speaking and listening. To make sense of what we hear we need to be able to divide the stream of speech up into units (for example, tone units, words and individual sounds) and to interpret what they mean. Very often in the rapid flow of speech, changes occur so that words can differ substantially from their citation forms. For example, we find weak forms (/ən/ for *and*, /fə/ for *for*), contracted forms (*mustn't've* for *must not have*), and other changes and deletions of individual sounds (/gɒm bəʊlɪn/ [*gom bowlin*] for *gone bowling*). It is important to remember that such changes are not 'careless speech' but are natural features of educated English. We only think of them as 'careless' if we judge speech using the standards we apply to formal written language. In the previous section, I suggested that certain features of

pronunciation, including weak forms and characteristics of connected speech (contractions, deletions, etc.) were of a lower priority than others in that they were less likely to cause communication difficulties if students got them wrong. I would go on to suggest, however, that it is important to include work on these in a language course to help students decode rapid speech and develop their listening skills. It is probably more important for less advanced students to recognise and understand such features than to produce them in their own speech, while more advanced students could be encouraged to include them as part of their pronunciation in order to become more fluent.

It is often thought that learners need to be able to discriminate between features of pronunciation before they can produce them in their own speech; for example, that they have to be able to hear a difference between /f/ and /v/ before they can say correctly the words *fan* and *van*. This connection is not always found, and it sometimes happens that learners are able to produce a difference without being able to hear it, and vice versa. However, it is a useful assumption to make that for most learners for most of the time an ability to hear features of pronunciation will be at least a useful starting point for developing their ability to produce them in their own speech.

For both these reasons, it is important to teach and test both *receptive* (listening) and *productive* (speaking) skills. While the activities in this book focus on productive aspects of pronunciation, in many of them there is a stage in which learners are encouraged to listen to features of pronunciation. This is intended to help them to improve their listening ability, and also to develop discrimination skills which provide a foundation for pronunciation improvement in their own speech.

Why and how should I test pronunciation?

The reasons for testing pronunciation are similar to those for testing language more generally: tests can give teachers an idea of students' present ability, where they need to improve, and how far they are away from their long-term target. The information gathered can be used to help establish priorities for future work, and a series of tests can provide a sense of achievement (assuming progress has been made!), which can be motivating for teachers and students alike.

However, a number of particular problems face us when testing pronunciation that are not encountered in testing other areas of language such as vocabulary and grammar. In teaching vocabulary, for example, we can select a certain set of words or phrases to be taught over a period and, at the end of this period, test how many of these students remember and are able to use. Similarly, in teaching grammar, we can introduce grammatical forms and functions individually and then test students' understanding and production. With pronunciation, however, all features (individual sounds, word stress, features of connected speech, intonation, etc.) will be present even in the very earliest lessons with beginner students, both in what they hear and in what they are required to say. It is not possible, then, to select, grade and gradually introduce features of pronunciation, testing understanding along the way. This suggests that two types of assessment of pronunciation will be of value. In one, a particular feature of pronunciation can be assessed. This might be used after lessons in which such features have been the focus of teaching. Activities 7.3–7.6 are examples of what might be done. The second type of assessment is of overall ability. This may be done in a general, impressionistic way (see Activity 7.1) or in a more systematic way, working with a checklist of pronunciation points that students get right or wrong (see Activity 7.2).

Second, we have seen that pronunciation has a role in both listening and speaking. Most pronunciation tests focus on testing pronunciation as a part of receptive skills (discriminating between sounds or minimal pairs of words, recognising placement of stress within words, etc.). Perhaps the main reason for this is that such tests are usually quick and easy to administer even to large classes. Testing production, however, usually involves assessing some part of the pronunciation of *individual* students. This means that teachers have to listen to individuals speaking (or listen to a recording of them) and make an assessment of certain features on the basis of particular criteria. This is clearly a much more time-consuming activity and in many teaching contexts, for example with large classes, it may be impracticable. Activities 7.3 to 7.6 have two versions, one testing receptive skills and the other testing productive skills, using the same or similar material. The second versions could be used if your teaching situation permits this kind of assessment.

In testing students' productive skills, two main sources of information are generally used: text read aloud, and more spontaneous speech gathered from sources such as interviews or stories told from a series of picture prompts. Both have advantages and disadvantages. The main advantage of text read aloud is that the language can be tightly controlled, so that particular features of pronunciation (sounds, word stress, etc.) can be built into the text. Also, if the same text is given to a number of students, a direct comparison between their relative strengths and weaknesses can be made. The main disadvantage is that writing may get in the way of pronunciation; a student may be able to pronounce a sound or word correctly, but have difficulties in decoding the written text (for example, working out how particular spellings should be said, or what meaning is intended) and this can interfere with how the text is read. Although spontaneous speech avoids this text-to-sound problem, there is no guarantee that the particular features of pronunciation that you wish to test will come up in what students say, or at least in sufficient numbers to make an assessment valid. Consequently, this kind of information can be incomplete, and also it may be time-consuming to gather and analyse. Clearly, then, neither source is ideal. Perhaps the most practical answer is to use text read aloud as the primary source of information (trying to make the vocabulary used as simple as possible to avoid some reading aloud difficulties), and to supplement this with an assessment of spontaneous speech. This approach is adopted in some of the activities in Chapter 7 (Testing pronunciation).

How can I integrate pronunciation into a teaching programme?

In some classes, pronunciation is given a lower priority than other components of language such as grammar and vocabulary, and is sometimes relegated to an 'end-of-the-day' activity or a five-minute filler to give students some light relief from the 'real' work of language learning. In some situations this relative neglect might be justified; for example, where students are learning English primarily to read it, or where an examination syllabus they are following emphasises reading and writing.

For most students, however, an understandable pronunciation will be an important part of their communication skills, and this justifies giving pronunciation a more central role in teaching by integrating it with other areas of language work. Perhaps the most obvious area for useful integration is work that connects vocabulary and pronunciation. There are good arguments for teaching the pronunciation of words (both the sounds and their stress) as they are introduced. If students have confidence that they can pronounce a word correctly, they are more likely to use it as they speak, and using words successfully aids memorisation. There is also evidence that knowing the stress pattern of a word (where it has more than one syllable) helps us to mentally 'store' words and retrieve them more easily.

Other links exist between grammar and pronunciation. For example, the past tense -ed endings can have different pronunciations (/d/ e.g. *played*, /t/

e.g. *stopped*, and /ɪd/ e.g. *wanted*) depending on the sounds that come before them. Highlighting and practising this feature can usefully be done when the simple past tense is introduced. The pronunciation of *going* is more frequently /gəʊɪn/ (*goin'*) than the citation form /gəʊɪŋ / (*going*), and this could be pointed out and practised when the *going to*-future is introduced. Suggested activities for integrating work on pronunciation with grammar and vocabulary (and a third area, spelling) are given in Chapter 6.

What principles should I adopt in teaching pronunciation?

Plan pronunciation teaching

Here are three main ways in which you can plan ahead:

- Be aware of the likely pronunciation difficulties of students with particular first-language groups and prepare activities that will focus on these problems. Some information about common problems is given in Appendix 2.
- If possible, diagnose your students' pronunciation weaknesses and plan activities that focus on these. Suggestions for diagnostic tests are given in Chapter 7.
- Look at the syllabus in the coursebook you are using and identify which parts lend themselves to work on particular areas of pronunciation. (Some coursebooks will already have integrated pronunciation work, which you might want to supplement.) For example, if you are teaching word formation, include an activity that looks at the relationship between suffixes and word stress (e.g. Activities 4.13 to 4.15).

React to opportunities for teaching pronunciation

Not all pronunciation teaching needs to be planned ahead. Look for opportunities to teach and practise pronunciation as they arise in the classroom. For example, during a lesson in which you have introduced a lot of new vocabulary, ask students to copy this into their books and mark stressed and unstressed syllables above each word, finding the words having the same stress pattern (e.g. Activity 4.5). As you become familiar with the activities in this book, it may be useful to build up a set of OHTs of the photocopiable material which you can use as the need arises.

Develop general techniques for modelling and correcting pronunciation

The basic cycle for presenting pronunciation used in many activities in this book is as follows:

- Model (say or play the recording).
- Choral repetition.
- Individual repetition.

The basic cycle for correcting an individual student's pronunciation used in many activities in this book is as follows:

- The student says or repeats the sound, word or phrase.
- Monitor (you listen to a particular pronunciation focus).
- If there are problems, model the sound, word or phrase.
- The student repeats after you.
- If necessary, give a number of opportunities for practice.

Develop a set of activities for recurring problems

Some pronunciation problems are likely to occur repeatedly, and it can be useful to develop a set of short, simple activities which don't require preparation, to use when these arise. For example, some students have problems producing or discriminating between particular vowels or particular consonants (see Chapter 2 for suggested activities).

Use a variety of activities

Different students learn things in different ways at different times, so using an unvarying approach to pronunciation teaching (for example, focusing only on minimal pairs) is unlikely to provide a variety of learning opportunities to the maximum number of students. The materials in this book try to demonstrate a wide range of activity types. Here are some of them:

- developing awareness (e.g. Activities 1.1 to 1.10)
- information transfer (e.g. Activity 2.6)
- games (e.g. Activity 2.12)
- analysis (e.g. sorting, Activity 6.1; matching, Activity 5.5; working out rules, Activity 6.5)
- prediction (e.g. Activity 3.9)
- reflection (e.g. Activity 1.1)
- using reference sources (e.g. Activity 8.1).

Recycle activities

Many of the activities in this book can be used repeatedly with students. Some can be used unchanged after a reasonable period of time, to revise and reinforce what has been learnt (e.g. Activity 2.4). In many, however, new language can be introduced so that while the same basic activity is used, different learning opportunities are created (e.g. Activities 4.15, 5.5). In the Extension section of some activities, specific suggestions are given on how this might be done (e.g. Activities 2.7, 4.7, 4.16).

The publisher has used its best endeavours to ensure that the URLs for external websites referred to in this book are correct and active at the time of going to press. However, the publisher has no responsibility for the websites and can make no guarantee that a site will remain live or that the content is or will remain appropriate.

1 Developing awareness of English pronunciation

1.1 Introducing features of pronunciation

This activity introduces some key terms (vowel, consonant, consonant clusters, word stress and intonation) and gets students thinking about differences between pronunciation in English and their first language.

Focus Key pronunciation terms

Level Elementary

Time 20–30 minutes

Preparation Copy the material in Box 1 onto a handout.

Procedure

1 Give a copy of the handout to each student and ask them to look at the section on vowels.
2 Present the examples in 1. Say the words and explain that vowel sounds are underlined.
3 Students do the exercise in 2 and check the answers.
4 Give students some time to think about the question in 3. They should talk about their answers to a partner or other students in a small group. (In a multilingual class, students in each pair/group should have different first languages if possible.)
5 Finally, discuss the answers with the class as a whole. Highlight similarities and differences between English and the students' first languages, and check that students have understood the key term (vowel) correctly.
6 Repeat the procedure for each of the key terms. Note that in the section on intonation, you will need to demonstrate the tones (fall, rise, rise-fall, and fall-rise) on the words in 1 or play the recording. Then say (or play) *No* with each of the four tones. You could add a step at this point where you get students to repeat, chorally and individually, the four tones on *No* after you.

Note

Consonant clusters are dealt with in more detail in Activity 1.4.

Box 1   Student handout

Vowels

1 Examples: j<u>o</u>b   g<u>i</u>ve   g<u>oo</u>d   c<u>ar</u>
2 Underline the vowel sounds in these words:
   fall   learn   way   road
3 Does your language have the same vowel sounds?
   Give example words: . . . .
   . . . .
   . . . .

Consonants

1 Examples: <u>m</u>y   <u>t</u>op   <u>w</u>or<u>k</u>   <u>th</u>is
2 Underline the consonant sounds in these words:
   shoe   rob   good   leave
3 Does your language have the same consonant sounds?
   Give example words: . . . .
   . . . .
   . . . .

Consonant clusters

1 Examples: <u>bl</u>ack   <u>dr</u>op   <u>tr</u>ip   <u>qu</u>een
2 Underline the consonant clusters in these words:
   space   play   climb   strong
3 Does your language have the same consonant clusters?
   Give example words: . . . .
   . . . .
   . . . .

Answer key

Vowels: f<u>a</u>ll, l<u>ear</u>n, w<u>ay</u>, r<u>oa</u>d
Consonants: <u>sh</u>oe, <u>r</u>o<u>b</u>, good, lea<u>ve</u>
Consonant clusters: <u>sp</u>ace, <u>pl</u>ay, <u>cl</u>imb, <u>str</u>ong
Syllables: helicopter (4), some (1), trousers (2), president (3)
Word stress: ba<u>na</u>na, <u>tea</u>cher, engi<u>neer</u>, a<u>lone</u>, <u>che</u>mistry
Intonation (as on the recording):   No↗ No↗ No↘ No↘

Box 1   continued

Syllables

1 Examples: bad (1 syllable)   arrive (2)   computer (3)   supermarket (4)
2 How many syllables do these words have?
   helicopter   some   trousers   president
3 Does your language have words with the same number of syllables?
   Give example words: . . . .
   . . . .
   . . . .

Word stress

1 Examples: <u>tra</u>ffic   a<u>bout</u>   <u>te</u>rrible   to<u>mo</u>rrow   conver<u>sa</u>tion
2 Underline the stressed syllable in these words:
   banana   teacher   engineer   alone   chemistry
3 Does your language have words with the same stress pattern?
   Give example words: . . . .
   . . . .
   . . . .

Intonation

1 Examples: Yes   Yes   Yes   Yes
2 Listen and mark the same tones in the word *No.*
   No   No   No   No
3 What are the words for *yes* and *no* in your language?
   Is it usual to say them with the same four tones? . . . .
   . . . .
   . . . .

1.2 Getting you thinking: a pronunciation questionnaire

In the early stages of a course, it is useful to encourage students to think about their current English pronunciation and particular problems; how important English pronunciation is to them, and how its importance might vary in different contexts; and what their pronunciation targets are. This can help students clarify their thoughts on important questions they may not have considered before, and it can help you to know where to aim in helping students improve. This questionnaire provides the basis for a discussion. If the terms used in the questionnaire aren't familiar to students, revise or introduce them first using Activity 1.1.

Focus	Grading pronunciation and identifying difficulties
Level	Elementary+
Time	30 minutes
Preparation	Copy the material in Box 2 onto a handout.

Box 2   Student handout

A How good is your English pronunciation?

1 Circle your answer: 1= high, 5 = low.

vowels	1 2 3 4 5
consonants	1 2 3 4 5
consonant clusters (e.g. cl-, fr-)	1 2 3 4 5
word stress (e.g. aGO, FOLLow)	1 2 3 4 5
intonation (e.g. Yes, Yes)	1 2 3 4 5

2 Note any particular problems you have with English.

vowels ....
....

consonants ....
....

consonant clusters (e.g. cl-, fr-) ....
....

word stress (e.g. aGO, FOLLow) ....
....

intonation (e.g. Yes, Yes) ....
....

B How important is it for you to have good English pronunciation?

Circle your answer: 1= high, 5 = low.

When you talk to your fellow students?	1 2 3 4 5
When you talk to your teacher?	1 2 3 4 5
When you talk to native speakers of English?	1 2 3 4 5
When you talk to other non-native speakers in English?	1 2 3 4 5

C Who would you like to sound like when you speak English? Why?

Procedure

1   Give a copy of the handout to each student and give them some time to complete it. (This might be best done as a homework activity.) Point out that the person they think of in C doesn't have to be a native English speaker. It could be, for example, someone who shares their first language, who they have heard speaking English.

2   Students report back their answers. Encourage comparison and discussion of differences. For example, students might feel they have different problems with English pronunciation, particularly in a multilingual class, or they might have different priorities, and this might become apparent when talking about the answers to question B. If students have selected both native and non-native English speakers for question C, talk about the relative difficulties of having one or the other as a 'target model'. You may also want to discuss which accents of English (again, either native or non-native speaker) they find more or less attractive and why this might be.

3   Keep a copy of the students' answers for your own records. You could use the information about particular problems for prioritising teaching.

4   Later in the course (if the course is of a reasonable length), ask students to repeat the exercise and compare their answers with those they gave earlier. Talk to them about whether and why their answers have changed.

1.3 Making vowel sounds

Focus	Position of organs of speech when making English vowel sounds
Level	Elementary+
Time	20 minutes
Preparation	Make a copy of the vowel chart[1] in Box 3 on an OHT or large piece of paper, and also make a small copy for each student.

---

[1]   Source: Underhill, A. (1994, pp. 10 and 15, adapted).

Procedure

1 Display the chart in Box 3. Point to /iː/ and say the word *me* a few times, elongating the vowel. Explain the chart by saying that when we say this vowel the tongue is 'high' in the mouth, nearly touching the roof of the mouth; that the tongue is pushed towards the 'front' of the mouth; and the lips are spread and less forward. Ask students to say the vowel until they become aware of these three features in their own mouths. Next, point to /ɒ/ and say the word *stop* a few times, elongating the vowel. Explain that when we say this vowel the tongue is 'low' in the mouth; that the tongue is pulled towards the 'back' of the mouth; and the lips are rounded and slightly forward. Ask students to say the vowel until they become aware of these three features in their own mouths.

2 Write on the board a list of the remaining simple vowels, randomly ordered, and example words which include them:

/ɪ/ sit, /ʊ/ stood, /uː/ you, /e/ pen, /ə/ <u>a</u>go, /ɜː/ bird, /ɔː/ more, /æ/ hat, /ʌ/ up, /ɑː/ car

3 Students should work in pairs or small groups to try to fill in the remainder of the chart. They should say the words/vowels to each other while they are doing this. During this time you should visit the pairs/groups and say the words/vowels at the students' request. When the pairs/groups have reached their decisions, collect answers from the class, fill in the rest of your chart, and talk about differences of opinion and difficulties. The completed chart, for your reference, is given in Box 4.

Note

If students are not familiar with phonetic symbols, use example words in the chart rather than symbols. (A full list of phonetic symbols is given in Appendix 1.)

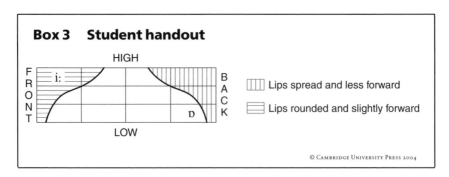

Box 3   Student handout

HIGH

FRONT · iː · BACK

▥ Lips spread and less forward

▤ Lips rounded and slightly forward

ɒ

LOW

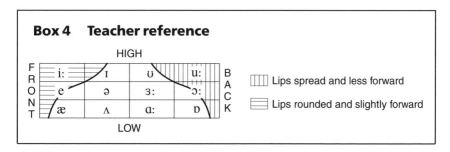

Box 4   Teacher reference

- ▥ Lips spread and less forward
- ▤ Lips rounded and slightly forward

1.4   Consonant clusters: English and first-language differences

The possible consonant clusters at the beginnings of words varies from language to language. This exercise builds awareness of what is possible in English and how this may be different from what is possible in the student's first language.

Focus Comparing consonant clusters in English and students' first language

Level Elementary+

Time 15 minutes

Procedure

1   Write a list of consonant clusters (comprising two or three consonant sounds) on the board. You could write these either as letters or using phonetic symbols. These should be a random mixture of possible and impossible combinations for the beginning of English words. (See Appendix 3 for possible combinations.) For example:

   possible: pl-, fr-, tr-, mu-, dw-, thr- scr-, spl- (*or* /pl/, /fr/, /tr/, /mj/, /dw/, /θr/, /skr/, /spl/)

   impossible: tl-, mr-, vr-, thl-, gw-, pw-, nl-, spw- (*or* /tl/, /mr/, /vr/, /θl/, /gw/, /pw/, /nl/, /spw/)

2   Students work in pairs to decide whether the clusters are possible in English, and to give an example word for each, and whether they are possible in their own first language. If you have a multilingual group, you could build up a list of possible and impossible combinations in different languages.

3   Write on the board the example English words for each cluster found by students. Students repeat these after you. Correct where necessary.

Extension

If you find clusters that are possible in English but not in a student's first language, it may well be that these will cause them pronunciation difficulties. Use this activity as a diagnostic exercise to identify clusters that may need attention.

1.5 Comparing slow and quick speech

Focus	Noticing differences between the way words are said at conversational speed and their citation forms (i.e. how they would be said in isolation, slowly and carefully)
Level	Elementary+
Time	25 minutes
Preparation	1 Record onto a cassette a short extract (15 seconds or so should be enough) of authentic conversation between native English speakers. Recording from radio or TV should give the high-quality recording needed for this activity. Alternatively, you could use the extract given on the recording.
	2 Identify short (maximum of about three seconds) sections within the extract used that are 'complete' in that they are either complete utterances or are part of a longer utterance but have a pause at the end. If possible, record these separately onto another cassette, with gaps in between. This makes it easier to play and replay. A 'gapped' extract is given on the recording.

Procedure

1 In the class, play the first utterance a couple of times and ask students as a group and then individually to repeat, trying to say it in exactly the same way.

2 Then ask 'What words did you say?' and write these on the board. Ask students to say how the pronunciation on the recording differs from the pronunciation of the words said slowly and carefully. The following examples are on the recording for this book:

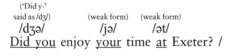

```
        ('Did y-'
      said as /dʒ/)      (weak form)   (weak form)
        /dʒə/              /jə/         /ət/
    Did you enjoy your time at Exeter? /
```

(weak form)
/wəz/
Erm. Yes, I did. Erm, because I was I <u>was</u> doing /

| (weak form) | (glottal stop (weak instead of /t/) form) | (linking sound between 'very' and 'interested') |

/ðə/   /ðəʔ/ /wəz/   /j/
on <u>the</u> whole subjects <u>that</u> I <u>was</u> ver<u>y</u> interested in doing /

(weak
form)
/ən/   (glottal stop
instead of /t/)
/wenʔ/
<u>and</u> I'd made up my mind before I <u>went</u> /

(weak
form)   (left out (weak
or 'unreleased') form)
/jə/   /d/ /tə/
<u>you</u> know what it was I wante<u>d</u> <u>to</u> do /

Extension
Repeat the activity using short sections of recordings you use for other purposes (e.g. in teaching listening or as model dialogues), to develop awareness of changes in pronunciation in connected speech.

1.6 Sounding English

The aim of this activity is to get students thinking about how other non-native speakers pronounce English and what pronunciations students value highly. If appropriate, you could make this more explicit at the end of the activity by asking why they have chosen particular students as having 'better' English pronunciation. What is it about these students' pronunciation they particularly like?

Focus Identifying good English pronunciation
Level Elementary+
Time Depends on size of class

Procedure
1 Organise the class into groups of five or six, and get students to stand in a line in their groups.
2 First demonstrate the activity with a group at the front of the class. Explain that you are going to find people with the best English pronunciation. Write on the board the letter vowels *A - E - I - O - U*. The student at the front of the line (S1) should say these letters to the person behind (S2), who then says them in reply. They should be said loudly

enough for the other members of the group to hear. The rest of the group decides (perhaps by a vote) who has the best English pronunciation of these two students. If S2 'beats' S1, they should move to the front of the line; otherwise, the order stays the same. S2 is then 'challenged' by S3. If S3 beats S2, they should move up the line and then challenge S1. This should continue until everyone has had a chance to challenge for first position or it becomes clear that the person with the best English pronunciation in the group is in this position.

3 When the person with the best English pronunciation has been found in each group, they could come to the front and perform. You could take a vote among the class as a whole on which of these 'winners' has the best English pronunciation.

4 Do the same for a number of features of English pronunciation:
  • Simple vowels: give students a list of words including simple vowels and ask them to focus their attention on these. Choose four or five from: *car, sat, bed, fit, sea, lot, four, book, food, her, sun.*
  • Complex vowels (diphthongs): give students a list of words including complex vowels and ask them to focus their attention on these. Choose four or five from: *my, now, day, bear, here, go, boy, sure.*
  • Consonants: give students a list of words beginning with single consonant sounds and ask students to focus their attention on these. Choose four or five from: *but, do, fill, good, hat, yes, cat, lose, me, no, put, run, soon, talk, very, win, zoo, ship, sin, cheap, thin, then, June.*
  • Consonant clusters: give students a list of words beginning with two consonant sounds, or three consonant sounds, and ask students to focus their attention on these. Choose four or five from: (two consonant sounds) *play, pray, pure, tree, Tuesday, twist, clock, cross, cube, quick, blue, brush, drip, glass, grow, news, fly, few, view, throw, slip, sweet, spill, start, snow, huge* (note that other consonant clusters are possible); or (three consonant sounds) *split, spray, strain, scream* (note that other consonant clusters are possible).

If you know that students in your group have particular English pronunciation problems because of interference from their first language(s), make these the focus of activities. (See Appendix 2 for information about this.)

1.7 Pronouncing names in English

	This activity is intended to raise awareness of pronunciation differences between English and students' first language by focusing on the students' first names.
Focus	Pronouncing first names in English
Level	Elementary+
Time	15 minutes

Procedure

1 Your students may:
   - have names with an equivalent used in English-speaking countries (i.e. with the same or nearly the same spelling, but different pronunciation); examples of names used in both English-speaking and other countries include David, Laura, Peter, Robert, Elizabeth and Martin
   - have names with no equivalent in English-speaking countries
   - have chosen an English name to use as their name in class.

   For all of these groups, make sure that students can pronounce their own and other students' names in an English-sounding way, as if they were English names. Demonstrate, ask students to repeat and correct where necessary. You might want to encourage students to use their English-sounding names in class.

2 Focus on a few of the names and ask students to observe what is different about the first-language pronunciation and the English pronunciation. Box 5 gives some examples involving equivalent names, but you could do a similar activity for names with no equivalent or chosen English names, too.

Box 5   Teacher reference

Name	English pronunciation	Example first-language pronunciation	What students might observe (and examples of questions you might ask to encourage more general awareness of English/first-language pronunciation)
David	/'deɪvɪd/	/dæ'vi:d/	1 The /eɪ/ vowel is different. (Is this vowel used in the students' first language? Can they think of example words where it is?) 2 Stress is different. (Do most English names have stress on the first syllable? Is this different in names in the first language?)
Elizabeth	/ɪ'lɪzəbəθ/	/elɪzæ'bet/	1 The /θ/ consonant is different. 2 Stress is different.
Laura	/'lɔ:rə/	/'laʊræ/	The /ɔ:/ vowel is different.

1.8 Pronouncing places, products and planets

The aim of this activity is to compare names (of cities, products, geographical features, etc.) that are often pronounced similarly (and are often written in the same or a similar way) in a number of languages. By comparing the usual (British) English pronunciation with the pronunciation in the students' language(s), more general differences in pronunciation can be highlighted.

Focus Comparing pronunciation of words in English and students' first language

Level Elementary+

Time	20 minutes
Preparation	Write on the board or display on an OHT one of the following lists (these are all on the recording): cities/states: *Paris, Moscow, Quebec, Budapest, Beijing, Seoul, Johannesburg, Edinburgh, Rio de Janeiro, Brussels, Siberia*; products/companies: *Coca-Cola, Microsoft, Toyota, Skoda, Ikea, Qantas, Volvo*; geographical features: *the Himalayas, the Urals, the Sahara Desert, the Pacific Ocean, Asia, Antarctica*; the planets: *Mercury, Venus, Mars, Jupiter, Saturn, Uranus, Neptune, Pluto*; elements: *Aluminium, Arsenic, Chlorine, Helium, Hydrogen, Iodine, Neon, Radium, Uranium, Xenon.*

Procedure

1   Students work in pairs or groups. In a multilingual class, try to have different first-language students working together. Point to the list on the board/OHT. Ask students to write down how each of the words are written in their first language and to note any differences.

2   Tell students to focus on those words that are written similarly or in the same way in English and their first language. Say (or play from the recording) words from the list, one at a time. After each, ask students to note down whether the pronunciation in English and in their language is nearly the same, different or very different for those words written the same or similarly.

3   Work with the whole class:

- Ask elementary students to say the words that are different or very different in pronunciation in their first language and in English.

- With more advanced students, talk about the differences in pronunciation in the words and whether these reflect more general differences between English and the first language. For example, in British English *Moscow* is pronounced /ˈmɒskəʊ/, in German it is written *Moskau* and pronounced close to /ˈmɒskaʊ/ and in Spanish it is written *Moscú* and pronounced close to /mɒsˈku/. You might note that the vowel sound /əʊ/ is not found in German or Spanish words. You might also note that while stress is on the first syllable in English, it is on the second in Spanish (although this does not represent a general feature of English and Spanish). In British English *(the) Himalayas* is pronounced /hɪməˈleɪəz/, while in French *Himalaya* is pronounced close to /ɪmæˈlæjæ/. Here you might note that the sound /h/ is not used in French.

Extension

For homework, ask students to list words from their first language that have been borrowed from English, or words in English that have been borrowed from their first language. In class, some or all students could write these words on the board and give the first language pronunciation and the English pronunciation of the borrowed word (or you may need to give this). For example, words in Japanese that have been borrowed from English include *sukebo* (skateboard), *poke beru* (= 'pocket bell' = a pager), *don mai* (= 'don't mind' = don't worry), *buruusu* (= blues, i.e. a kind of music). Talk about any differences between English and Japanese pronunciation that have led to the different spellings. In other languages, words are borrowed from English and spelt the same but with different pronunciations. For example, *video* is written *vídeo* in Spanish and pronounced close to /ˈbɪðeɪəʊ/.

1.9 Impersonations

Focus	Developing awareness of differences in how native and non-native speakers position their organs of speech when they speak English
Level	Elementary+
Preparation	Find an audio or (preferably) a video recording of an actor or other well-known native speaker of English. Take a short section (around 10 to 15 seconds) of what they say and write it out. Put it on a handout for students or on an OHT. Alternatively, use the extract on the recording.
Time	25 minutes

Procedure

1 Explain to students that they are going to see and listen to [name of well-known person] and try to imitate their accent. Before playing the recording, find out what students know about the person and how they feel about the way the person speaks. For example, what country they are from, whether they are easy or difficult to understand, whether students like the way they speak, and perhaps whether they can detect any regional accent.

2 Display the OHT or give out the handout. Play the recording a few times while students follow the written text. The following extract is on the recording for this book. The speaker is the well-known British actor, Michael Caine.

'People say to you, well how do you do this? I say well I just do it. I don't know how I do it. And then I found out that I did know a lot of things that I could impart.'

Form pairs and ask them to say, first one student and then the other, what was said, as far as possible in exactly the same way as the person in the recording. If you have willing volunteers – perhaps students who are happy to 'throw themselves into the part' – ask a few of them to perform their impersonation to the rest of the class.

3 Then ask students to reflect on any differences they perceived when imitating a native speaker compared to when they speak English with their usual accent. Without being too technical, try to elicit differences in how they position their lips or tongue, or how rigidly they hold their jaw. They might also comment on other facial and body gestures: do they move the muscles around the eyes more or use greater hand movements when they imitate?

4 If appropriate, to follow up, ask students to spend a little time at home imitating another native speaker that they see on television or have recordings of, including songs.

Notes

1 It is not intended, of course, that students should try permanently to sound like the well-known person used. For the vast majority of learners, a native-speaker-like pronunciation is an unachievable goal and, in any case, few would aspire to this. (See the discussion in the Introduction, pp. 13–14.) Rather, students should be encouraged to develop an awareness of how the general position of the speech organs (the 'articulatory setting') differs in the spoken English of native speakers and of learners. The idea is that if learners can to some extent move towards the articulatory setting of native speakers, this can make the pronunciation of English easier.

2 You would obviously need to conduct this activity with sensitivity. Some students may be reluctant to imitate in this way in public. If this is the case, encourage them to do the exercise at home, perhaps in front of a mirror, to develop their awareness.

Extension

This activity has suggested imitating just one native speaker. You could develop it by using recordings of more native speakers with a variety of accents (British, North American, Australian, etc. and regional accents within countries) and also fluent non-native speakers of English. The latter would perhaps be most appropriate when you are working with students sharing a first language; the recording could be of a non-native with the same first language as the student.

1.10 Intonation in print

In this activity, students are asked to interpret how speech represented in novels might sound when said aloud. The aim is to raise awareness of the significance of intonation in conveying emotion, attitude, etc. However, intonation is only one aspect of this, although an important part. Other aspects are such things as loudness, overall pitch level, gesture and facial expression. It is important in this activity not to insist on a 'correct' way of saying things – many interpretations are obviously possible. The examples in this activity are taken from children's books, which are a good source of this kind of material.

Focus Significance of intonation in conveying emotion and attitudes

Level Advanced

Time 45 minutes

Preparation Copy the material in Box 6 onto a handout or an OHT. Copy the material in Box 7 onto a handout.

Procedure

1 Introduce by presenting the material in Box 6 to students. Ask them to work in pairs and decide how the utterances in quotation marks in extracts 1–3 might be said. Encourage them to say the utterances aloud to each other. It is important to make it clear throughout this exercise that there is no correct answer.

2 Choose a few students to perform each extract aloud and point out (and perhaps talk about) differences. For example, the utterance in extract 1 might be said (among many ways of saying it):

WHO'S been EATing my PORRidge *or*
WHO'S been EATing MY porridge

The first example might be said by the first bear when they find their porridge eaten, but the second example said by the second or third bear (*porridge* is no longer 'news' and so is not prominent).

3   Repeat the procedure for extracts 4–7. In these extracts, clues to how the reported speech might be said come from punctuation (*!* and *?*), reporting verbs (*screamed*, *hissed*, *demanded*), italics for emphasis (*day*), and adverbs (*knowingly*).

4   Give out the handout (Box 7). Ask students to read the extract quietly. Answer any questions about vocabulary.

5   Students then work in groups of three. One student takes the role of the narrator, and the other two take the roles of Mr and Mrs Foster (underlined in the extract). (If this is difficult, students could work in pairs, with one taking the role of the narrator and Mr Foster, and the other Mrs Foster.) They should act out the speech (i.e. as if it were conversation rather than words read aloud) as they did with the material in Box 6.

6   After they have worked through the text, you take the role of narrator, and select individual students to take the parts of Mr and Mrs Foster. You might choose a number of students to contribute in a single read-through. Ask students to offer alternative readings of utterances and again talk about differences.

Box 6   Student handout

1   Bear: 'Who's been eating my porridge?'

(from *Goldilocks and the Three Bears*)

2   Cinderella: 'Am I invited to the ball, too?'
Stepmother: 'No, of course not. Who would want to invite you?'

(from *Cinderella*)

3   LRRH: 'What big teeth you have, Grandma.'
Wolf: 'All the better to eat you with!'

(from *Little Red Riding Hood*)

4   'It bit me!' he screamed.[2]

5   Then there was a click of the front door opening.
'Your grandad?' hissed Kirsty.

6   'Are you going to stand around all *day*?' Kirsty demanded.

7   'Ah,' said Yo-less, knowingly. 'It's like that, is it?'

---

[2]   Extracts 4–7 all from Terry Pratchett, *Johnny and the Bomb* (Corgi, 1996): 4 = p. 85;
5 = p. 72; 6 = p. 84; 7 = p. 133.

Box 7   Student handout

From *The Way up to Heaven*, a short story by Roald Dahl[3]

Mr and Mrs Foster are rich, elderly New Yorkers. Mrs Foster has a terrible fear of being late for appointments, while Mr Foster seems to enjoy seeing her become worried and irritated and finds ways to delay her. Mrs Foster has to catch a plane to take her to Paris to stay with her daughter and family. The day before, the plane was cancelled because of fog. Now she is trying again to get to the airport . . .

———————

Next morning, Mrs Foster was up early, and by eight-thirty she was downstairs and ready to leave.

Shortly after nine, her husband appeared. 'Did you make any coffee?' he asked.

'No, dear. I thought you'd get a nice breakfast at the club. The car is here. It's been waiting. I'm all ready to go.'

They were standing in the hall – they always seemed to be meeting in the hall nowadays – she with her hat and coat and purse, he in a curiously cut Edwardian jacket with high lapels.

'Your luggage?'

'It's at the airport.'

'Ah yes,' he said. 'Of course. And if you're going to take me to the club first, I suppose we'd better get going fairly soon, hadn't we?'

'Yes!' she cried. 'Oh, yes – *please!*'

'I'm just going to get a few cigars. I'll be right with you. You get in the car.'

She turned and went out to where the chauffeur was standing, and he opened the car door for her as she approached.

'What time is it? she asked him.

'About nine-fifteen.'

Mr Foster came out five minutes later, and watching him as he walked slowly down the steps, she noticed that his legs were like goat's

———————

3 Roald Dahl, *The Way up to Heaven*. In *The Great Automatic Gammatizator and other stories* (Penguin, 1996, pp. 164–181).

Box 7   continued

legs in those narrow stovepipe trousers that he wore. As on the day before, he paused half-way down to sniff the air and to examine the sky. The weather was still not quite clear, but there was a wisp of sun coming through the mist.

'Perhaps you'll be lucky this time,' he said as he settled himself beside her in the car.

'Hurry, please,' she said to the chauffeur. 'Don't bother about the rug. I'll arrange the rug. Please get going. I'm late.'

The man went back to his seat behind the wheel and started the engine.

'*Just* a moment!' Mr Foster said suddenly. 'Hold it a moment, chauffeur, will you?'

'What is it, dear?' She saw him searching the pockets of his overcoat.

'I had a little present I wanted you to take to Ellen,' he said. 'Now, where on earth is it? I'm sure I had it in my hand as I came down.'

'I never saw you carrying anything. What sort of present?'

'A little box wrapped up in white paper. I forgot to give it to you yesterday. I don't want to forget it today.'

'A little box!' Mrs Foster cried. 'I never saw any little box!' She began hunting frantically in the back of the car.

Her husband continued searching through the pockets of his coat. Then he unbuttoned the coat and felt around in his jacket. 'Confound it,' he said. 'I must've left it in my bedroom. I won't be a moment.'

'Oh, *please*!' she cried. 'We haven't got time! *Please* leave it! You can mail it. It's only one of those silly combs anyway. You're always giving her combs.'

'And what's wrong with combs, may I ask?' he said, furious that she should have forgotten herself for once.

'Nothing, dear, I'm sure. But . . .'

'Stay here!' he commanded. 'I'm going to get it.'

'Be quick, dear! Oh, *please* be quick!'

She sat still, waiting and waiting . . .

Sounds: vowels, consonants and consonant clusters

Vowels (2.1–2.5)

Correcting particular vowels

When you use Activities 2.1 to 2.5, you may need to give some explicit guidance to help students form the vowel sounds correctly. Here are some suggestions for teaching strategies to use when students have problems pronouncing particular vowels:

/iː/ (*eat*), /uː/ (*you*), /æ/ (*am*), /ɔː/ (*more*), /ɜː/ (*fur*), /ɑː/ (*arm*)

- Focus on lip position. Demonstrate that:
  /iː/ (*eat*) has lips 'smiling'
  /uː/ (*you*) has lips rounded and pushed forward
  /æ/ (*am*) has lips open
  /ɔː/ (*more*) has lips rounded and more open than /uː/
  /ɜː/ (*fur*) has lips relaxed/neutral
  /ɑː/ (*arm*) has lips rounded and wide open.
- If possible, students use mirrors to look at lip position. Alternatively, represent lip shape on the board:

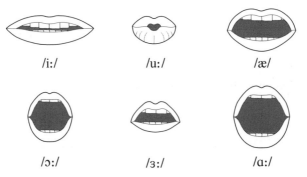

| /iː/ | /uː/ | /æ/ |

| /ɔː/ | /ɜː/ | /ɑː/ |

- Say the vowels silently; students try to guess which vowel you are 'saying' from lip position. Students could try this in pairs.

- Students alternate sounds to become aware of lip position. For example:
  /iː/ vs /uː/: *eeee – oooo – eeee – oooo – eeee – oooo*
  /ɔː/ vs /ɜː/: *orrrr – errrr – orrrr – errrr – orrrr – errrr*
- To practise /ɑː/, ask students to produce the sound that doctors ask you to make when they want to look at your throat.

Long vowels /iː/ (*eat*), /uː/ (*you*), /ɑː/ (*arm*), /ɔː/ (*more*), /ɜː/ (*fur*) vs short vowels /ɪ/ (*it*), /e/ (*end*), /æ/ (*am*), /ʌ/ (*up*), /ɒ/ (*stop*), /ʊ/ (*would*)

- Focus on vowel length and give a visual demonstration of this. Gradually open arms wider as you say *eeeeeeeeeeeat* (*eat*) and contrast this with a much shorter, rapid arm movement as you say *it*.
- Students alternate sounds to become aware of different length. For example:
  /iː/ vs /ɪ/: *eeee – i – eeee – i – eeee – i – eeee*
  /uː/ vs /ʊ/: *oooo – u – oooo – u – oooo – u – oooo*

Front vowels (made with the front part of the tongue near the front of the mouth) /iː/ (*eat*), /e/ (*end*), /æ/ (*am*) vs back vowels (made with the back of the tongue near the back part of the mouth) /uː/ (*you*), /ɔː/ (*more*), /ɒ/ (*stop*)

- Focus on the position of the tongue. Draw head cross-sections and show the position of the tongue in the vowels:

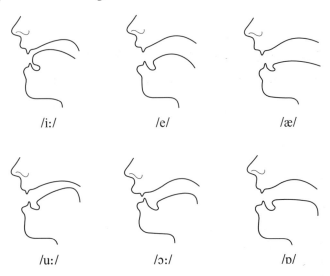

/iː/   /e/   /æ/

/uː/   /ɔː/   /ɒ/

- Students alternate sounds to become aware of different tongue positions. For example:

/i:/ vs /u:/: *eeee – oooo – eeee – oooo – eeee*

/e/ vs /ɔ:/: *e – orrrr – e – orrrr – e – orrrr*

Diphthongs /aɪ/ (e<u>y</u>e), /aʊ/ (<u>ou</u>t), /eɪ/ (d<u>ay</u>), /eə/ (<u>air</u>), /ɪə/ (<u>ear</u>), /əʊ/ (<u>o</u>pen), /ɔɪ/ (b<u>oy</u>), /ʊə/ (s<u>ure</u>)

- Separate the diphthong into its two parts, practise these separately, and then join them together. (Note that the separate components are not exactly the simple vowels used in English, so the vowels given below are an approximation.)

/aɪ/ (e<u>y</u>e): /ɑ:/ (<u>ar</u>m) and /i:/ (<u>ea</u>t)

/aʊ/ (<u>ou</u>t): /æ/ (<u>a</u>m) and /u:/ (y<u>ou</u>)

/eɪ/ (d<u>ay</u>): /e/ (<u>e</u>nd) and /i:/ (<u>ea</u>t)

/eə/ (<u>air</u>): /e/ (<u>e</u>nd) and /ə/ (<u>a</u>go) [or /ɜ:/ (f<u>ur</u>)]

/ɪə/ (<u>ear</u>): /i:/ (<u>ea</u>t) and /ə/ (<u>a</u>go) [or /ɜ:/ (f<u>ur</u>)]

/əʊ/ (<u>o</u>pen): /ə/ (<u>a</u>go) and /u:/ (y<u>ou</u>)

/ɔɪ/ (b<u>oy</u>): /ɔ:/ (m<u>ore</u>) and /i:/ (<u>ea</u>t)

/ʊə/ (s<u>ure</u>): /u:/ (y<u>ou</u>) and /ə/ (<u>a</u>go) [or /ɜ:/ (f<u>ur</u>)]

For example, students say or repeat:

aaaa – eeee – aaaa – eeee – aaee – aaee

to produce /aɪ/ (e<u>y</u>e).

2.1 Matching vowel sounds: a family tree

	Students match the vowel sounds in people's names to construct a family tree.
Focus	Matching vowel sounds in names
Level	Elementary – Intermediate
Time	20 minutes
Preparation	Copy Box 8 onto a handout for each student, and also Box 10 if you are going to do the extension activity.

Procedure

1 If necessary, explain the idea of a family tree and the ways of showing children, brothers and sisters, and 'married to' (═══). For example, draw on the board the following section from a family tree and explain that Ken is married to Becky, and they have two children, Sam and Patrick:

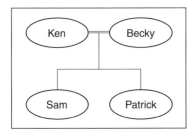

2   Give out the handout (Box 8). Explain that in this family all brothers and sisters have the same first vowel sound in their name and that family members only get married to people with the same first vowel sound in their name. They should work in pairs to use this information to complete the family tree with the names in the list at the bottom of the handout. Ask the name of David's wife (Answer: Rachel) to check that they have understood.

3   Before starting, students repeat after you, or the recording, the names already in the family tree and then the names in the list.

4   Students report back their answers (e.g. Jack is married to Carol; Daniel and Jack are brothers). The answers are in Box 9. Check that the vowel sounds in the names are pronounced correctly, and correct where necessary.

Extensions

1   Give out Box 10. Ask students to prepare a family tree on the same principles – both a full version and a gapped version with the missing names underneath – for other students to complete, and use some of these with the class at a later time. (Note that the names used in the main activity are included in Box 10 and could be used again.)

2   Alternatively, ask students to give as many male and female names as they can think of, and write these on the board. Then give out a handout based on Box 10, leaving out all the names. Students then write the names from the board on their handout. There should be at least two male and two female names for each vowel sound. If there are gaps, try to elicit additional names, or provide names from those in Box 10. Then follow the procedure in Extension 1.

Box 8   Student handout

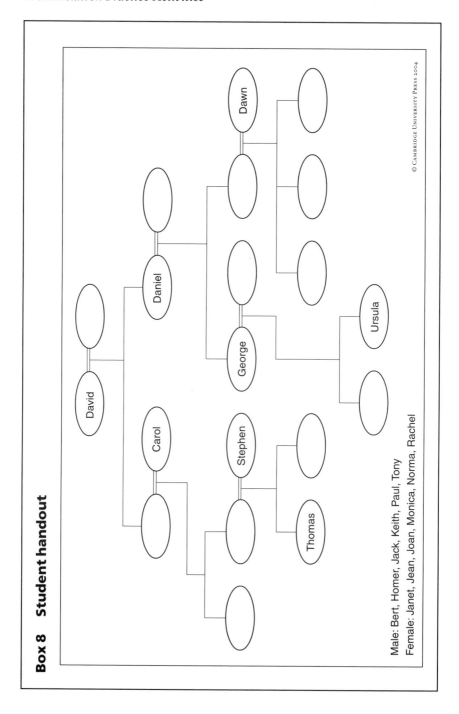

Male: Bert, Homer, Jack, Keith, Paul, Tony

Female: Janet, Jean, Joan, Monica, Norma, Rachel

© CAMBRIDGE UNIVERSITY PRESS 2004

Box 9   Teacher reference

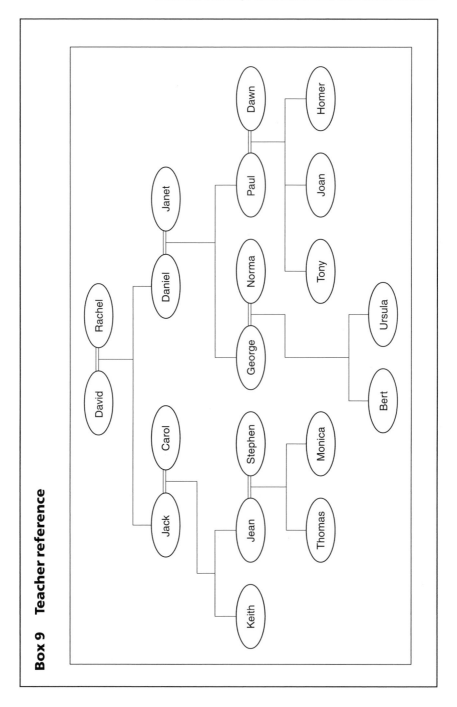

Box 10   Student handout

First vowel sound	Male names	Female names
/ɑː/ (as in *part*)	Charles, Mark, Martin	Barbara, Charlotte, Margaret
/æ/ (as in *black*)	Barry, Daniel, Patrick	Carol, Frances, Janet
/aɪ/ (as in *drive*)	Nigel, Clive, Guy	Di, Eileen, Irene
/e/ (as in *pen*)	Derek, Gerald, Henry	Beverly, Edna, Heather
/eɪ/ (as in *day*)	David, James, Ray	Daisy, Rachel, Kay
/ɪ/ (as in *sit*)	Chris, Richard, Vincent	Bridget, Linda, Hilda
/iː/ (as in *see*)	Keith, Peter, Stephen	Celia, Jean, Sheila
/ɒ/ (as in *stop*)	Colin, John, Tom	Florence, Monica, Olive
/əʊ/ (as in *phone*)	Homer, Joseph, Tony	Joan, Rose, Sophie
/ɔː/ (as in *more*)	George, Gordon, Paul	Dawn, Maureen, Norma
/uː/ (as in *choose*)	Bruce, Hugh, Luke	Judith, Susan, Ruth
/ɜː/ (as in *bird*)	Bert, Herbert, Percy	Bernadette, Gertrude, Ursula

---

2.2 Finding words including the same vowel sound: word routes[1]

Focus	Identifying words that have the same vowel sound
Level	Elementary – Intermediate
Time	30 minutes
Preparation	Copy Box 11 and Box 12 onto separate handouts, one for each student. It would also be useful to copy Box 11 onto an OHT.

---

[1] Based on ideas in Hancock, M. (1995).

Procedure

1 Begin by teaching or revising compass points: *north, south, east, west, north east, north west, south east, south west.* As a reminder, draw a compass with these points on the board.

2 Give out the Box 11 handout.

3 Explain that in this game you move from one square to another depending on the vowel sound in each word. For example, if you start at the word *black* and hear the word *go* then you move to the word *slow* because *go* and *slow* have the same vowel. From there, if you hear the word *floor* you move to *sort* because *floor* and *sort* have the same vowel. The final move is a compass direction, so from *sort* if you hear *north east* you move to *paid* because it is north east of *sort*. And the aim of the game is to find the word in this final square. Point to this word route on the OHT if one is available.

4 Give a full demonstration. Go from *make* to *cat*. Use the words in Box 12 as prompts for the word route. (Don't show this to students.) The corresponding words in the two boxes have the same vowel sound.
   You say: 'Start at *make*.' Then give the route using words from Box 12: '*sure* → *know* → *but* → *scared* → *south east*'
   Students move: *make* → *poor* (the same vowel sound as *sure*) → *soap* (the same vowel sound as *know*) → *sun* (the same vowel sound as *but*) → *chair* (the same vowel sound as *scared*) → *cat* (= the answer)
   Point to this word route on the OHT if available.

5 Make up some more word routes and at the end of each one students get a point for a correct answer. After each word route, ask if any students got 'lost' and find out where problems occurred, focusing on the pronunciation of the vowels in words along the route. Get students to repeat problem words, and correct and repeat vowel sounds if necessary.

6 After doing this a few times as a class activity, organise students into pairs. They should put Box 11 in front of them (or this should be displayed on the OHT). Give Student A a copy of the Box 12 handout. They should keep this hidden from Student B. Student A should decide on a start word and an end word on Box 11, and write the prompt words down (from Box 12) for the route, keeping the list secret from Student B. They should then take Student B on a word route from the start word to the end, as demonstrated in step 4 above. If students go wrong, encourage them to talk about the route, focusing on vowels and any difficulties in pronouncing or hearing them. Students do this a few times, and then swap roles.

Box 11   Student handout

black	slow	room	paid	pure	stop
car	wash	sort	bit	chair	horse
leave	dear	spend	sound	sun	cat
bird	high	poor	soap	beach	climb
start	make	will	book	you	well
wood	bear	real	drum	first	voice

Box 12   Student handout

fat	home	blue	take	cruel	watch
half	soft	more	still	scared	born
cheap	clear	tell	mouse	but	tap
turn	right	sure	know	deep	lie
large	way	fill	full	who	best
push	wear	ear	run	girl	boy

Note

You or the students can make the activity more demanding by having longer word routes.

2.3 Hearing and saying differences between vowels and between consonants: minimal pairs

Minimal pairs are two words which have a different meaning when only one sound is changed (see p. 3). Below are five different simple activities you can use to help students discriminate between sounds in minimal pairs. All of the activities have a stage of pairwork. During this stage, encourage students to discuss wrong answers – is the problem with the hearing of one student or the pronunciation of the other? Correct and ask students to repeat after you where necessary.

Focus Discriminating between sounds in minimal pairs

Level Elementary+

Time 5–20 minutes

Procedure

Same or different?

1 Students write *1* to *10* in their notebooks. Say pairs of words, either the same word (e.g. *tree–tree*) or minimal pairs (e.g. *tree–tray*; *bear–pear*). Students write *S* if the words are the same and *D* if the words are different. When you check the answers, get students to repeat pairs of words after you if they have had difficulty.

2 Students work in pairs. Give a list of minimal pairs to one of the students in the pair, and they repeat the procedure in step 1 with their partner. After a time, students exchange roles.

Box 13 includes some examples of minimal pairs that you could use in this activity, showing the focus of the difference in each set.

Box 13   Teacher reference

Vowels (/ɪ/ vs /iː/)	Vowels (/eɪ/ vs /æ/)	Consonants (/b/ vs /d/)	Consonants (/θ/ vs /s/)
1 bead/bid	1 pad/pad	1 bark/dark	1 thank/sank
2 chip/cheap	2 made/mad	2 door/door	2 sick/thick
3 seat/seat	3 bake/back	3 drain/brain	3 thing/sing
4 it/eat	4 snake/snake	4 big/big	4 sink/think
5 list/list	5 plane/plane	5 buy/buy	5 thumb/some
6 sheep/ship	6 tap/tape	6 bent/dent	6 pass/path
7 fit/feet	7 ate/at	7 dead/bed	7 mouse/mouse
8 still/still	8 hat/hat	8 brown/drown	8 tenth/tense
9 leave/leave	9 rain/ran	9 double/double	9 fourth/fourth
10 wheel/will	10 lack/lake	10 beside/decide	10 worth/worse

Vowels (/e/ vs /ɒ/)	Vowels (/ʌ/ vs /əʊ/)	Consonants (/tʃ/ vs /ʃ/)	Consonants (/p/ vs /f/)
1 neck/knock	1 come/come	1 chair/share	1 wipe/wife
2 trod/tread	2 boat/boat	2 wish/witch	2 four/pour
3 net/net	3 none/known	3 chip/chip	3 packed/fact
4 loft/loft	4 robe/robe	4 sheep/sheep	4 chief/chief
5 leg/log	5 home/home	5 cheat/sheet	5 prize/fries
6 get/got	6 bun/bone	6 cash/cash	6 past/past
7 stop/step	7 flood/flood	7 chew/shoe	7 leap/leap
8 pot/pot	8 most/most	8 watch/watch	8 fan/pan
9 less/less	9 fun/phone	9 she's/cheese	9 pool/fool
10 wreck/wreck	10 note/nut	10 shows/shows	10 phrase/phrase

Column A or column B?

1   On the board or an OHT give a list of minimal pairs in two columns, headed *A* and *B*, as in Box 14.
2   Say each word and students repeat after you. Correct pronunciation where necessary.

3   Say one of the words in a minimal pair and students say whether they hear the word from column A or B.

4   Organise the students into pairs and ask them to repeat the procedure in step 3 with first one student taking the teacher's role and then, after a time, the other.

Box 14 includes some examples of minimal pairs that you could use in this activity, showing the focus of the difference in each set.

Box 14   Teacher reference

Vowels /ɪ/ vs /e/		Vowels /eɪ/ vs /ʌ/		Consonants /l/ vs /r/		Consonants /p/ vs /b/	
A	B	A	B	A	B	A	B
1 spill	spell	1 same	sum	1 lane	rain	1 pear	bear
2 did	dead	2 blade	blood	2 glass	grass	2 simple	symbol
3 pin	pen	3 days	does	3 collect	correct	3 pie	buy
4 bill	bell	4 hate	hut	4 climb	crime	4 pack	back
5 lift	left	5 made	mud	5 lead	read	5 pat	bat
6 disc	desk	6 came	come	6 lane	rain	6 cap	cab
7 wrist	rest	7 place	plus	7 light	right	7 pride	bride
8 will	well	8 rain	run	8 glow	grow	8 rip	rib
9 tin	ten	9 game	gum	9 cloud	crowd	9 played	blade
10 lid	led	10 lake	luck	10 lied	ride	10 pea	bee

Minimal pair 'Bingo!'

1   On the board or an OHT give a list of minimal pairs in columns. Begin by asking students to repeat all the words after you. Correct pronunciation where necessary. Then, students select a given number of words from the list at random (tell them how many they should choose) and write them down. Say the words at random and students cross words off their own lists as they hear them. (Keep a note of which words you have said.) The winner is the one who crosses out all their words first and then shouts *Bingo!* Check the answers carefully. Ask the 'winning' student to say their words aloud and to point to them on the board. Correct any mistakes.

Box 15 gives possible sets of words that you could select from, or you could use a selection from Boxes 13 and 14. The lists in Box 15 focus on three sounds in each case (you could of course focus on only two, or more than three).

2　Students work in groups (three or more) and repeat the procedure in step 1. They should take it in turns to be 'caller'.

Box 15　Teacher reference

Vowels (/aʊ/ vs /aɪ/ vs /ɔɪ/)			Vowels (/æ/ vs /ɪ/ vs /e/)		
found	find		shall		shell
sound	signed		gas		guess
loud	lied		sat	sit	set
crowd	cried		than		then
mouse	mice		fat	fit	
	buy	boy	swam	swim	
	tie	toy	as	is	
	pint	point	thank	think	
owl		oil		wrist	rest
bow (=/baʊ/)		boy		litter	letter
				miss	mess

Consonants (/s/ vs /z/ vs /ʃ/)			Consonants (/θ/ vs /t/ vs /d/)		
sour		shower	thin	tin	din
suit		shoot	thaw	tore	door
seat		sheet	thread	tread	dread
sip		ship	threw	true	drew
peace	peas		thigh	tie	die
price	prize		fourth	fought	ford
loose	lose		thrill		drill
place	plays		three		tree
rice	rise		both	boat	
	zoo	shoe	thinner		dinner
	zip	ship	worth		word
	zone	shown			

Same word or different word?

1   On the board or an OHT write a numbered list of words that come from minimal pairs. Ask students how many times they hear the word in the set of words they will hear. For example:

Write on board/OHT: *man*

You say: *man – mine – man – mine*

Answer: 2

You could use the following to practise a variety of simple vowels:

Write on board/OHT: 1 *leap* 2 *met* 3 *till* 4 *sit* 5 *love* 6 *men* 7 *many* 8 *wet* 9 *ran* 10 *top* 11 *not* 12 *luck* 13 *bus* 14 *books*

You say: 1 *leap – lip – lip – lip*

Answer: 1

Continue in the same way using the words in Box 16.

2   Organise students into pairs and give each student a copy of the material in Box 16. Hiding their paper from their partner, students should write a number between 0 and 4 above each word, totalling 4 for each pair of words. For example:

3   1   0   4   2   2
1 *leap/lip*   2 *met/meat*   3 *till/tell*   etc.

Student A should then say, for each item, four words corresponding to the numbers they have written. For example,

3   1
for 1 *leap/lip*

they might say:

1 *leap – leap – lip – leap* (i.e. *leap* = three times, *lip* = once).

Student B should say how many times they heard the first word (Answer: 3). Once Student A has worked through their list, they should exchange roles.

3   As a variation on this activity, say four words, one of which is different from the others, for example: 1 *lip – lip – leap – lip*. Students should say the number of the word which is different (Answer: 3/third).

Box 16   Student handout

1 leap/lip	5 love/live	9 ran/run	13 bus/boss
2 met/meat	6 men/man	10 top/tap	14 books/box
3 till/tell	7 many/money	11 not/nut	
4 sit/sat	8 wet/what	12 luck/look	

Minimal pairs in context

1 Copy the material in Box 17 onto a handout for each student or put it on an OHT. It focuses on /eɪ/ (as in *may*) vs /aɪ/ (as in *my*) minimal pairs.

2 Read the sentences aloud (or play the recording), completing them with the words/phrases in either column A or B. The following examples are given on the recording:

    1 She thinks she's going today. (A)

    2 I don't want to pay. (A)

    3 I'd like a try, please. (B)

    4 My house is at the end of the lane. (A)

    5 The workers were very unhappy in the mine. (B)

    6 I didn't like the wait. (A)

    7 I wasn't certain that it was time. (B)

    8 It covers a big area, Lake Washington. (A)

Students tick a word/phrase in column A or B. If you are using an OHT, they should write *A* or *B* in their notebooks. Check the answers.

3 Ask one of the students to take your role and repeat the activity with the class. Then students work in pairs to do the activity again.

Box 17   Student handout

/eɪ/ (*may*) vs /aɪ/ (*my*)	A	B
1 She thinks she's going	today	to die
2 I don't want	to pay	a pie
3 I'd like a ...., please.	tray	try
4 My house is at the end of the	lane	line
5 The workers were very unhappy in the	main	mine
6 I didn't like the	wait	white
7 I wasn't certain that it was	tame	time
8 It covers a big area, ... Washington.	Lake	like

---

Boxes 18–20 provide similar materials to use in the same way.

Box 18   Student handout

/ɪ/ (*it*) vs /iː/ (*eat*)   A   B

1 I can't .... without it.   live   leave
2 He .... me on the leg.   bit   beat
3 There's nothing to ....   it   eat
4 I can't find the .... anywhere.   lid   lead
5 He emptied the .... all over the floor.   bins   beans
6 I wanted .... in the garden.   to sit   a seat
7 Peter had the ....   list   least
8 Don't .... on the floor.   slip   sleep

© Cambridge University Press 2004

Box 19   Student handout

/l/ (*lose*) vs /r/ (*run*)   A   B

1 I went for a walk in the ....   lane   rain
2 There was a .... in the field.   lamb   ram
3 She had a watch on her ....   list   wrist
4 I'm sure it won't fit. It looks .... to me.   long   wrong
5 Don't walk on the ....   glass   grass
6 He couldn't sail the boat. He hadn't got a .... clue crew
7 She drew a picture of a ....   clown   crown
8 Can you .... the report for me?   collect   correct

© Cambridge University Press 2004

Box 20   Student handout

/p/ (*p*ut) vs /b/ (*b*ut)

		A	B
1	There was a .... under the tree.	pear	bear
2	It was a really good	pie	buy
3	There was dirt all over the	peach	beach
4	I'll make sure they're in the	pack	back
5	Can you bring the .... over here?	pole	bowl
6	He had always hated	peas	bees
7	I've never had a	pet	bet
8	There was a towel lying next to the	path	bath

© CAMBRIDGE UNIVERSITY PRESS 2004

2.4 Communicating with single vowel sounds[2]

Focus	Using single vowel sounds in communication
Level	Intermediate+
Time	35 minutes
Preparation	Copy the material in Box 21, preferably onto an OHT, and as a handout for students. Copy the material in Box 22 as a handout for students.

Procedure

1 Explain that a number of vowel sounds can be used alone to give a particular meaning. Give an example: try to turn on a piece of electrical equipment (a cassette recorder, an overhead projector, etc.) which doesn't work – before the class, make sure that it is unplugged! Say 'Ah (/ɑː/), I see what's wrong. It's not plugged in.' Show item 1 of the OHT to illustrate the example.

2 Uncover the 'Common meaning' column of item 2, keeping the other three columns covered. Ask students what single vowel sound can be used to express the idea that something is really pretty or nice. Continue with the rest of the items. Talk about differences between the use of the various sounds in British English and in the students' first language(s).

---

[2] Based on material in Celce-Murcia, M., Brinton, D.M. and Goodwin, J.M. (1996, pp. 122–123).

When you have gone through all the items, give a copy of the material in Box 21 and Box 22 to the students. (Note that these sounds can be used to express other meanings, too.)

3 Students work in pairs to suggest which of the sounds in Box 21 is most likely to fill each gap in the dialogues in Box 22. Discuss the answers with the whole class.

Box 21   Student handout

Common meaning	Pronunciation	Written	Example
1 Now I understand.	/ɑ:/ (short; falling tone)	ah	'It's not working because it's not plugged in!' 'Ah, of course.'
2 That's really pretty or nice.	/ɑ::/ (long; falling tone)	ah *or* aah	'And here's a photo of my baby daughter.' 'Ah, isn't she pretty.'
3 That hurts.	/aʊ/ (falling tone)	ow	'Ow, I've cut myself.'
4 I'm disappointed.	/əʊ/ (falling tone)	oh	'Sorry, Jim's already left.' 'Oh, what a pity.'
5 I'm thinking about what to say next.	/ɜ:/ (level tone)	er	'What do you want to do now?' 'Er, I'm not sure.'
6 That's horrible/ disgusting.	/ɜ::/ *or* /i::/ (both long; falling tone)	urgh ee	'This cheese has gone mouldy. Look!' 'Urgh, it smells revolting.'
7 I'm looking forward to something.	/u:/ (falling tone)	ooh	'Shall we go out for a meal?' 'Ooh, that would be nice.'
8 Angrily getting someone's attention, usually to stop them doing something they shouldn't.	/ɔɪ/ (falling tone; usually said loudly)	oi	'Oi! Get off my bike!'

Box 22   Student handout

1   A: Put your hand in this bag.
    B: .... , it feels disgusting. What is it?

2   A: Do you want to come over for dinner?
    B: .... , that would be great.

3   A: Have you seen our new kitten?
    B: .... , isn't it cute!

4   A: Come with me!
    B: .... , you're hurting me.

5   A: We've just eaten all the dinner. Sorry.
    B: .... , that's a shame.

6   A: The children from next door are stealing apples again.
    B: .... , get out of my garden!

7   A: Brian's already gone home.
    B: .... , I'm sorry I missed him.

8   A: This wire should go into the second hole.
    B: .... , yes, I see now.

9   A: What's the answer to question 3?
    B: .... , let me think about that.

10 A: Watch out for the low ceiling.
    B: .... , I banged my head.

11 A: I wonder why there's no one here.
    B: .... , there's a note on the door that says the class has been
    cancelled.

12 A: How old do you think Joan is?
    B: .... , I've no idea.

13 A: There's someone trying to break into your car.
    B: .... , get away from there!

14 A: This is a photo of my two-year-old son holding his baby sister.
    B: .... , aren't they sweet.

15 A: Watch out for the puddle!
    B: .... , the water's gone into my shoes.

16 A: Would you like some chocolate?
    B: .... , yes please.

2.5 Classifying words according to their first vowel

This activity focuses on the vowels /æ/, /ɑː/, /ʌ/ and /ɪ/, but you could devise a similar activity with other vowels or with consonants (see the Extension section below).

Focus Classifying words according to their first vowel sound
Level Intermediate+
Time 20 minutes
Preparation Copy the material in Box 23 onto the board, an OHT or a handout.

Procedure

1 Ask students (individually, in pairs or in groups) to complete the table in Box 23 with the names of an animal/bird, household object, etc. Make sure that students understand that they are looking for words with the given vowel *sound*, and not a particular vowel letter. The *first* vowel sound (not necessarily the first sound) in each word should be the one given. You could give a time limit. The winner is the one who has filled in most squares correctly.

2 When students report back their answers, monitor the vowel sounds /æ/, /ɑː/, /ʌ/ and /ɪ/, and correct and repeat where necessary.

Variation
To make the activity easier, give students answers written randomly on the board and ask them to put them in the correct square.

Extension
Here are some other possible words for different sets of vowels and initial consonants:

1 /eɪ/, /aɪ/, /əʊ/, /aʊ/ (all long vowels)
animals/birds: *crayfish, bison, mole, owl*
household objects: *table, lights, toaster, shower*
parts of the body: *brain, eyes, nose, mouth*
food or drink: *raisins, wine, doughnuts, flour*

2 /s/, /f/, /v/, /ʃ/ (all fricatives)
   animals/birds: *snake, frog, vulture, sheep*
   household objects: *sofa, frying pan, vase, sheets*
   parts of the body: *stomach, finger, veins, shin*
   food or drink: *sultanas, flan, vegetables, sugar*

Box 23   Student handout

	/æ/ (bl<u>a</u>ck)	/ɑ:/ (p<u>ar</u>t)	/ʌ/ (l<u>u</u>ck)	/ɪ/ (s<u>i</u>t)
animal or bird				
household object				
part of the body				
food or drink				

© Cambridge University Press 2004

Answer key

Example answers: animals: camel, shark, monkey, giraffe; household objects: matches, armchair, cup, fridge; parts of the body: back, arm, stomach, rib; food: carrots, garlic, onions, figs.

Consonants (2.3; 2.6–2.9)

Correcting particular consonants

When you use activities 2.3 (on consonants in minimal pairs) and 2.6 to 2.9, you may need to give some explicit guidance to help students form the consonant sounds correctly. Here are some suggestions for teaching strategies to use when students have problems pronouncing particular consonants:

Strong consonants (/p/, /t/, /k/, /tʃ/) and weak consonants (/b/, /d/, /g/, /dʒ/)

- Students place their hand or a piece of paper in front of their mouths. When they produce the strong consonants, they should be able to feel a puff of air and the paper should move. The weak consonants are produced with less force, with no noticeable puff of air. Otherwise the pairs of sounds /p/–/b/, /t/–/d/, /k/–/g/, /tʃ/–/dʒ/ are produced with mouth and tongue in a similar position. Students alternate the sounds /p/ – /b/ – /p/ – /b/ (etc.) until they can feel the difference. (Note: When the sounds are used in context the difference in force between them is much less marked. However, isolating them and exaggerating the difference can help develop students' awareness of how the sounds are made.)

- If students have special problems with /tʃ/, ask them to shape the mouth as if they were going to produce /t/. Then to push the lips forward and round them; flatten the tongue a little against the top of the mouth; build up pressure in the mouth and release it suddenly. To produce /dʒ/, do the same but with less pressure, making sure that the sound is voiced (see next section).

- Some learners produce initial /j/ as /dʒ/ (saying *yet* as *jet*, for example). If they do this, ask them to say the word *yet* beginning with a long /iː/ vowel *eeeee – et* and repeat, gradually reducing the length of the initial vowel. The result should be *ee –et*, and sound close to *yet*.

Fricative sounds: 'voiceless' /f/, /θ/ (<u>th</u>in), /s/, /ʃ/ (<u>sh</u>ip) and 'voiced' /v/, /ð/ (<u>th</u>en), /z/, /ʒ/ (u<u>su</u>al)

- Students place their hands gently on their throats. When they produce the voiced sounds they should be able to feel a vibration through their hand; with the unvoiced sound there should be no vibration. Otherwise the pairs of sounds /f/–/v/, /θ/–/ð/, /s/–/z/ and /ʃ/–/ʒ/ are produced with mouth and tongue in a similar position. Students alternate the sounds /f/ – /v/ – /f/ – /v/ (etc.) until they can feel the difference.

/w/ vs /v/

- Demonstrate the different starting lip positions: /w/ is produced with lips rounded and pushed forward (as if saying *oo*); /v/ is produced with the top teeth on the bottom lip. Students alternate the sounds /w/ – /v/ – /w/ – /v/ (etc.) and then put them into words *wet – vet – wet – vet* (etc.) until they become aware of the difference.
- As the external shape of the mouth is different, ask students to look in mirrors to observe this.

/b/ vs /v/

- Demonstrate the different starting lip positions: /b/ is produced with lips together; /v/ is produced with the top teeth on the bottom lip. Students alternate the sounds /b/ – /v/ – /b/ – /v/ (etc.) and then put them into words *bat – vat – bat – vat* (etc.) until they become aware of the difference.
- Demonstrate that /b/ is 'short' (i.e. the air is released and the sound ends) while /v/ is a 'continuing' sound (i.e. it can be continued indefinitely – or at least until you run out of air!). Students alternate the sounds /b/ – /vvvvv/ – /b/ – /vvvvv/ (etc.) until they become aware of this.

/r/ vs /l/

- Help students become aware of the position of the tip of the tongue in producing these sounds. /l/ is produced with the tongue touching the alveolar ridge (behind the teeth). With the tongue in this position and the mouth open a little, ask students to blow; they should feel the air moving down the sides of their tongue. /r/ is produced with the tip of the tongue a little further back in the mouth (as in /t/), but the tongue should not touch the top of the mouth. Students alternate the sounds /r/ – /l/ – /r/ – /l/ (etc.) and then put them into words *right – light – right – light* (etc.) until they become aware of this.
- Drawing head cross-sections to show the two sounds can help some students.

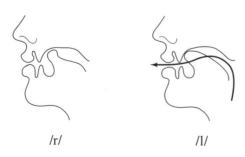

/r/   /l/

initial /h/

- Some learners produce a *kh* sound instead of an initial /h/. To produce initial /h/ correctly, tell students to make the noise they would make if they were trying to steam up a mirror by breathing on it.
- Students alternate words with and without initial /h/: *it – hit – it – hit* (etc.) or *at – hat – at – hat* (etc.) until they become aware of the difference.

2.6 Who lives where? Minimal pair names[3]

The activities described here use the material in Box 24, focusing on the sounds /w/, /v/, /r/ and /l/. People's names and the places where they live are given in each square, and these names and places are minimal pairs (e.g. John <u>L</u>eece/<u>R</u>ees, <u>W</u>ighton/<u>R</u>yton).

Focus Sounds /w/, /v/, /r/, /l/

Level Elementary+

Time 20–30 minutes

Preparation Version 1: copy the material in Box 24 onto an OHT or a handout. Version 2: copy the material in Box 24 twice onto two OHTs or two handouts: in the first, include Part A and a version of Part B with the *places* omitted; in the second, include Part A and a version of Part B with the *names* omitted. Version 3: copy the material in Box 24 twice onto two handouts: in the first, include Part A and a version of Part B with half of the names and places omitted at random; in the second, include Part B and the other half of the names and places omitted instead.

Procedure

Version 1

1 Give out or display the material in Box 24. Students repeat the names and places given in Part A after you or the recording. Correct and repeat where necessary.

2 Focus students on Part B. Explain that the place where a person lives is given under their name. Make statements such as 'Mark Vaughan lives in Ridcombe' and students write or say *True* or *False*.

3 Repeat step 2 with different students making the statements. Then organise students into pairs to repeat the activity again. During this stage, monitor their pronunciation of /w/, /v/, /r/ and /l/, and correct where necessary.

---

[3] Based on an idea from Michael Vaughan-Rees.

Version 2

1 Show the OHT or give out the copies of the first version of Box 24. Students repeat the names and places in Part A after you or the recording.

2 Make statements such as 'Mark Vaughan lives in Ridcombe' and students write down the places in the chart in Part B or in their notebooks. Choose places at random and keep a note of where you have said people live.

3 Students report back their answers. Correct and repeat names and places where necessary.

4 Show or give out the second version of Box 24. Students work in pairs, to repeat steps 2 and 3 above. One in each pair should take the teacher's role (selecting names at random) and their partner should add names to their chart, checking the answers at the end. During this stage monitor their pronunciation of /w/, /v/, /r/ and /l/, and correct where necessary.

Version 3

1 Students work in pairs. Give the first version of the handout to one student in each pair and the second version to the other. They should keep these hidden from their partner. Students repeat the names and places in Part A after you or the recording. Correct and repeat where necessary.

2 In pairs, students then ask each other questions such as 'Where does Mark Vaughan live?' and 'Who lives in Ryton?' to complete their version of Part B. During this stage monitor their pronunciation of /w/, /v/, /r/ and /l/, and correct where necessary. At the end, students should compare the information they have on their completed handouts and talk about any differences.

Extension

You could write similar material focusing on other consonants or vowels, depending on the sounds your students find problematic. Here are two possibilities:

1 Focus on /p/, /b/, /t/ and /d/:

John Payne – John Dain	Phil Dab – Phil Babb	Helen Tar – Helen Parr
Carol Penney – Carol Denny	Julie Drew – Julie Brue	Darren Tatton – Darren Patten
Keith Purdon – Keith Durden	Tim Dayle – Tim Bail	Laura Tandy – Laura Pandee

Pinmoor – Dinmore	Bagnall – Dagnell	Tadberry – Padbury
Perivale – Derryvale	Bail – Dale	Tadlow – Padloe
Purton – Derton	Bierton – Dearton	Torcross – Pawcross

66

Box 24   Student reference

Part A

John Leece – John Rees	Mark Warne – Mark Vaughan	Alison Ray – Alison Way
Betty Lawson – Betty Rorson	Paul Wayne – Paul Vane	Les Right – Les White
Peter Lowe – Peter Roe	Ann Whicker – Ann Vicker	Susan Wain – Susan Rayne

Loxwood – Rockswood	Vines Cross – Whines Cross	Ryton – Wyton
Lorton – Rawton	Vorden – Warden	Ridcombe – Widcombe
Lambsgate – Ramsgate	Venby – Whenby	Rateby – Waitby

Part B

John Leece	Mark Warne	Betty Rorson
Wyton	Widcombe	Waitby
Paul Wayne	Alison Ray	Ann Whicker
Loxwood	Vines Cross	Lambsgate
Alison Way	Betty Lawson	Les White
Whines Cross	Rateby	Lorton
John Rees	Susan Wain	Paul Vane
Ryton	Vorden	Rockswood
Mark Vaughan	Les Right	Peter Lowe
Ridcombe	Rawton	Venby
Peter Roe	Ann Vicker	Susan Rayne
Whenby	Ramsgate	Warden

2 Focus on /æ/, /ɑː/, /ɪ/ and /iː/:

Ed Catlow –	Sharon Hills –	Liam Patch –
Ed Cartlow	Sharon Heals	Liam Peach
Emily Danley –	Patrick Lim –	Hannah Radburn –
Emily Darnley	Patrick Leem	Hannah Reedburn
Jack Gadden –	Diane Mickin –	Harry Sacker –
Jack Garden	Diane Meekin	Harry Seeker

Fanmoor – Farnmore	Histon – Heeston	Lackford – Leakford
Hadfield – Hardfield	Kilby – Keelby	Manton – Meanton
Tanbrook – Tarnbrook	Pithill – Peathill	Napton – Neepton

2.7 Lip-reading

In this activity students focus on the visible features of sound production to be able to discriminate between the sounds. The idea is to make both 'hearer' and 'speaker' more aware of how the sounds are articulated, and of differences between pairs of sounds. This activity focuses on the sounds /s/, /z/, /f/, /v/, /θ/ and /ð/.

Focus Articulation of the sounds /s/, /z/, /f/, /v/, /θ/ and /ð/

Level Elementary+

Time 15 minutes

Preparation Copy the material in Box 25 onto the board or an OHT, or as a handout for students.

Procedure

Give a demonstration. Focus students on the first pair of words in Box 25. Face the class and silently say either *sat* or *fat*. Ask students if you said word a or b. Repeat until they clearly understand the activity and then ask them to work in pairs to complete the activity.

Extension

You can do the same kind of activity with any pairs of sounds that have a visible difference. In addition to the /s/ vs /f/, /f/ vs /θ/, /s/ vs /θ/, /s/ vs /ð/, /θ/ vs /v/, /f/ vs /z/ practised in the material in Box 25, other possible contrasts and some example minimal pairs are:

- /w/ vs /v/: west – vest, wine – vine, wet – vet, worse – verse
- /m/ vs /w/: me – we, might – white, make – wake, met – wet
- /p/ vs /f/: pat – fat, pit – fit, pride – fried, pool – fool
- /b/ vs /d/: bad – dad, big – dig, buy – die, bark – dark

- /w/ vs /r/: wear – rare, wise – rise, weed – read, way – ray
- /f/ vs /ʃ/: fair – share, fade – shade, fine – shine, folder – shoulder
- /f/ vs /s/: fin – sin, fit – sit, found – sound, fine – sign
- /v/ vs /b/: vet – bet, vote – boat, vest – best, very – berry
- /θ/ vs /t/: thin – tin, three – tree, through – true, thank – tank
- /θ/ vs /s/: thank – sank, think – sink, thaw – saw, thick – sick
- /ð/ vs /d/: than – Dan, they – day, their – dare, then – den
- /t/ vs /p/: tea – pea, tie – pie, ten – pen, tower – power
- /t/ vs /tʃ/: talk – chalk, test – chest, tip – chip, toes – chose
- /l/ vs /r/: lace – race, late – rate, lay – ray, lock – rock

---

Box 25   Student handout

	a	b		a	b		a	b
1	sat	fat	6	threw	view	11	bath	bars
2	fat	that	7	some	thumb	12	death	deaf
3	sing	thing	8	sort	thought	13	path	pass
4	say	they	9	few	zoo	14	that	sat
5	sink	think	10	than	van	15	there	fair

© CAMBRIDGE UNIVERSITY PRESS 2004

2.8 Classifying words according to their first consonant

This activity focuses on the consonants /t/, /d/, /k/, /g/, /p/ and /b/, but you could devise a similar activity with other consonants or with vowels (see Extension activities below).[4]

Focus Sounds /t/, /d/, /k/, /g/, /p/, /b/
Level Elementary+
Time 15 minutes
Preparation Copy the pictures in Box 26 onto an OHT or a handout.

Procedure

Focus students on the pictures in Box 26. Explain that Tom, Deborah, Kathy, Gary, Pam and Barbara are thinking about the presents they would like for their birthday. Tom wants things that begin with the sound /t/, Deborah things that begin with /d/, Kathy things that begin with /k/, and so on. Students should decide what presents each person wants and make sentences like: *Tom wants some trousers. Deborah wants a dictionary.* Monitor and correct the sounds /t/, /d/, /k/, /g/, /p/ and /b/ where necessary.

---

4 From Hewings, M. (1993, p. 14).

Box 26   Student handout

© CAMBRIDGE UNIVERSITY PRESS

Extensions

1 Ask students to suggest other presents for the same characters on the same principle as above.
2 Give students the names of people that begin with sounds you know your students find difficult. Students repeat the names after you. Then ask them to suggest appropriate presents for these people.

2.9 Getting rid of unwanted vowels

Focus	Correcting the addition of vowels before and after words
Level	Elementary+
Time	10 minutes
Preparation	Version 1: copy the material in Box 27 onto an OHT or a handout.
	Version 2: copy the material in Box 28 onto an OHT or a handout.

Procedure

Version 1

This is for learners who add a vowel (usually /ə/ or sometimes /e/) before a word beginning with a consonant (usually a consonant cluster such as /st/) producing, for example, *estart* for *start*. (Speakers of Brazilian Portuguese, Spanish, Catalan, Farsi and Arabic may have particular problems with this.)

1 Focus students on the material in Box 27. Students repeat after you a word from column A, followed by the corresponding phrase from B, then the corresponding word from C.

2 Ask students to do the same again, but this time don't provide a model for repetition.

3 If students add an initial /ə/ (e.g. *espan*), ask students to elongate the *s* sound – *Thisssssspan* – when they repeat phrases in B, then omit *Thi* until they produce *sssspan*. Then reduce the length of *s* until they produce *span*.

Box 27   Student handout

A	B	C
pan	This pan.	span
park	This park.	spark
pin	This pin.	spin
port	This port.	sport
table	This table.	stable
tool	This tool.	stool
top	This top.	stop
trip	This trip.	strip
can	This can.	scan
car	This car.	scar
cot	This cot.	Scot
kid	This kid.	skid

Version 2

This is for learners who add a vowel (usually /ə/) after a word ending with a consonant producing, for example, *what-er* for *what* or *yes-er* for *yes*. (Speakers of Italian, Japanese, Chinese and Korean may have particular problems with this.) The first half of the material is for words ending with /s/ and /z/; the second half is for words ending with plosive sounds e.g. /t/ and /d/.

1 Focus students on the material in Box 28. Students repeat after you a phrase from column A and then the corresponding word from B.
2 Ask students to do the same again, but this time don't provide a model for repetition.
3 If students add a final /ə/ to words in column B (e.g. *pass-er*), ask students to repeat the phrase in A a few times (perhaps holding the /s/ or /z/ for a little time in the first examples) and then concentrate on dropping *it*, leaving the word without the final /ə/.

Box 28   Student handout

A	B
Pass it.	Pass.
Force it.	Force.
Race it.	Race.
Is it.	Is.
Saws it.	Saws.
Was it.	Was.
Read it.	Read.
Write it.	Write.
Stop it.	Stop.
Kick it.	Kick.
Keep it.	Keep.
Guard it.	Guard.

Consonant clusters (2.10–2.12)

2.10 Word chains

Focus	Words beginning with a consonant cluster
Level	Elementary+
Time	15 minutes

Procedure

1   Demonstrate the principle of the activity on the board. Build up the word chain below and explain that each word must begin with a consonant cluster (two or more consonant sounds). The cluster must contain *one* of the consonant sounds from the cluster at the beginning of the previous word.[5]

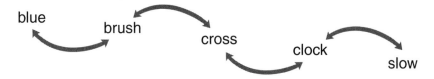

blue   brush   cross   clock   slow

2   Continuing from *slow*, go round the class with each student (or pair/group) adding a new word. Don't write these on the board, so that the focus is on sounds rather than spelling. Give a limited thinking time (longer or shorter depending on the ability of the class). If students fail to provide a new word, provide a word that doesn't begin with an appropriate consonant cluster, or provide a word that has already been used, they are 'out' and the turn passes to the next student(s). Continue until there is a winner or until you feel they have had enough. Alternatively, set a goal for the class as a 'team' to achieve: ten or fifteen words in a sequence, for example. Keep a note of how many words they have produced as they add to the chain.

---

5   From Hewings, M. (1993, p. 28).

2.11 Definitions quiz

	Box 29 focuses on words beginning with the clusters /bl/, /br/, /pl/ and /pr/, and Box 30 on /sl/, /sp/, /sk/ and /st/.
Focus	Words beginning with a consonant cluster
Level	Intermediate+
Time	15 minutes

Procedure

1 Using either letters or phonetic symbols, write the target consonant clusters (given above for Boxes 29 and 30) on the board before the exercise.

2 Read out word definitions at random and ask students to supply the correct word.[6] The class can repeat the word chorally, and then ask a few students to repeat individually. Make this a 'quick-fire' activity so that students are saying the target words frequently. Correct any cluster problems. Repeat definitions randomly until the students tire of the activity.

Extension

Devise your own material. When you identify particular consonant clusters that are causing problems for your students, find a number of words beginning with those clusters and prepare simple dictionary-type definitions of them (in fact, these could be taken straight from a monolingual or, if your students share a first language, a bilingual dictionary). Use easier or more difficult vocabulary depending on the ability of your students.

---

[6] The definitions are loosely based on those in the *Cambridge Learner's Dictionary*.

Box 29   Teacher reference

/bl/

to close and open your eyes quickly *(blink)*
unable to see *(blind)*
a cover on a bed to keep you warm *(blanket)*
the darkest colour *(black)*
describing a person with fair hair *(blonde)*
red liquid in your body *(blood)*
the colour of the sky on a sunny day *(blue)*
the opposite of sharp *(blunt)*

/br/

the organ inside your head *(brain)*
what makes a car go more slowly *(brakes)*
part of a tree *(branch)*
showing no fear *(brave)*
a food made from flour, water and yeast *(bread)*
air that goes in and out of your lungs *(breath)*
something you make houses out of *(bricks)*
a woman who is getting married *(bride)*

/pl/

a living thing that grows in earth *(plant)*
a flat dish *(plate)*
to take part in a game *(play)*
to make someone happy *(please)*
a piece of plastic that fits into the hole in a bath *(plug)*
the opposite of minus *(plus)*
enough or a large amount *(plenty)*
things like Mars, Mercury and the Earth *(planets)*

/pr/

to say that something will happen in the future *(predict)*
to like one thing more than another *(prefer)*
not the past or future *(present)*
the title of the head of the USA *(president)*
the son of a king *(prince)*
the opposite of public *(private)*
the head of a university department *(professor)*
to show that something is true *(prove)*

Box 30 Teacher reference

/sl/
to close something with great force *(slam)*
the part of a shirt that covers your arm *(sleeve)*
feeling tired *(sleepy)*
to hit with the flat part of your hand *(slap)*
soft shoes worn in the house *(slippers)*
a flat piece of food such as bread *(slice)*
a vehicle used for travelling across snow *(sledge)*
not fast *(slow)*

/sp/
the area outside the Earth *(space)*
an insect with eight legs *(spider)*
to say something using your voice *(speak)*
your backbone *(spine)*
an old-fashioned word for glasses *(spectacles)*
a round mark *(spot)*
to use money to buy or pay for something *(spend)*
to turn around and around quickly *(spin)*

/sk/
the outer layer of your body *(skin)*
equipment for measuring weight *(scales)*
to frighten someone *(scare)*
the area where you can see clouds *(sky)*
a place where children go to be educated *(school)*
a piece of women's clothing worn around the waist *(skirt)*
a country north of England *(Scotland)*
a piece of cloth worn around the neck *(scarf)*

/st/
the raised area in a theatre where plays are performed *(stage)*
a long, thin piece of wood *(stick)*
a piece of paper stuck on a letter *(stamp)*
the organ in your body where your food goes *(stomach)*
to begin doing something *(start)*
a building where trains stop *(station)*
to finish doing something *(stop)*
the gas produced when you heat water *(steam)*

2.12 **Consonant cluster towers**

The aim of this activity is for students to keep adding single consonant sounds at the beginning or end of a word until they can't add any more.

Focus Consonant sounds at the beginning and end of words

Level Intermediate+

Time 20 minutes

Procedure

1 Demonstrate the activity. Say one of the following vowels aloud a few times: /æ/ (as in _am_); /ɑ:/ (_car_); /aɪ/ (_my_); /aʊ/ (_how_); /eɪ/ (_pay_); /eə/ (_care_); /ɪ/ (_it_); /e/ (_egg_); /i:/ (_eat_); /ɒ/ (_on_); /əʊ/ (_go_); /ɔ:/ (_more_); /ɔɪ/ (_boy_); /u:/ (_you_); /ɜ:/ (_fur_); /ʌ/ (_up_).

2 Students make a word by adding a single consonant *sound* (not necessarily a single letter) to either the beginning or end of the word: e.g. /æ/ → _am_. Write this word on the board. Students then try to make a new word by adding another single consonant sound to this word, either at the beginning or the end: e.g. _am_ → _ram_. Write this above _am_ to start building the cluster tower. This continues until no new words can be made. There should be no additional vowel sounds between the consonant clusters at the start and end of the words. For example:

tramples /træmplz/

trample /træmpl/

tramp /træmp/

tram /træm/

ram /ræm/

am /æm/

/æ/

3 This could be a competitive activity between two halves of the class. One half makes the first word, the other the second, and so on. The half that makes the final 'top' word is the winner of the round and gets a point. Alternatively, it could be a co-operative activity where the aim is for the class as a whole to try to build as high as possible. Obviously, some towers might be quite short. When a tower is finished, chorally and individually repeat the words and correct pronunciation where necessary.

There are some examples of possible towers on p. 78. Of course, the same base vowel could in each case lead to totally different towers, depending on the knowledge and originality of the students. Other base vowels and possible first words in the tower are given in step 1.

scarfs		
scarf	mines	
calf	mine	house
car	my	how
/ɑ:/	/aɪ/	/aʊ/
		splits
spades		split
spade	scared	spit
paid	scare	sit
pay	care	it
/eɪ/	/eə/	/ɪ/

3 Connected speech

Links between words (3.1–3.4)

3.1 Matching adjectives and nouns: consonant to vowel links

Focus	Consonant–vowel links
Level	Elementary
Time	15 minutes

Procedure

1 Ask students (giving clues if necessary) to suggest singular countable nouns that begin with a vowel *sound* and end with a consonant *sound* (e.g. *animal*, *egg*). Notice that the words may or may not begin and end with vowel and consonant *letters* (e.g. *unit* begins with the vowel letter *u* but the consonant sound /j/; *apple* ends with the vowel letter *e* but the consonant sound /l/). Write the words that students give you on the right half of the board.

2 Now ask for similar adjectives (e.g. *American*, *unsafe*). Write these on the left side of the board. Write the word *an* to the left of these.

3 Students chorally and individually repeat all the words after you. Correct pronunciation where necessary.

4 Give students a few minutes to study the lists and write down as many meaningful (though possibly amusing!) *an* + adjective + noun combinations as they can. Then invite them to suggest their examples. Make sure that the word final consonants flow smoothly into the following word initial vowels. If necessary, illustrate this by marking the link on the board. For example:

    an intelligent elephant   an overweight uncle

After a student suggests an example and pronounces it with smooth consonant–vowel link, ask others to repeat. Monitor the links and correct where necessary.

Variation

Instead of eliciting adjectives and nouns from students, copy Box 31 onto a handout or an OHT and do steps 3 and 4.

Box 31   Student handout

an	awful endless enjoyable excellent impossible incorrect informal innocent intelligent Irish old open overweight underground unfinished	address aeroplane airport animal apple apricot arm example egg elephant evening exam example ice cream illness office omelette onion orange uncle

© CAMBRIDGE UNIVERSITY PRESS 2004

3.2 Changing sounds: consonant to consonant links

This exercise focuses on changes in the pronunciation of the final consonant in words ending with a vowel + /t/, /d/ or /n/ when they are followed by a word beginning with another consonant (e.g. *hot potato*, *red bag*, *ran quickly*). The sounds /t/ and /d/ are sometimes left out when they are in the middle of a consonant cluster formed when a word ending with consonant sounds is followed by a word beginning with consonant sounds (e.g. *I asked Gary*, *We told Peter*). This feature is highlighted and practised in Activity 3.11.

Focus Consonant-final changes in words followed by a consonant at the beginning of the next word

Level Intermediate+

Time 15 minutes

Preparation Copy the material in Box 32 onto a handout or an OHT.

Procedure

1   Explain that some consonant sounds at the end of a word change when they are followed by a consonant at the beginning of the next word. Illustrate by writing on the board:

   that   that sort   that cat

and saying each item. Demonstrate that in the first two items the final *t* in *that* is pronounced /t/, but that before *cat* the *t* is pronounced something like /g/. Students repeat each word/phrase after you and try to make the sound change in *that cat*. (Note that before the sound /s/ the /t/ might also be 'unreleased' or replaced with a 'glottal stop'. This is the closure in the throat we make as we begin a cough, just before we make a coughing sound. You could encourage either a /t/ sound or a glottal stop before /s/.)

2   Organise students into pairs and give out or show the material in Box 32. Students say the words and phrases in each row to each other and decide which of the underlined final consonants in columns B or C is said in the same or nearly the same way as in column A. They should put a ✓ next to this. Demonstrate with the first row: in column C, *t* will be pronounced as in *hot*, but in column B it will be pronounced something like /p/.

3   Give the students an opportunity to check their answers. Say (or play from the recording) the items in each row: 'hot – a hot pizza – a hot oven', etc. Make sure that you say the items in columns B and C fairly quickly so that the consonant-final changes take place.

4   Students report back their answers by saying the two similar pronunciations first and then the different one. For example:

hot (= ho/t/) – a hot oven (= ho/t/) – a hot pizza (= ho/p/)

The phrase in which there is a change in the final consonant (and the type of change) is given in the Answer key below Box 32.

5   Check the answers and then ask the class and individuals to repeat after you or the recording.

Extensions

1   Ask students to suggest when /t/, /d/ and /n/ change and when they do not, and how they change.

Answer key

/t/, /d/ and /n/ sound like /p/, /b/ and /m/ respectively before /p/ and /b/.

/t/, /d/ and /n/ sound like /k/, /g/ and /ŋ/ respectively before /k/ and /g/.

/t/, /d/ and /n/ don't change before a vowel sound, /l/, /w/, /r/ or /s/ (although /t/ and /d/ are sometimes unreleased or replaced with a glottal stop before these sounds).

---

2   Keep a note of items that are commonly said as one 'unit' (i.e. without a pause between), such as compound nouns, in which the first element ends in /t/, /d/ or /n/. Ask students to repeat these items making the sound changes practised above where necessary. Examples of compound nouns are: (with sound changes) *credit card, output, feedback, broadcast, godmother, handball, pedestrian crossing, downpour, input*; (without

sound changes) *part-exchange, handout, godfather, tin opener, downstream.* Can students think of more? Encourage them to look out for examples in their own reading or listening, and also their own speech.

Box 32   Student handout

	A	B	C
1	ho<u>t</u>	a ho<u>t</u> pizza	a ho<u>t</u> oven
2	goo<u>d</u>	a goo<u>d</u> excuse	a goo<u>d</u> price
3	seve<u>n</u>	seve<u>n</u> languages	seve<u>n</u> people
4	shor<u>t</u>	a shor<u>t</u> boy	a shor<u>t</u> way
5	re<u>d</u>	a re<u>d</u> bike	a re<u>d</u> apple
6	brow<u>n</u>	a brow<u>n</u> suit	a brow<u>n</u> beard
7	whi<u>te</u>	whi<u>te</u> wine	whi<u>te</u> coffee
8	ba<u>d</u>	a ba<u>d</u> cold	a ba<u>d</u> illness
9	te<u>n</u>	te<u>n</u> cars	te<u>n</u> letters
10	ligh<u>t</u>	ligh<u>t</u> rain	ligh<u>t</u> green
11	wi<u>de</u>	a wi<u>de</u> river	a wi<u>de</u> gap
12	gree<u>n</u>	a gree<u>n</u> sofa	gree<u>n</u> grass

© CAMBRIDGE UNIVERSITY PRESS 2004

Answer key

1 B a ho/p/ pizza, 2 C a goo/b/ price, 3 C seve/m/ people, 4 B a shor/p/ boy, 5 B a re/b/ bike, 6 C a brow/m/ beard, 7 C a whi/k/ coffee, 8 B a ba/g/ cold, 9 B te/ŋ/ cars, 10 C li/k/ green, 11 C a wi/g/ gap, 12 C gree/ŋ/ grass.

3.3 Predict the linking sounds: vowels linked with /j/ (y) and /w/

Focus	/j/(y) and /w/ links between words ending with a vowel sound followed by words beginning with a vowel sound
Level	Intermediate+
Time	25 minutes
Preparation	Copy the material in Box 33 onto a handout or an OHT.

Procedure

1 Explain that when a word that ends in a vowel sound is followed by a word beginning with a vowel sound, a very short /w/ or /j/ (*y*) linking sound is sometimes put between them. Illustrate by writing on the board:

two eggs three eggs
  w   y

Students repeat the phrases after you a few times.

2 Give out the handout or display the OHT. Students work in pairs to decide whether the links marked in the sentences in column B are *w* or *y*. They should say the phrases aloud quietly to each other as they do this.

3 Students repeat the phrases in column B after you or the recording and check their answers.

4 Students match the questions in column A and answers in column B. Check by asking the questions and students give the answers. Then students work in pairs, saying the complete dialogue. Monitor the students as they do this and check that they are using *w* and *y* links. Correct where necessary.

5 Take a dialogue from the textbook you are currently using. Ask students to mark where they think *w* and *y* links should be. Students then read the dialogue aloud, making sure that the links are included.

Extensions

1 Ask students to identify the two *w* and *y* links in the questions in column A. (Answer: 4 Who is he? *w*; 12 Why an umbrella? *y*.)

2 For more advanced students you could ask them to work out when, in general, *w* links and *y* links are used. (Answer: The choice of *w* or *y* depends on the vowel that ends the first word. If the vowel is produced with the highest part of the tongue close to the *front* of the mouth e.g. /i:/ [as in see], /eɪ/ [day], /aɪ/ [my], /ɔɪ/ [boy], then the linking sound will be /j/ [y]. If the vowel is produced with the highest part of the tongue close to the *back* of the mouth e.g. /u:/ [you], /aʊ/ [now], /əʊ/ [go] then the linking sound will be /w/ [w].)

Box 33   Student handout

A

1 Where are you going?
2 When?
3 Why?
4 Who is he?
5 Have you got cousins there, too?
6 How will you get there?
7 How long will it take?
8 Have you been there before?
9 How long will you be there?
10 Why don't you stay longer?
11 Will you take Adam a present?
12 Why an umbrella?

B

a By air.
b I grew up there.
c Yes, a new umbrella.
d He asked me for one.
e Tomorrow afternoon.
f I'll stay a week.
g They all live in France.
h It's too expensive.
i To see Adam.
j A few hours.
k My uncle.
l To Austria.

Answer key

1 l To Austria. *w*
2 e Tomorrow afternoon. *w*
3 i To see Adam. *y*
4 k My uncle. *y*
5 g They all live in France. *y*
6 a By air. *y*
7 j A few hours. *w*
8 b I grew up there. *w*
9 f I'll stay a week. *y*
10 h It's too expensive. *w*
11 c Yes, a new umbrella. *w*
12 d He asked me for one. *y*

3.4 Matching opposites and words that go together: vowels linked with /r/

In some accents of English, such as southern British or 'BBC English', words that end in vowel + the letter *r* or vowel + the letters *re* end with a vowel sound (e.g. *car* is pronounced /kɑː/, *care* is pronounced /keə/). These accents are sometimes called *non-rhotic*. In other accents, such as North American, Scots and the west of England, these words end with a /r/ sound (e.g. /kɑːr/ and /keər/). These accents are sometimes called *rhotic*. This exercise is intended to be used only if you have a non-rhotic accent.

Focus /r/ link between words ending -*r*/-*re* followed by words beginning with a vowel sound

Level Elementary/Intermediate+

Time 25 minutes

Preparation For elementary students, copy the material in Box 34 onto a handout or an OHT. For intermediate students, copy the material in Box 35 onto a handout or an OHT.

Procedure

1 Write the following on the board:

> four – four elephants   another – another ice cream
> poor – poor example   more – more apples   were – were open
> somewhere – somewhere else

Say each pair in turn or play the recording. Explain that when said alone, the -*r* or -*re* words end in a vowel sound, but when they are followed by another word beginning with a vowel sound an *r* is inserted. For example:

> four – four elephants   (/fɔː/ – /fɔːrelɪfənts/)
> ‿
> r

Alternatively, say the pairs (perhaps exaggerating the *r* link a little) and ask them what they observe about the pronunciation of *four, another,* etc., in context. Students should then say the pairs after you. Check that they are adding the *r* links.

(For elementary students)

2 Give out the handout (Box 34) or display the material on the OHT.

3 Students work in pairs to match opposites in A and B.

85

4 Ask students for their answers. They should say, for example:

    before and after
      ⌣
      r

giving the words from A first. Then get the class or individuals to repeat after you. Monitor the use of linking *r* and correct where necessary.

(For intermediate+ students)

2 Give out the handout (Box 35) or display the material on the OHT.

3 Students work in pairs to match words in A and B that commonly go together. (You could use the term *collocate* if the students know it.) Give or ask for a couple of examples: *amateur orchestra, bitter enemy.* Make clear that the words need a linking *r*:

    amateur orchestra   bitter enemy
        ⌣   ⌣
        r   r

4 Ask students for suggestions and then get the class or individuals to repeat after you. Monitor the use of linking *r* and correct where necessary.

Extension

If you have a non-rhotic accent (see above), play the recording of the same pairs listed in step 1 *(four – four elephants, another – another ice cream,* etc.) said with a North American accent. Ask students if they notice a difference between British and North American English. They should observe that in North American English -*r* and -*re* words said alone are pronounced with an *r* sound at the end. For example, in North American English, *four* said alone is /fɔːr/ and in British English it is /fɔː/.

Box 34   Student handout

A

before	better	bigger
brother	enter	future	here
major	mother	near	teacher
under	war		

B

after	exit	far	father
minor	over	past	peace
sister	smaller	student	
there	worse		

Answer key

before and after, better and worse, bigger and smaller, brother and sister, enter and exit, future and past, here and there, major and minor, mother and father, near and far, teacher and student, under and over, war and peace

---

Box 35   Student handout

A

amateur   bitter   car   clever
end-of-year   fair   fire   inner
leather   newspaper   rare   rear
regular   severe   sour   upper

B

alarm   animal   arm
armchair   article   ear
earthquake   enemy   engine
estimate   exams   exercise
exit   idea   orange   orchestra

© Cambridge University Press 2004

Answer key

Likely answers: amateur orchestra, bitter enemy, car alarm, clever idea, end-of-year exams, fair estimate, fire engine, inner ear, leather armchair, newspaper article, rare animal, rear exit, regular exercise, severe earthquake, sour orange, upper arm. Other answers are possible (e.g. rear engine, fair exercise, clever animal).

Contracted forms (3.5–3.7)

3.5 Dialogues

Focus	Contracted forms
Level	Elementary+
Time	45 minutes
Preparation	Copy the material in Box 36 and Box 37 onto separate handouts or OHTs.

Procedure

1 Give out or display the material in Box 36. Say the sentences in A or play the recording, and students repeat each one, first chorally and then individually. Do the same with the sentences in B and C.

87

2   If necessary, explain how contractions are formed by writing on the board, for example:

It is blue. → It *is* blue. → It's blue.

3   Ask students to look at A again. Then ask the questions in random order from D in Box 37. Students answer with sentences from A. Do the same for the questions in E and answers in B, and then the questions in F and answers in C. Monitor contracted forms and correct where necessary.

4   Give out or display the material in Box 37. Chorally and individually, students repeat the questions in D, E and F after you or the recording. (Note there are no contracted forms in the questions in F.) Then students work in pairs to ask and answer questions. Monitor contracted forms and correct where necessary.

5   Ask pairs of students to write a short two-part question-answer dialogue, similar to those practised so far. The two parts should be labelled *A* and *B* and written on separate pieces of paper. There must be at least one contracted form in each part. Collect the papers, mix them up, and distribute them randomly around the class. Ask for a volunteer with an *A* part to read out their sentence. Any students who think they have the corresponding *B* part should read out their sentence. Students should continue reading out the sentences until the class (and you) are happy that all the pairs have been found. This may need some discussion if mistakes are made. Make sure students use contracted forms when they read out their sentences, and correct where necessary. Alternatively, do this as an activity where students move around the class looking for their 'partner'.

Box 36   Student handout

A	B	C
It's blue.	He's gone home.	No, I don't.
There's some here.	I've cut it.	No, he doesn't.
That's right.	It's disappeared.	No, I wasn't.
They're in my bag.	You've left it on your desk.	No, she can't.
I'm tired.	I've forgotten them.	No, I won't.

Box 37   Student handout

D	E	F
What colour's your bag?	Where's Sam?	Do you like coffee?
Where's the chalk?	What've you done	Does Tom like tea?
You're French,	to your finger?	Were you in town
aren't you?	Where's your ruler?	yesterday?
Where're your books?	Where's my pen?	Can Pat swim?
What's wrong?	Where're your books?	Don't forget your
		book tomorrow.

A	B	C
It's blue.	He's gone home.	No, I don't.
There's some here.	I've cut it.	No, he doesn't.
That's right.	It's disappeared.	No, I wasn't.
They're in my bag.	You've left it on your desk.	No, she can't.
I'm tired.	I've forgotten them.	No, I won't.

© Cambridge University Press 2004

3.6 Talking about families[1]

Focus	Contracted forms
Level	Elementary+
Time	20 minutes
Preparation	Copy the picture in Box 38 onto a handout or an OHT.

Procedure

1   Give out or display the handout. Focus on Picture 1. Say the sentences below aloud or play them on the recording. Students repeat chorally and individually. Make sure they produce contracted forms.

Judy's 34. Adrian's 35. They've been married for five years. They've got two children. Pat's three and David's two.

2   Ask students to make similar sentences about the family in Picture 2. Monitor the contracted forms and correct where necessary.

3   Make wrong sentences about the family in Picture 1. Elicit corrections from the students as in the following examples:

A: Judy's 35.
B: No, she's not (*or* she isn't). She's 34.

[1]   Based on Hewings, M. (1993, p. 74).

A: They've been married for seven years.

B: No, they haven't. They've been married for five years.

A: They've got three children.

B: No, they haven't. They've got two children.

Repeat for Picture 2. Then students work in pairs, making wrong sentences and correcting. Monitor contracted forms and correct where necessary.

4 Ask students to tell you about themselves and their own families using similar sentences with contracted forms. For example:

I'm 18. I'm (not) married. I've got two children/brothers/sisters.

They're 16 and 21. My brother's called Marcus. He's married to Jenny.

They've been married for three years. They haven't got any children.

Monitor contractions and correct where necessary.

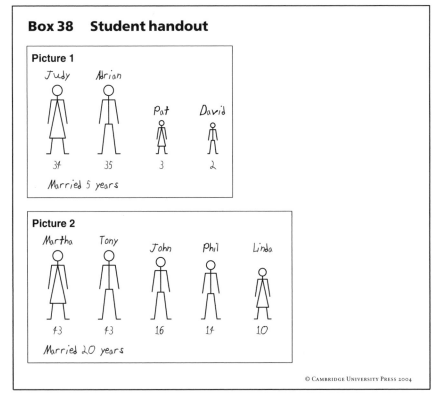

Box 38   Student handout

Picture 1

Judy Adrian   Pat   David

34   35   3   2

Married 5 years

Picture 2

Martha Tony John Phil Linda

43   43   16   14   10

Married 20 years

3.7 Comparing speech and writing

Focus	Marking possible contracted forms in written dialogues; saying contracted forms
Level	Intermediate+
Time	60 minutes
Preparation	Copy the material in Box 39 onto a handout. Copy the material in Box 40 onto a separate handout or an OHT.

Procedure

1   Give out the handout (Box 39). Students work in pairs to decide where contracted forms would be used in the dialogues if they were said at normal conversational speed. You may find it useful to introduce the idea of written contractions (= reductions such as *he's, I'll, we've,* etc. that are represented in writing) and blending (= reductions found in speech that may be, but are not often, represented in writing, such as *this'd [this would], why're [why are], couldn't've [could not have;* although *couldn't have* is found in writing], etc. In this activity students are asked to mark all contracted forms, both written contractions and blending.

2   Check answers. You might ask students when auxiliary verbs (e.g. *have, will, would*) are *not* normally contracted (in *yes/no* questions, e.g. *Have you seen the time?*, and when they occur at the end of a sentence, e.g. *Yes, I am sure it will*).

3   Give out the second handout with the contracted versions on (Box 40). Go through each dialogue a sentence at a time, asking students to repeat after you or the recording, chorally and individually. Check that the contracted forms are produced.

4   Students work in pairs, reading the dialogues. Monitor the contracted forms and correct where necessary.

5   Students work in pairs to write short, four-line dialogues like the ones practised so far. They should try to include at least one contracted form in each line and represent the contraction in the dialogue. (You could discuss later whether these are likely to be represented in written English.) The dialogues should be given to different pairs of students, who practise and then perform them to the class.

Box 39   Student handout

1

A: Where have you put the coffee?

B: It is in the cupboard.

A: There is none left.

B: Sorry. I would have bought some more if I had known.

2

A: What are you doing in the summer?

B: Tom and Mary have asked me to stay.

A: That will be nice.

B: Yes, I am sure it will.

3

A: Okay, let us go.

B: I am not ready.

A: Have you seen the time? We are going to be late.

B: Do not panic. The party will not have started yet.

4

A: Ann is coming over later.

B: How will she get here?

A: I do not know. She might have asked Ken for a lift.

B: I have not met Ken. It would be good to see him.

5

A: What is wrong?

B: I have lost my bike.

A: John might have borrowed it.

B: No, he would have asked me first.

A: I suppose he would.

6

A: I have made these biscuits. Would you like one?

B: That is kind. Urgh, they are so sweet.

A: I must have put too much sugar in.

B: Richard would like them. He will eat anything.

Box 40 Student handout

1

A: Where've you put the coffee?

B: It's in the cupboard.

A: There's none left.

B: Sorry. I'd've bought some more if I'd known.

2

A: What're you doing in the summer?

B: Tom and Mary've asked me to stay.

A: That'll be nice.

B: Yes, I'm sure it will.

3

A: Okay, let's go.

B: I'm not ready.

A: Have you seen the time? We're going to be late.

B: Don't panic. The party won't've started yet.

4

A: Ann's coming over later.

B: How'll she get here?

A: I don't know. She might've asked Ken for a lift.

B: I haven't met Ken. It'd be good to see him.

5

A: What's wrong?

B: I've lost my bike.

A: John might've borrowed it.

B: No, he'd've asked me first.

A: I suppose he would.

6

A: I've made these biscuits. Would you like one?

B: That's kind. Urgh, they're so sweet.

A: I must've put too much sugar in.

B: Richard'd like them. He'll eat anything.

Weak and strong forms of grammar words (3.8–3.10)

3.8 Comparing weak and strong forms

Focus	Comparing weak and strong forms of common grammar words
Level	Elementary+
Time	25 minutes
Preparation	Copy the material in Box 41 onto a handout or an OHT. Use either the left column or the right column (see step 2 below).

Procedure

1 If students aren't already familiar with the idea of weak and strong forms of common grammar words, introduce the idea. Write the following dialogue on the board:

   A: I've just had a letter.
   B: Who's it from? (i)
   A: It's from Jim. (ii)

   Say the dialogue. Ask students to listen to (i) and (ii) and note the pronunciation of *from* in each. In (i) it is pronounced with its strong form /frɒm/, and in (ii) it is pronounced with its weak form /frəm/. Explain that many short 'grammar' words have both a weak and a strong form: *have* (/hav/ vs /həv/), *can* (/kæn/ vs /kən/), *but* (/bʌt/ vs /bət/), etc.

2 Give out the material in Box 41. (The left column is easier, with only the weak forms omitted. The right column is more challenging with sentence beginnings and endings omitted. Choose *one* of these for your students.)

3 Play the sentences in Box 42 from the recording (making sure that the weak forms of the underlined words are used in the gaps in Box 41). Ask students to fill in the gaps in the sentences by writing what they hear.

4 Check the answers (see Box 42). Ask students to give complete sentence answers with weak forms. Don't ask them to say the individual words they have written as these will then be produced with their strong forms. If there are problems, demonstrate the weak forms in the whole sentence said aloud.

5 Say the sentences or play them on the recording. Students repeat chorally and individually. Monitor the weak forms and correct where necessary. Note that many of the weak forms marked could be said in their strong form depending on context, particularly if the word is being contrasted with another, or given stress for emphasis. For example: A: Did he throw the ball to you? B: No, he threw the ball at (/æt/) me. (contrast); You must (/mʌst/) come over for dinner soon. (emphasis)

Box 41   Student handout

1 .... threw the ball .... me.	1 .... threw the ball ....
2 You .... come over .... dinner soon.	2 .... come ....
3 Bill .... Mark .... left.	3 .... Mark ....
4 .... got more .... Tom?	4 .... got more ....
5 I .... home .... five o'clock.	5 .... home ....
6 .... talk about it .... lunch.	6 .... talk about it ....
7 Ask .... come .... the party.	7 .... come ....
8 .... tell .... now?	8 .... tell ....
9 .... going .... park.	9 .... going ....
10 When .... get the results .... tests?	10 .... get the results ....
11 .... in .... box.	11 .... more in ....
12 When .... taking .... see ....?	12 .... taking ....

Box 42   Teacher reference

(Sentences with weak forms marked)

1 He threw the ball at me.	/hi/ ... /ət/ ...
2 You must come over for dinner soon.	... /məs/ ... /fə/ ...
3 Bill and Mark have left.	... /ən/ ... /əv/ ...
4 Have you got more than Tom?	/həv ju/ ... /ðən/ ...
5 I was at home from five o'clock.	... /wəz ət/ ... /frəm/ ...
6 We could talk about it at lunch.	/wi kəd/ ... /ət/ ...
7 Ask them to come to the party.	... /ðəm tə/ ... /tə/ ...
8 Can you tell us now?	/kən ju/ ... /əs/ ...
9 We were going to the park.	/wi wə/ ... /tə ðə/ ...
10 When do you get the results of your tests?	... /də jə/ ... /əv jə/ ...
11 There should be some more in the box.	/ðə ʃəd bi səm/ ... /ðə/ ...
12 When are you taking him to see her?	... /ə ju/ ... /ɪm tə/ ... /ə/

3.9 Predicting weak and strong forms

This activity can be used after students are familiar with the idea that some common grammar words have weak and strong forms.

Focus Identifying when to use weak and strong forms of common grammar words

Level Intermediate+

Time 35 minutes

Preparation Copy the material in Box 43 onto a handout or an OHT.

Procedure

1 Give out the handout or display the OHT (Box 43). Students work in pairs to decide whether the underlined words are likely to be pronounced with their strong or weak form in each pair of dialogues (one will be pronounced with the strong form and the other the weak form).

2 Play the recording of the dialogues for students to check their predictions. As an alternative to using the recording, you could ask students to read the A parts and you read the B parts.

3 Say the B parts aloud. Students repeat chorally and individually. Then ask students to perform the dialogues. Monitor the weak and strong forms of the underlined words and correct when necessary.

4 Tell students that words like the ones underlined are normally said with their weak forms, but there are four situations in which they are given their strong forms. Ask them to work out when, using the information in the dialogues.

Extension

Write on the board some other words that have weak and strong forms, such as *them, at, to, can, have*. Students choose a word and work in pairs to write two short dialogues like those in Box 43, one in which the word is likely to be pronounced with its strong form and the other with its weak form.
Distribute these to other pairs of students, who practise and perform them.

Box 43   Student handout

1 a A: That cake smells good. B: Do you want <u>some</u>?
   b A: I'm hungry. B: There's <u>some</u> soup in the fridge.
2 a A: My music teacher is George Bush. B: Not *<u>the</u>* George Bush, surely.
   b A: Which is your house? B: It's <u>the</u> one on the right.
3 a A: Did you enjoy the film? B: I thought it <u>was</u> great.
   b A: I didn't see you at the meeting. Why weren't you there? B: I <u>was</u> there.
4 a A: Did you get any questions wrong? B: Just one. I spelt '<u>could</u>' C-U-L-D.
   b A: I'm going to the conference, too. B: Maybe we <u>could</u> go together.
5 a A: What are you reading? B: It's a letter <u>from</u> Alice.
   b A: Is this a present for Bob? B: No, it's <u>from</u> Bob.
6 a A: I'm going to Hungary next week. B: Are you going on <u>your</u> own?
   b A: Why did you put 'Mistake' here? B: You've written '<u>your</u>' instead of 'you'.
7 a A: I like those flowers. B: They're <u>for</u> Jane.
   b A: Have you got any matches? B: What do you need them <u>for</u>?
8 a A: What time do you have to be at work tomorrow? B: Well, I *<u>should</u>* be there by 7.30, but I don't like getting up early.
   b A: My new printer doesn't work properly. B: You <u>should</u> take it back.

Answer key
Strong forms are generally used: when the words come at the end of a sentence (1a, 7b); when the word is given special emphasis (2a, 8a); when the word is contrasted with another word (a special kind of emphasis) (3b – *weren't* vs *was*, 5b – *for* vs *from*); when the word is 'quoted' (4a, 6b).

3.10 Listening to weak forms

Focus	Identifying the number of weak forms in sentences
Level	Elementary
Time	15 minutes
Preparation	Copy the material in Box 44 onto a handout.

Procedure

1 Give students the handout (Box 44).

2 Say the full sentences (see Answer key) aloud or play the recording. Students write the number of unstressed words (not the words themselves) in the gaps.

3 Check the answers and then students repeat the sentences after you or the recording.

Box 44   Student handout

1 I wanted .... stay.
2 She went .... room.
3 When will you give .... back?
4 I knew .... did it.
5 It dropped .... floor.
6 What time .... here?
7 I dropped .... floor.
8 I asked .... money.
9 When will you give .... back?
10 She wanted .... stay.
11 We went .... room.
12 What time .... get here?
13 I asked .... money.
14 I knew .... did it.

© CAMBRIDGE UNIVERSITY PRESS 2004

Answer key

1 I wanted <u>her to</u> stay. (2)
2 She went <u>up to her</u> room. (3)
3 When will you give <u>them</u> back? (1)
4 I knew <u>that he</u> did it. (2)
5 It dropped <u>on the</u> floor. (2)

6 What time <u>can you be</u> here? (3)
7 I dropped <u>it on the</u> floor. (3)
8 I asked <u>him for</u> money. (2)
9 When will you give <u>me them</u> back? (2)
10 She wanted <u>to</u> stay. (1)
11 We went <u>to her</u> room. (2)
12 What time <u>does he</u> get here? (2)
13 I asked <u>him for some</u> money. (3)
14 I knew <u>she</u> did it. (1)

Leaving out sounds (3.11–3.12)

3.11 Leaving out consonants: /t/ and /d/ in clusters

See also Activity 3.2 for changes to the sounds /t/ and /d/ when they are at the end of a word and between a vowel and a consonant.

Focus Omitting /t/ and /d/ sounds in consonant clusters
Level Intermediate+
Time 25 minutes
Preparation Copy the material in Box 45 onto a handout or an OHT.

Procedure

1 Explain that words with consonant clusters are sometimes simplified because they are difficult to say. Write the word *mostly* on the board and show that the *t* is not usually pronounced when it is said at normal speed. Cross out the *t*, say the word a few times and ask students to repeat. Point out that /t/ and /d/ are the sounds most commonly missed out in clusters.

2 Give out the handout or display the OHT. Ask students to look at Part A. Say each word or play the recording. Students repeat chorally and individually. Monitor that the /t/ or /d/ is left out.

3 Students look at Part B. Explain that /t/ and /d/ are also sometimes left out when consonant clusters occur across word boundaries. Write *last month* on the board and illustrate the omission of *t* (in *last*) as you did in step 1. Ask students to work in pairs to decide in which of the phrases the word-final /t/ or /d/ are likely to be left out (they can indicate this by crossing out the *t* or *d* letters) and in which they are likely to be included. They should say the phrases quietly to each other as they do this.

4 Say the phrases (making sure that the /t/ or /d/ sounds are left out where this is likely) or play the recording. Students check their answers.

5 Students repeat the phrases chorally and individually. Monitor the /t/ and /d/ sounds and correct where necessary.

Extension

You could ask students to suggest rules for when /t/ and /d/ are *not* left out when they are the final consonant in a cluster at the end of a word. This exercise gives a partial picture. The full rules are that /t/ and /d/ are not left out: before a word beginning with a vowel, or the letters *l, w, h, y* or *r*; in the clusters *-lt, -nt, -rt, -rd* and *-red* (pronounced /rd/).

Box 45   Student handout

Part A

postman   correctly   wastepaper   facts   restless   lastly   exactly
friendly   kindness   handshake   hands   landscape   blindness
grandmother

Part B

1 It was next morning.	13 Did I hurt you?
2 Hold tight.	14 We reached Berlin.
3 She's world champion.	15 She arrived there.
4 It was just him.	16 We crossed over.
5 It's in first gear.	17 I phoned Keith.
6 Take a left turn.	18 It moved towards us.
7 I heard singing.	19 They're second hand.
8 She changed clothes.	20 He finished first.
9 I'll send Lucy.	21 I slept badly.
10 It was hard work.	22 I found Ruth.
11 They kept quiet.	23 I understand this.
12 It looked good.	24 I felt bad.

Answer key

1 It was nex~~t~~ morning.	9 I'll send Lucy.	17 I phone~~d~~ Keith.
2 Hol~~d~~ tight.	10 It was hard work.	18 It move~~d~~ towards us.
3 She's worl~~d~~ champion.	11 They kep~~t~~ quiet.	19 They're second hand.
4 It was just him.	12 It looke~~d~~ good.	20 He finishe~~d~~ first.
5 It's in firs~~t~~ gear.	13 Did I hurt you?	21 I slep~~t~~ badly.
6 Take a lef~~t~~ turn.	14 We reache~~d~~ Berlin.	22 I found Ruth.
7 I heard singing.	15 She arrive~~d~~ there.	23 I understan~~d~~ this.
8 She change~~d~~ clothes.	16 We crossed over.	24 I fel~~t~~ bad.

3.12 Leaving out vowels in words

Focus	Omitting vowel sounds in words
Level	Intermediate+
Time	20 minutes
Preparation	Copy the material in Box 46 onto a handout.

Procedure

1 Explain that in some words, vowel sounds that are pronounced when the word is said slowly and carefully are left out when the words are said at normal speed in conversation. Illustrate by writing the word *average* on the board. First say it slowly and carefully with its full form /ˈævərɪdʒ/ and then its usual, reduced form /ˈævrɪdʒ/. Cross out the sound that is omitted: *av~~e~~rage*.

2 Give out the handout (Box 46). Focus on Part A. Students work in pairs to predict and cross out the vowel sound which is left out of each word in its usual pronunciation.

3 Check the answers. Then say each word in its reduced form or play the recording. Students repeat chorally and individually. Monitor and correct when necessary.

4 Focus on Part B. Students should use the words in Part A to complete the phrases in Part B.

5 When students report their answers they should say the complete phrase and use the reduced form of the words. Monitor and correct where necessary.

Box 46   Student handout

Part A

camera   definite   every   factory   family   favourite   history
marvellous   police   recovery   reference   secretary   separate
similar   strawberry   traveller

Part B

1 A .... friend.
2 Modern ....
3 A .... plant.
4 A car ....
5 .... time.
6 A great ....
7 Remarkably ....
8 A personal ....

9 A .... officer.
10 A digital ....
11 Absolutely ....
12 A frequent ....
13 A .... book.
14 A .... answer.
15 Entirely ....
16 An amazing ....

© CAMBRIDGE UNIVERSITY PRESS 2004

Answer key

Part A: cam$e$ra, def$i$nite, ev$e$ry, fact$o$ry, fam$i$ly, favo$u$rite, hist$o$ry, marv$e$llous, p$o$lice, recov$e$ry, ref$e$rence, secret$a$ry, sep$a$rate, sim$i$lar, strawb$e$rry, trav$e$ller.
Most likely answers for Part B: 1 family, 2 history, 3 strawberry, 4 factory,
5 Every, 6 favourite, 7 similar, 8 secretary, 9 police, 10 camera, 11 marvellous,
12 traveller, 13 reference, 14 definite, 15 separate, 16 recovery.

Syllables, word stress and stress in phrases

Syllables (4.1–4.3)

4.1 How many syllables?

Focus	Identifying the number of syllables in words
Level	Elementary
Time	15 minutes
Preparation	Prepare a list of words familiar to students. There should be the same number of words with one, two, three, four and five syllables. Write them randomly on the board, a handout or an OHT. Alternatively, use the words in Box 47.

Procedure

1 Focus students on the list of words. Students group the words according to the number of syllables. Tell them they should find the same number of words in each group, or tell them how many words with the same number of syllables they should find (four for each group in Box 47).
2 Elicit from students the five lists of words with the same number of syllables. Correct pronunciation where necessary.

Box 47   Student handout

pedestrian   university   umbrella   cow   winter   potato
supermarket   magazine   accommodation   dress   country
information   difficult   congratulations   boat   ago   upstairs
cook   January   communication

Answer key
1 syllable: cow, dress, boat, cook
2 syllables: upstairs, winter, country, ago
3 syllables: umbrella, potato, magazine, difficult
4 syllables: information, supermarket, January, pedestrian
5 syllables: university, accommodation, congratulations, communication

Extension

Students work in pairs to produce a new version of Box 47, using words from their coursebook or their own ideas. They could write this on the board or an OHT, and then repeat the procedure above. They should also produce an answer key, listing the words with the same number of syllables.

4.2 The same or different number of syllables?

	For intermediate students, follow the Variation.
Focus	Identifying the number of syllables in pairs of words
Level	Elementary/Intermediate
Time	15–20 minutes
Preparation	Prepare a list of ten pairs of words. The words in each pair should have the same or a different number of syllables. Alternatively, use the words in Box 48. Don't give students a written list of the words.

Procedure

1 Students write the numbers *1* to *10* in their notebooks. Say the pairs of words and students write *S* if they hear the same number of syllables and *D* if they hear a different number. Check the answers.

2 Students work alone or in pairs to produce their own list of ten pairs of 'same' and 'different' words. Then follow step 1, with each student reading out their ten pairs and the rest of the class writing the answers.

Box 48   Teacher reference

		Answer
1 sandwich (2) – April (2)	S
2 majority (4) – exercise (3)	D
3 pollution (3) – competition (4)	D
4 horse (1) – choose (1)	S
5 guitar (2) – homework (2)	S
6 twice (1) – colour (2)	D
7 helicopter (4) – American (4)	S
8 museum (3) – abroad (2)	D
9 before (2) – computer (3)	D
10 timetable (3) – afternoon (3)	S

(The number of syllables in each word is given in brackets.)

Variation

For intermediate students, follow the same procedure, but use short phrases or sentences. You may need to repeat each one, two or three times. Example material is given in Box 49. Don't give students a written list of the phrases/sentences.

Box 49   Teacher reference

		Answer
1	Tom's in Spain. (3) – She's inside. (3)	S
2	What are you afraid of? (6) – Nice to see you again. (6)	S
3	Give these to Pauline. (5) – She's over there. (4)	D
4	Can I try it on? (5) – I saw it on TV. (6)	D
5	Highly unlikely. (5) – Hang on a minute. (5)	S
6	Put it on the top shelf. (6) – We should be going. (5)	D
7	I've got nothing to do. (6) – Absolutely fantastic. (7)	D
8	A coffee, please. (4) – In the summer. (4)	S
9	I want to go tomorrow. (7) – The homework was difficult. (7)	S
10	Leave it in the kitchen. (6) – Some time on Tuesday. (5)	D

(The number of syllables in each phrase/sentence is given in brackets.)

4.3 Eliminating words

	For intermediate students, follow the Variation.
Focus	Identifying the number of syllables in words
Level	Elementary/Intermediate
Time	15 minutes
Preparation	Prepare a list of 15–20 words familiar to students. There should be about the same number of words with two, three, four and five syllables. Write them randomly on the board. You could use some of the words from Box 47.

Procedure

1 Chorally and individually, practise the pronunciation of the words on the board.

2 Call out numbers from two to five. Students find a word on the board with that number of syllables. The first student to raise a hand and give a correct answer or shout out a word with that number of syllables gets one point (for themselves or their group). That word is then

deleted from the list and the game continues until all the words are crossed out.

3   Ask pairs of students to write down four words (different from those used so far), with two, three, four and five syllables. Collect these in and write a selection on the board. Repeat the procedure in steps 2 and 3 above.

Variation

For intermediate students, follow the same procedure, but include some words that may be said with either three syllables, or two when they are at normal conversational speed. Students only get a point if they can say the word with the number of syllables that they claim it has. You could use some words from Box 46, and below are a few more examples. The vowel sounds left out when the word is spoken at conversational speed are in square brackets.

comf[or]table   caref[u]lly   nurs[e]ry   p[e]rhaps (pronounced *praps*)
prob[ab]ly   rest[au]rant   sev[e]ral

Word stress (4.4–4.15)

4.4 Demonstrating syllable length

	This activity is intended to demonstrate that stressed syllables are longer than unstressed syllables.
Focus	Identifying stressed and unstressed syllables in words
Level	Elementary+
Time	5 minutes

Procedure

1   Say a number of words familiar to students. These should have a variety of number of syllables (always more than one) and stress patterns. For example, you could take words from Box 66 (p. 133). As you say each word, do a short, quiet clap for each unstressed syllable, and a longer, louder clap for each stressed syllable. Students repeat and make the same clapping movements with you.

2   Write a few more words on the board. Individuals say them aloud and clap at the same time, demonstrating the number of syllables and stress pattern. Correct where necessary.

Variations

1 Instead of clapping, use a thick elastic band. Hold the elastic band at two ends, pulling it a little at each unstressed syllable and pulling it a lot at each stressed syllable.[1]

2 Demonstrate syllable length by writing words with the unstressed syllables in squashed-together lower case letters and stressed syllables in spread-out capital letters. For example:

S E N T ence   par T I C ularly   after N O O N

4.5 Matching words with their stress patterns

Focus	Identifying words by their stress pattern
Level	Intermediate
Time	20 minutes
Preparation	Copy the material in Box 50 onto a handout or an OHT.

Procedure

1 Give out the handout (Box 50) or display the OHT. Ask students to focus on the words in the box at the top and to repeat them after you or the recording. (Alternatively, ask them to say the words to themselves, paying attention to the stress pattern; if they are unsure about stress in any of the words they should check this in their dictionary.)

2 Students complete each sentence in Box 50 with one of the words at the top that has the stress pattern indicated at the end of the sentence. Warn them that they can't guess the answers only from the meaning of the sentences as there is more than one possibility each time. They need to check the stress pattern to find the correct word.

3 Read out the answers for students to check. Students then repeat the dialogues after you before saying them in pairs. Monitor and correct stress placement where necessary.

---

[1] This idea comes from Judy Gilbert. See for example, Gilbert, J. B. (2001).

Box 50   Student handout

| above   accountant   biology   calculation   economics |
| engineer   experiment   guitar   over   trumpet |

1 A: Where did you put John's photo? B: It's .... the door. oO

2 A: What's Sue doing at college? B: She's studying .... ooOo

3 A: What does Pat do? B: He's an .... oOo

4 A: David's quite musical, isn't he?
   B: Yes, he plays the .... oO

5 A: What do you like best at school? B: I really like .... oOoo

6 A: What did you do in maths today?
   B: A really difficult .... ooOo

7 A: Was Jack hurt when he fell off his bike?
   B: He just got a small cut .... his left eye. Oo

8 A: What was the exam like?
   B: We had an easy .... to do. oOoo

9 A: Do you play any musical instruments?
   B: I used to play the .... Oo

10 A: What does Maria want to do when she leaves university?
   B: She wants to be an .... ooO

Answer key

1 above, 2 economics, 3 accountant, 4 guitar, 5 biology, 6 calculation, 7 over,
8 experiment, 9 trumpet, 10 engineer.

4.6 Group the words

Focus	Classifying words according to their stress pattern
Level	Elementary+
Time	15 minutes
Preparation	List 20 or so recently learned words with more than one syllable and compounds, making sure that there are a number of words with each stress pattern. (Alternatively, use the ones in Box 51.)

Procedure

Write the words/compounds randomly on the board, or write and display them on an OHT. Students classify them according to their stress pattern. They should group them under patterns such as: Oo, oO, Oo, ooO, etc. When they report back their answers, correct pronunciation if necessary, focusing on any wrong stress placement.

Extension

For more advanced students, include some examples where there are alternative stress patterns, and discuss these. You could include words such as *Japanese* which have shifting stress (see Introduction, p. 5). For example, the word *Japanese* might be said with stress on the third or the first syllable. The stress in *She's <u>Japanese</u>* is likely to be o oo<u>O</u>, while in *She's a <u>Japanese</u> author* it may be either o o <u>Ooo</u> Oo or o o oo<u>O</u> Oo. So the stress pattern of the words said in isolation might best be represented as OoO. Some more examples of words and compounds with variable stress like this are given in Activities 4.20 and 4.21. You could also include words such as *object*, which have different stress patterns depending on whether they are used as verb or noun: *object* (oO) = verb; *object* (Oo) = noun. Some more examples of words like this are given in Activity 4.11.

Box 51   Teacher reference

Example words	*Stress pattern*
curtains, flower, tea towel	Oo
around, giraffe, guitar	oO
basketball, countryside, furniture, frying pan, traffic jam	Ooo
December, hot chocolate, museum, romantic	oOo
incorrect, understand	ooO
primary school, supermarket, windscreen wipers	Oooo

4.7 Country names

> Students need first to be familiar with representing syllables and word stress using O for stressed and o for unstressed syllables,
> e.g. *language* = Oo; *pronunciation* = oooOo.

Focus Identifying words by their stress pattern

Level Elementary+

Time 25 minutes

Procedure

1 Write on the board the following series of stress patterns:
    Oo → ooOo → oOoo → oO → O → ooO → Ooo → oOo
   and the following country names in random order:
    Estonia, France, Germany, Japan, New Zealand, Norway, Singapore, Venezuela

2 Say the country names and students repeat after you.

3 Explain that Jane is a businesswoman who travels all over the world. In the last year she has visited eight different counties. The students need to find out what order she visited the countries listed above. The stress patterns written on the board show the order. Her first trip was to Norway (Oo). (Answer: Norway [Oo] → Venezuela [ooOo] → Estonia [oOoo] → Japan [oO] → France [O] → Singapore [ooO] → Germany [Ooo] → New Zealand [oOo].)

4 Ask a few students to give their answers, and correct any wrong pronunciations and stress patterns.

5 Write some more examples on the board and repeat the procedure in steps 1–4. Use the information about country names and their stress patterns given below.

1 syllable		2 syllables		3 syllables		4 syllables	
Wales	O	Belgium	Oo	Angola	oOo	Algeria	oOoo
Greece	O	China	Oo	Zimbabwe	oOo	Nigeria	oOoo
Chad	O	Finland	Oo	Austria	Ooo	Venezuela	ooOo
Spain	O	Taiwan	oO	Canada	Ooo	Madagascar	ooOo
		Sudan	oO	Cameroon	ooO	Azerbaijan	oooO
		Nepal	oO	Mozambique	ooO	Uzbekistan	oooO

Extensions

1 Students write their own versions of the exercise, using different countries and making sure there is only one country having each stress pattern. Other students or the whole class try to solve these new versions.

2 Use the same procedure in different contexts. For example, people standing in a queue at a bus stop all had different jobs. What order were they in? For example, write:
    Oo → Ooo → oOo → ooO → oOoo → Oooo
   and the jobs:
    solicitor, hairdresser, teacher, engineer, decorator, mechanic
   (Answer: teacher [Oo] → hairdresser [Ooo] → mechanic [oOo] → engineer [ooO] → solicitor [oOoo] → decorator [Oooo].)

Here are some more jobs with their stress patterns:

1 syllable		*2 syllables*		*3 syllables*		*4 syllables*	
judge	O	artist	Oo	carpenter	Ooo	receptionist	oOoo
chef	O	dentist	Oo	astronaut	Ooo	librarian	oOoo
nurse	O	farmer	Oo	detective	oOo	economist	oOoo
vet	O	doctor	Oo	optician	oOo	psychologist	oOoo
		cashier	oO	accountant	oOo	politician	ooOo
		masseur	oO			dietician	ooOo
						electrician	ooOo

3   Include compounds for more advanced students. You could add some of
    the jobs below to those given above. Note that some of these have two
    main stresses (see Introduction, pp. 4–5).

3 syllables		*4 syllables*		*5+ syllables*	
bus driver	Ooo	shop assistant	Oooo	safety officer	Ooooo
street sweeper	Ooo	taxi driver	Oooo	refuse collector	Ooooo
farm worker	Ooo	research worker	oOoo	civil engineer	OoooO
art dealer	Ooo	civil servant	OoOo	police officer	oOooo
				security guard	oOooo
				personnel officer	ooOooo

4.8 At the supermarket

Focus	Identifying words by their stress pattern
Level	Elementary+
Time	10 minutes
Preparation	Prepare a list of about ten items found in a supermarket. These should all have different numbers of syllables or stress patterns. Include two-word compounds with one main stress (e.g. *washing powder* [Oooo]), and for intermediate students include two-word compounds with two main stresses (e.g. *chocolate biscuits* [OoOo]). Don't include items with the pattern *a ... of ...* (e.g. *a bottle of wine*). Possible examples (together with their stress patterns) for elementary students are: *soap* (O), *butter* (Oo), *shampoo* (oO), *pineapple* (Ooo), *potatoes* (oOo), *lemonade* (ooO), *washing powder* (Oooo), *tomato juice* (oOoo), *avocados* (ooOo). Possible examples (together with their stress patterns) for intermediate students are: *carrots* (Oo), *courgettes* (oO), *apricots* (Ooo), *sultanas* (oOo), *margarine* (ooO), *paper plates* (OoO), *chocolate biscuits* (OoOo), *blackcurrant jam* (OooO), *coriander* (ooOo), *sun-dried tomatoes* (OooOo).

Procedure

1   Write the prepared list of words on the board in random order. Write just the words, not the stress patterns. Give students a few minutes to try to remember the words.

2   Rub the words out, and in random order write up the stress patterns of the words (oOo, oO, etc.). It can help to write a number next to each one. Students point to a pattern (or say the number) and then give the word from the list having that pattern. If correct, they score a point and the pattern is rubbed off the board. Continue until all the patterns are removed. The winner is the person/team with most points.

Variations

1   After step 1, rub the words out and write up only the stress patterns in a numbered order.

Start with this: End with only this:

1 lemonade	5 shampoo		1 ooO	5 oO
2 pineapple	6 potatoes	→	2 Ooo	6 oOo
3 soap	7 butter		3 O	7 Oo
4 washing powder	8 tomato juice		4 Oooo	8 oOoo

The first student begins: 'I went to the supermarket and bought some lemonade' (stress pattern 1). The second student continues: 'I went to the supermarket and bought some lemonade and a pineapple' (stress patterns 1 and 2). The remaining students continue in the same way, remembering what has come before and adding an item to the list. They are eliminated if they make a mistake (either in remembering the word or getting the wrong stress pattern) and the turn moves to the next student. Students may substitute words not in the original list, provided that they have the correct stress pattern.

2   Don't use a pre-set list of words for the 'I went to the supermarket...' memory activity. Instead, write a list of numbered stress patterns on the board (such as the possible list opposite) and ask students to suggest items themselves which they can buy in a supermarket and which match these patterns. You could use some of the examples given above, but some other example items (with only one main stress) are given opposite.

Possible list of stress patterns:

1 ooO	6 Oooo	11 oO
2 Oo	7 oOoo	12 Oo
3 oOoo	8 oOo	13 Ooo
4 oOo	9 Oooo	14 Oo
5 Ooo	10 Ooo	15 ooO

Example items:
Oo: coffee, ice cream, sugar, apples
Ooo: marmalade, cabbages, oranges, shower gel
oOo: salami, tomatoes, spaghetti, satsumas
ooO: mayonnaise
Oooo: tonic water, talcum powder
oOoo: deodorant

4.9 Stress patterns in -*ty* and -*teen* numbers (1): Bingo

	We usually distinguish between -*ty* and -*teen* numbers (e.g. *30* vs *13*, *90* vs *19*) more on the basis of stress (THIRTy vs thirTEEN) than on the *n* sound at the end of -*teen*. Activities 4.9 and 4.10 focus on this feature.
Focus	Distinguishing between -*ty* and -*teen* numbers on the basis of stress pattern
Level	Elementary+
Time	15 minutes

Procedure

1 Write the numbers *13, 14, 15, 16, 17, 18, 19, 30, 40, 50, 60, 70, 80, 90* on the board. Each student chooses six of the numbers and writes them on a piece of paper. Call the numbers out at random and students cross them off their lists when they hear them. Make sure that you stress the second syllable in the -*teen* numbers (thirTEEN, fourTEEN, etc.) and the first in the -*ty* numbers (THIRTy, FORTy, etc.). The first student to cross out all six numbers shouts out *Bingo*, and they are the winner if they have crossed out the correct numbers.

2 Check by asking the winner to read back their numbers.

Variations

1   Instead of just saying the numbers, say sentences with the numbers in context. Some possible sentence frames are given in Box 52. Use the numbers at the end of sentences or followed by an unstressed word. Make sure that you stress the second syllable in the *-teen* numbers (thirTEEN, fourTEEN, etc.) and the first in the *-ty* numbers (THIRTy, FORTy, etc.). (See Variation 2 for the reason.)

2   As in Variation 1, say sentences with the numbers in context. This time, however, include examples of *-teen* numbers with stress shift when they are followed by a stressed syllable. If you use the *-teen* numbers followed by a word beginning with a stressed syllable, the stress usually shifts to the first syllable. Compare:

   fifTEEN   but   FIFteen YEARS

(For more details, see Introduction, p. 5.)

Some possible sentence frames for this are given in Box 53. You could replace some of the frames in Box 52 with these.

Box 52   Teacher reference

1   His office is number (13/30).
2   Next birthday he'll be (13/30).
3   There were (13/30) of them.
4   Do questions 1 to (13/30) for homework.
5   Turn to page (13/30).
6   It costs 4 dollars, (13/30).
7   She'll be (13/30) on Friday.
8   The plane leaves from gate (13/30).

Box 53   Teacher reference

1   It costs (13/30) dollars. (... THIRteen DOLLars / THIRTy DOLLars)
2   I've got (13/30) cousins. (... THIRteen COUSins / THIRTy COUSins)
3   There are (13/30) children in the class. (... THIRteen CHILDRen / THIRTy CHILDRen ...)
4   The book only has (13/30) pages. (...THIRteen PAGes / THIRTy PAGes ...)
5   There were (13/30) thousand people in the crowd. (... THIRteen THOUSand / THIRTy THOUSand ...)

4.10 Stress patterns in *-ty* and *-teen* numbers (2): talking about accommodation

Focus	Distinguishing between *-ty* and *-teen* numbers on the basis of stress pattern
Level	Intermediate
Time	25 minutes
Preparation	Copy the material in Box 55 (for half the class) and 56 (for the other half) onto separate handouts. For the demonstration, write the information about house 1 in just one copy of Box 55.

Procedure

1 Write the following on the board:

O o   o O
She's thirty.   She's thirteen.

O o O o o   O o O o o
She was thirty yesterday.   She was thirteen yesterday.

Students repeat the sentences after you, chorally and individually. Point out (if the students don't already know) that stress can be shifted in the *-teen* words: *She's thirTEEN* vs *She was THIRteen YESterday*. (For more information, see Activity 4.9 or Introduction, p. 5.) Repeat a few times with some of the 14/40, 15/50, etc. pairs (up to 19/90).

2 Do a quick listening quiz. Say sentences such as 'She's ninety', 'She was fourteen yesterday', etc., and students write down the numbers they hear: *90, 14*, etc. You could use the frames in Box 52 (without stress shift) and Box 53 (with stress shift).

3 Organise the students into Student A/B pairs. Give one of the handouts (Box 55) to Student A and the other (Box 56) to Student B.

4 Explain the context: Students A and B are looking for accommodation to rent together while studying at college / university / a language school (whichever is relevant to your context). They have each found different things out about advertised accommodation and are now back home sharing this information (the address, the rent per week, the distance from the college/university/school, the bus number, and the time the bus journey takes). They have to complete their table by asking each other questions.

5 Demonstrate the activity. Call one of the students to the front and give them the copy of Box 55 that you prepared earlier with the added information about house 1. You take one of the blank copies. Ask this

student questions abut house 1 and write the information you get on your handout. Show that answers can be checked if necessary by saying 'Sorry, did you say… or …?' The conversation might go, for example:

Teacher (T): What's the address of the first house?

Student (S): 80, Black Road.

T: Sorry, did you say 80 (EIGHty) or 18 (eighTEEN)? S: 80.

(You then write down the answer.)

T: How much does it cost? S: 116 pounds a week.

T: How far is it from the college? S: 18 kilometres.

T: Sorry, did you say 80 (EIGHty) or 18 (eighTEEN)? S: 18.

T: How long does it take? S: 40 minutes.

T: What's the bus number? S: 17.

T: Sorry, did you say 70 (SEVenty) or 17 (sevenTEEN)? S: 17.

6 The rest of the class should add the information to their sheets at the same time. At the end of the demonstration, ask students to check any information they didn't get or weren't sure about, with the student at the front. Encourage them to use the 'Sorry, did you say … or …?' pattern demonstrated.

7 Students then work in pairs, asking each other questions to complete their handouts. When they have finished, they should compare handouts and check that they have the correct information. During this time, monitor and correct stress in numbers.

Extensions

1 At the end of the activity, ask students to discuss which accommodation they would prefer to have and why. If they don't make the *-teen/-ty* numbers clear in the discussion, ask 'Sorry, did you say … or …?', and encourage other students to do the same.

2 Having formally introduced and practised this point of pronunciation in the activity, try to repeat it as the occasion arises in the classroom. For example, when asking students to open their books at a particular page, give them the opportunity to check numbers:

T: Can you turn to page 70 (mumbled, or said quietly), please?

S: Sorry, did you say 70 or 17?

or to clarify numbers for you:

T: What room is your next class in? S: G13.

T: Sorry, did you say G13 or G30?

Box 54   Teacher reference

Accommodation	1	2	3	4	5
Address	80, Black Rd	50, Blue Rd	19, Green Rd	16, Red Rd	40, White Rd
How much?	£116/wk	£70/wk	£117/wk	£180/wk	£60/wk
Bus number?	17	60	13	14	90
How far?	18 km	19 km	14 km	16 km	13 km
How long?	40 min	50 min	30 min	40 min	60 min

Box 55   Student A handout

Accommodation	1	2	3	4	5
Address		50, Blue Rd	19, Green Rd		
How much?		£70/wk			£60/wk
Bus number?			13	14	
How far?			14 km	16 km	
How long?		50 min			60 min

Box 56   Student B handout

Accommodation	1	2	3	4	5
Address				16, Red Rd	40, White Rd
How much?			£117/wk	£180/wk	
Bus number?		60			90
How far?		19 km			13 km
How long?			30 min	40 min	

4.11 Stress in noun–verb pairs

Focus	Identifying different stress patterns when the same word is used as a noun or a verb
Level	Advanced
Time	20 minutes
Preparation	Copy the material in Box 57 onto a handout.

Procedure

1 Give out the handout (Box 57) and ask students to look at Part A. Explain that some words, such as the three in the box, have different stress patterns when they are used as a noun or a verb. Say the sentences aloud or play them on the recording, and ask students to use the sentences to complete the rule at the bottom of Part A.

2 Focus on Part B. Students decide whether the words given are used as a noun or verb in each sentence and where stress should be placed.

3 Students say the sentences aloud. Say each sentence after the student (or play the recording) and ask other students to check whether the student was using the correct stress in the target word.

Extension

Prepare a similar exercise with other words that have this feature: *combine, compound, conflict, contest, contrast, convict, decrease, defect, extract, insult, misprint, perfect, produce, protest, rebel, reject, survey, upset.* Note that the nouns *export* and *import* are stressed on the first syllable: EXport, IMport. As verbs these words usually have stress on the second syllable: exPORT, imPORT, but may be stressed on the first syllable with stress shift (see Introduction, p. 5): We EXport SHOES / They IMport CARS.

Answer key

Part A: 1 noun: CONtract, 2 verb: conTRACT, 3 noun: PERmit, 4 verb: perMIT, 5 noun: RECord, 6 verb: reCORD.

Rule: used as nouns – stress on the first syllable; used as verbs – stress on the second syllable.

Part B: 1 verb: conDUCT, 2 noun: PRESent, 3 noun: SUSpect, 4 noun: OBject, 5 noun: PROduce, 6 verb: preSENT, 7 verb: disCOUNT, 8 noun: CONduct, 9 verb: proDUCE, 10 verb: susPECT, 11 verb: obJECT, 12 noun: DIScount.

Box 57   Student handout

Part A

contract	permit	record

1. They won the contract to build the new museum.
2. As they cool, metals contract.
3. You need a permit to fish here.
4. The rules don't permit mobile phones in the school.
5. The time was a new world record.
6. I asked if I could record her lecture.

Rule
When these words are used as nouns they have stress on the
.... syllable, and when they are used as verbs they have
stress on the .... syllable.

Part B

conduct	discount	object	present	produce	suspect

1. I've always wanted to conduct an orchestra.
2. She gave me a watch as a present.
3. Thomas was the main suspect in the crime.
4. What's that strange object on the top shelf?
5. The vegetable shop sold only local produce.
6. It's my pleasure to present Dr Stevens.
7. We can't discount the possibility that John has had an accident.
8. The children's conduct during the concert was excellent.
9. I have to produce the report by the end of the week.
10. When she asked for money I began to suspect her honesty.
11. Would anyone object if we finish the meeting early?
12. Will you give me a discount on the price if I buy three?

4.12 Rules of word stress in two-syllable nouns, adjectives and verbs

Focus	Identifying stressed and unstressed syllables in two-syllable nouns, adjectives and verbs
Level	Elementary to Intermediate
Time	15 minutes
Preparation	Copy the material in Box 58 onto the board, an OHT or a handout. If you use the board or an OHT, you should start by asking students to copy the noun / verb / adjective columns and the gapped rule into their notebooks. If you are going to do the extension, copy the material in Box 59 onto an OHT or a handout. (It could go on the same handout as Box 58.)

Procedure

1 Give or show students the material in Box 58. Ask them to write the two-syllable words in the box under the correct heading: Noun, Verb or Adjective.

2 Say the words (all the nouns first: *bottle, brother, pencil, pocket*; then the verbs: *carry, forget, begin, happen*; and finally the adjectives: *famous, happy, lovely, yellow*). Students check their answers. Repeat and ask students to mark the syllables in the words as stressed or unstressed (for example, by putting O over the stressed syllable and o over the unstressed).

3 Students use the information in the table to complete the general rule about stress in two-syllable words. Tell them that the gaps should be filled with the words *nouns, verbs* and *adjectives*. (Answer: nouns, adjectives, verbs.)

Extension

Give or show students the text in Box 59 and ask them to identify all two-syllable nouns and adjectives. Remind them that the rule they have just learned applies to most, but not all, nouns and adjectives. Ask them which ones don't follow the rule. (Note that verbs are not highlighted here as the tendency in verbs is less definite than with nouns and adjectives, as the second sentence of the rule in Box 58 shows.) Read the text aloud or play the recording. Students check their answers.

Box 58   Student handout

bottle	brother	carry	forget	famous	happy
lovely	pencil	pocket	begin	happen	yellow

Noun	Verb	Adjective
....	....	....
....	....	....
....	....	....
....	....	....

Rule

Most two-syllable .... and .... have stress on the first syllable. Some two-syllable .... are stressed on the first and some on the second syllable.

Box 59   Student handout

I had a letter from my brother Paul yesterday. He was very angry and upset. He's a guitarist and he was going to Japan to give some concerts. But at the airport his guitar was stolen. He called the police, of course. They were very polite and friendly and took his address, but told him he would be very lucky to get it back. He still had his passport and tickets, but couldn't go without his guitar.

Stress and word formation (4.13–4.17)

Activities 4.13 to 4.15 look at the relationship between pronunciation and word stress. Although English word-stress rules are complicated, generalisations can be made that relate word formation, particularly suffixes, to stress and pronunciation. Some of these are presented in Appendix 4. While it would be difficult to learn every application of these rules in total, it can be useful to focus on particular words with particular suffixes or groups of suffixes. By the time they do the suggested activities below, students should already be familiar with the idea that words are divided into syllables (e.g. Activity 4.1) and that one of these syllables takes main stress (e.g. Activity 4.4). They should also have been taught a way of marking main stress (e.g. Activity 4.7) and should have had experience of looking up word stress in a dictionary (e.g. Activity 8.1). Rules of word stress associated with suffixes are probably best taught at post-intermediate levels as the vocabulary involved is likely to be very difficult for lower-level students.

4.13 Rules of word stress: prefixes and suffixes

This activity is a general introduction to the relationship between word stress and prefixes and suffixes. It should be used before Activities 4.14 and 4.15, which look in more detail at particular aspects of word stress and suffixes.

Focus Identifying the influence of suffixes on word stress
Level Upper-intermediate
Time 40 minutes
Preparation Copy the material in Box 60 onto a handout. For this activity, each student should have access to a dictionary that shows stress patterns in words.

Procedure

1 Explain that some common word suffixes influence word stress. Some
usually cause the syllable before the suffix to be stressed and others don't.
Illustrate with:

O o   o Oo   O o o   o O oo

athlete *but* athletic   infinite *but* infinity

(so the suffixes *-ic* and *-ity* cause the syllable before the suffix to be
stressed)

O o   O o o o

fashion *and* fashionable

(so the suffix *-able* doesn't change the stress from that in the 'root'
word)

If you feel that your students lack confidence in understanding stress
markings in dictionaries, ask them to look up the six words and note how
stress is represented.

2 Give students the handout (Box 60). Ask them to:

- underline the suffixes

- give the 'root' word for each (you could just say 'Find the word these
  come from')

- say which ones are like *-ic* (i.e. they cause the syllable before the suffix
  to be stressed) and which ones are like *-able* (i.e. they don't usually
  change stress placement).

Encourage students to use their dictionaries, particularly for the last task.

3 Check the answers. Finally, say the words aloud, or play the recording,
and students repeat.

Box 60   Student handout

historical   consistency   solidify   managerial
punishment   rapidly   politeness   ability   political
presidency   bottomless   beautiful   acidify   investigation
uniformity   willingness   powerless   conservation   purposeful
government   substantial   immediately

Answer key

Suffixes that usually cause the syllable before the suffix to be stressed include: *-ity, -ial, -ion, -ical,* and *-ify.* These words with their roots are: *uniform–uniformity, able–ability; substance–substantial, manager–managerial; investigate–investigation, conserve–conservation; history–historical, politics–political; solid–solidify, acid–acidify*

Suffixes that don't usually change stress placement from that in the 'root' word include: *-cy, -ful, -ment, -less, -ly,* and *-ness.* These words with their roots are: *president–presidency, consistent–consistency; purpose–purposeful, beauty–beautiful; punish–punishment, govern–government; bottom–bottomless, power–powerless; rapid–rapidly, immediate–immediately; polite–politeness, willing–willingness*

4.14 Suffixes and word stress: words ending *-ian*[2]

Students should have done Activity 4.13 before this one. Activity 4.13 is a general introduction to the relationship between word stress and prefixes and suffixes, while this activity looks in particular at the suffix *-ian.*

Focus Identifying the relationship between the suffix *-ian* and word stress

Level Upper-intermediate+

Time 25 minutes

Preparation Copy the material in Box 61 onto a handout; or write the words at random on the board and students copy them into their notebooks.

Procedure

1 Focus students on the words in Box 61. In pairs, students mark above each word a small circle for an unstressed syllable and a larger circle for the main stressed syllable, as in the example. If students can't agree, they should check stress placement in a dictionary.

2 Check class answers quickly by eliciting the number of syllables each word has and the syllable taking main stress. So, for example, the answers for *musician* would be *three* and *second.* Note that *library* and *history* can be said with either two syllables or three: (/laɪbri/ or /laɪbrəri/; /hɪstri/ or /hɪstəri/).

---

[2] This activity is based loosely on one in Celce-Murcia, M., Brinton, D. M. and Goodwin, J. M. (1996, p. 149).

3   Ask students if they can see any patterns in stress placement in the words. They should notice that all the *-ian* words have main stress in the syllable before *-ian*. This is the general rule that you should highlight. (*-ian* words often refer to 'people who are members of a particular group'.) Students might also note that the other words all have stress in the first syllable. Accept this, of course, but as this doesn't represent a general rule, don't focus attention on it.

4   Students continue to work in pairs. Student A should 'be' one of the *-ian* words, and Student B tries to guess what they are by asking questions: 'Do you do magic?' 'Are you involved in politics?' etc. They should include words on the handout (*magic, politics*) in their questions, but for some roles (*physician, pedestrian*) they will need to use additional vocabulary either because they do not have a corresponding 'root' word (*pedestrian*) or because a corresponding word has a different meaning (a physician is a doctor, not someone who studies or works with physics). Demonstrate the activity with one student in front of the class before starting the pairwork.

5   In monitoring and correcting while the pairwork is in progress, focus only on stress placement in the words on the handout.

Extensions

1   Ask students (perhaps for homework) to collect other *-ian* words and check whether they follow the general rule introduced in the activity.

2   At a later date, you could do the same kind of activity with the material in Box 62. Here the focus is on the *-er/-or* noun suffix, used in the names of jobs. With this suffix, words have the *same* stress as in the corresponding 'root' verb (DECorate/DECorator, comPOSE/comPOSer, etc.). Note that some of the jobs have corresponding verbs, and others don't (e.g. *hairdresser, author*), so that in the guessing stage students will have to use additional vocabulary, as in step 4 above.

Box 61   Student handout

o O o

musician politician diet magic vegetarian library music physician

dietician historian politics grammar electricity pedestrian

vegetables history librarian grammarian electrician magician

Answer key

o O o   o oOo   Oo   O o   o oOoo   O oo   O o   o O o

musician, politician, diet, magic, vegetarian, library, music, physician,

ooOo   o Ooo   O oo   O   o oo   Ooo   o O oo

dietician, historian, politics, grammar, electricity, pedestrian,

O   oo   O oo o Ooo   o   Ooo oo O o   o O o

vegetables, history, librarian, grammarian, electrician, magician.

Box 62   Student handout

conduct   actor   composer   conductor   hairdresser   decorator

edit   translator   decorate   translate   astronomer   editor

act   author   compose

4.15 Suffixes and word stress: words ending *-ic* and *-ical*

Students should have done Activity 4.13 before this one. Activity 4.13 is a general introduction to the relationship between word stress and prefixes and suffixes, while this activity looks in particular at the suffixes *-ic* and *-ical*.

Focus Identifying the relationship between the suffixes *-ic* and *-ical* and word stress

Level Advanced

Time 40 minutes

Preparation Copy the material in Box 63 onto a handout.

Procedure

1 Give out the handout (Box 63) and focus on Part A. Ask students to work in pairs and underline the main stress in each word, using a dictionary where necessary to check stress, pronunciation and meaning.

2 Say the words with the stress indicated below or play them on the recording. Students repeat and check their answers.

MICroscope	microSCOPic	ALPHabet	alphaBETical
ATHlete	athLETic	aNALysis	anaLYTical
aPOLogy	apoloGETic	GRAMMar	graMMATical
aROMa	aroMATic	CYLinder	cyLINDrical
ICEland	IceLANDic	Irony	iRONical
caTAStrophe	catasTROPHic	phiLOSophy	philoSOPHical

3 Ask students to look for a pattern in the stress placement in words ending *-ic* and *-ical*. (Answer: In these words, stress is placed on the syllable immediately before *-ic* and *-ical*.)

4 Then focus attention on Parts B and C. In pairs, students should first use the sets of words in Part B to complete the gaps in the sentences in Part C. The four words in each set fill the four spaces in each pair of sentences.

5 Students then report back by reading out their full sentence answers. Monitor stress in the words they have written in the spaces and correct where necessary, reminding them of the *-ic/-ical* rule where appropriate. Ask a number of students to say each sentence, in order to give plenty of practice.

Box 63   Student handout

Part A

microscope	microscopic	alphabet	alphabetical
athlete	athletic	analysis	analytical
apology	apologetic	grammar	grammatical
aroma	aromatic	cylinder	cylindrical
Iceland	Icelandic	irony	ironical
catastrophe	catastrophic	philosophy	philosophical

Part B

drama – dramatic   politics – political
theatre – theatrical   energy – energetic

diplomat – diplomatic   science – scientific
enthusiasm – enthusiastic   theory – theoretical

technology – technological   geography – geographical
practice – practical   history – historical

Part C

1 a The course is a mixture of the .... and the ....
   b In .... it takes three hours, but in .... it takes much longer.
2 a He didn't know anything about .... or the ....
   b The performance was .... and extremely ....
3 a My best subjects at school were .... and ....
   b Although it was a novel, it had both .... and .... accuracy.
4 a The best teachers are full of .... and .... for their subject.
   b She must be both .... and .... to have such an important job and bring up a family, too.
5 a They're trying to get more young people interested in .... and ....
   b They are among the first patients to benefit from recent .... and .... advances in medicine.
6 a Jane Winters is the .... and .... correspondent for the *Daily News*.
   b He claims to be the only .... who has no interest in ....

Answer key
Part C:
1a theoretical, practical; b theory, practice
2a drama, theatre; b dramatic, theatrical
3a geography, history; b geographical, historical
4a energy, enthusiasm; b energetic, enthusiastic
5a science, technology; b scientific, technological
6a political, diplomatic; b diplomat, politics
Note that the order of the words added can be reversed in 1a (... *the practical and the theoretical*), 1b, 2b, 3a, 3b, 4b, 5a (although the order *science and technology* is more usual), 5b and 6a.

4.16 Stress in phrasal verbs and related nouns

Focus	Identifying word stress in phrasal verbs and related nouns
Level	Upper-intermediate+
Time	25 minutes
Preparation	Copy the material in Box 64 onto a handout.

Procedure

1 Give out the handout (Box 64) and focus on Part A. Point out that some phrasal verbs (you could just call them 'two-word verbs' if students don't know the term 'phrasal verb') have related nouns, but that the stress in each is different. The verbs are commonly stressed in both component words, while the noun has just one stress, usually on the first syllable. In the table in Part A, stressed syllables are marked in capital letters.

2 Say the verbs and nouns, or play the recording, and students repeat.

3 Reinforce the stress and pronunciation by: saying one of the words and asking students which number word you said (e.g. PRINTout = 12); saying a number and asking a student to say the word(s) (correcting stress placement if necessary).

4 In pairs, students then use the words to complete the pairs of sentences in Part B.

5 When students report their answers back, monitor that they are saying the verb/noun they have written with correct stress. Extend the practice by asking a number of students to say each sentence.

Box 64   Student handout

Part A

Verb		*Noun*	
1	BREAK OUT	2	BREAKout
3	COVer UP	4	COVer-up
5	GET toGETHer	6	GET-together
7	HIDE aWAY	8	HIDEaway
9	LIE DOWN	10	LIE-down
11	PRINT OUT	12	PRINTout
13	SEND OFF	14	SEND-off
15	SET BACK	16	SETback
17	STOP OVER	18	STOPover
19	TURN OUT	20	TURNout

Part B

1 a I must *send off* this parcel before the post office closes.
   b We gave him a good *send-off* before he left for Australia.
2 a He couldn't .... from his parents any longer.
   b The robbers had a .... in the mountains.
3 a I'm not feeling very well. I'm going to have a ....
   b I'm tired. I think I might go and ....
4 a The government is accused of a .... of events at the demonstration.
   b There's no point trying to .... the mistake. You'll just have to admit it.
5 a We've got a spare room if you need a place to ....
   b My ticket to Sydney includes a .... in Singapore.
6 a There's a .... of the report next to the computer.
   b I'll .... the report and give you a copy.
7 a He felt a cold sweat .... on his forehead.
   b There's been a .... from the prison.
8 a My brothers and I try to .... every month or so.
   b We're having a .... on Friday. Would you like to come?
9 a There was a .... of 95% in the election.
   b The play didn't .... to be a great success.
10 a Ronaldo suffered a .... yesterday as he tried to get fit for the World Cup.
   b The flooding .... work on the building by weeks.

Answer key

Part B

2 a hide away; b hideaway

3 a lie-down; b lie down

4 a cover-up; b cover up

5 a stop over; b stopover

6 a printout; b print out

7 a break out; b breakout

8 a get together; b get-together

9 a turnout; b turn out

10 a setback; b set back

Extension

Here are some other verb–noun pairs with the same stress pattern, which you could use later in a similar exercise: *break down / a breakdown, break in / a break-in, buy out / a buyout, change over / a changeover, climb down / a climbdown, flare up / a flare-up, get away / a getaway, hold up / a hold-up, let down / a letdown, let up / a letup, mix up / a mix-up, sell out / a sell-out, takeaway / a takeaway, work out / a workout.*

4.17 Rules of stress in compound nouns

Focus	Identifying word stress in compound nouns
Level	Upper-intermediate+
Time	20 minutes
Preparation	Copy the material in Box 65 onto a handout or an OHT.

Procedure

1 If necessary, explain that compound nouns are made up of two separate words (either noun + noun, or adjective + noun) and are often written as two words (e.g. *credit card*). Others are written as a single word (e.g. *toothpaste*) or with the words joined by a hyphen (e.g. *cross-section*).

2 Give out or show students the sentences in Box 65 and ask them to underline all the compound nouns (each sentence has two). Ask them whether the main stress is in the first or second part of the compound.

3 Read the sentences aloud or play the recording. Students check their answers. Ask them to say what is the usual pattern. (Main stress is in the first part of most compound nouns, but occasionally in the second.)

Extension

Ask students to take a text that they have been using for other purposes, identify the compound nouns and note whether the pattern they observed in the activity can be found.

Box 65   Student handout

1 I went out during the lunch hour and bought a newspaper.
2 When I have tea with my grandparents, they always give me jam sandwiches.
3 I'm meeting my girlfriend at the bus station in an hour.
4 I've only got a tape recorder, so I can't play CDs.
5 I never do any housework on weekdays.
6 It gets so hot in the sitting room that we've had to fit an air-conditioner.
7 He works as a shop assistant in the city centre.
8 My housemate is terrified of fireworks.

Answer key
(Main stress is on the syllable in capital letters)

1 LUNCH hour – NEWSpaper
2 GRANDparents – jam SANDwiches
3 GIRLfriend – BUS station
4 TAPE recorder – cDS (i.e. 'CDs')

5 HOUSEwork – WEEKdays
6 SITting room – AIR-conditioner
7 SHOP assistant – city CENtre
8 HOUSEmate – FIREworks

Stress in phrases (4.18–4.22)

4.18 Same or different stress patterns?

This activity is intended to help students become aware of stress patterns in phrases and short sentences. The first step introduces the activity by looking at stress in words. You may decide that your students don't need this introductory step, so you could start at step 2.

Focus Identifying stress patterns in words, phrases and short sentences

Level Elementary

Time 20 minutes

Preparation Prepare a list of pairs of words for step 1, each pair having the same number of syllables, but either the same or different stress pattern (alternatively use the pairs in Box 66; these are on the recording); for step 2, prepare a list of pairs of phrases and short sentences, each pair having the same number of syllables, but either the same or different stress pattern (alternatively use the pairs in Box 67; these are on the recording). Note that many of the phrases and sentences could have different stress patterns, depending on context.

Procedure

1   Say pairs of words with more than one syllable (either from your list or Box 66, which is on the recording) and ask whether they have the same stress pattern (i.e. the same number of syllables and stress placement) or a different one. For example:

   around – below (= same: oO)
   computer – overseas (= different: oOo / ooO)

2   Do the same using pairs of phrases or short sentences as in Box 67. For example:

   She told me her name. – A litre of milk. = same: oOooO
   He went by car. – Over the hill. = different: oOoO / OooO

3   Students work in pairs to produce one or two pairs of phrases or short sentences, each pair having the same number of syllables. Students can choose whether these will be said with the same or different stress pattern. Students say their pairs aloud, and the rest of the class decides whether they are the same or different.

Box 66 Teacher reference	
	(S)ame or (D)ifferent?
1 around – below	S: oO
2 computer – overseas	D: oOo/ooO
3 furniture – tomorrow	D: Ooo/oOo
4 timetable – granddaughter	S: Ooo
5 education – scientific	S: ooOo
6 moustache – ugly	D: oO/Oo
7 journalist – wonderful	S: Ooo
8 politics – overweight	D: Ooo/ooO
9 Argentina – biology	D: ooOo/oOoo
10 pyjamas – attractive	S: oOo

Box 67   Teacher reference

		(S)ame or (D)ifferent?
1	She told me her name. – A litre of milk.	S: oOooO
2	He went by car. – Over the hill.	D: oOoO/OooO
3	He plays the guitar. – I'll try to find out.	S: oOooO
4	On holiday. – A chest of drawers.	D: oOoo/oOoO
5	They live in a flat. – It's against the law.	D: oOooO/ooOoO
6	What does it look like? – She's really angry.	D: OooOo/oOoOo
7	I'm afraid I can't. – In the afternoon.	S: ooOoO
8	She's meeting her boyfriend. – It's under the table.	S: oOooOo
9	She's completely exhausted. – He wants to be a doctor.	D: ooOooOo/oOooooOo
10	She's expecting a baby. – I was looking for David.	S: ooOooOo

4.19 Find your partners

Focus Identifying sentences with the same stress pattern

Level Intermediate

Time 30 minutes

Preparation Prepare small cards/pieces of paper, each of which has one of the two-part (A+B) dialogues from Box 68 written on it. You could photocopy the material and cut out the dialogues (in the left column) that you want to use. Don't give the stress pattern (in the right column) to students. The dialogues are organised so that all three dialogues in each set (there are six sets in total) have the same stress pattern in the B parts of the dialogues. Note that the A parts are just designed to put the B parts in context and are not spoken by students in this activity. Prepare enough so that there are at least two from each set. So, for example, if you have a class of 12 students, you could use two dialogues from each of the six sets, or all three dialogues from four sets. You can give the same dialogue to more than one student if you have large numbers. For the Variation, prepare a handout or an OHT with the material from Box 69.

Procedure

1 Distribute at random to each student one of the cards/pieces of paper you have prepared.

2 Students walk around the room and find others who have B parts with the same stress pattern (i.e. the same number of syllables with stress on the same syllables). To do this, Student 1 says the B part on their card and Student 2 says theirs. If the two B parts don't have the same stress pattern, the students move on to another student and do the same thing. If the two parts are the same, the students form a pair and together they go to find other students with the same stress pattern. This continues until all students have formed into groups. First demonstrate the procedure carefully with a few students at the front of the class.

3 Check the answers by saying the A parts for each set of dialogues. The student with the appropriate B part responds. If the students who respond to the A parts in each set are standing together, then they have found their partners correctly. If they are not, ask them to say their parts again and discuss with the other members of the class where they should be. Continue until you and the class are happy that the correct groups are formed.

Variation

If it is not practical for students to walk around the classroom, give all the dialogues to all students on a handout (Box 69). They should work in pairs to categorise the B parts according to their stress pattern.

Box 68   Teacher reference

Stress pattern for B parts:

A: Where's their office?
B: On the seventeenth floor.

A: Why are you having a party tonight?
B: It's my birthday today.   ooOooO

A: Where does Becky always sit?
B: At the back of the class.

A: How do you like your coffee?
B: With milk and sugar.

A: What are you going to eat?
B: A plate of pasta.   oOoOo

A: What did Francis say when you phoned her?
B: She didn't answer.

A: What languages do you speak?
B: English and Spanish.

A: Where are you going to hang that picture?
B: Over the window.   OooOo

A: When did you learn to ski?
B: When I was younger.

A: Where did you get your new coat from?
B: I bought it in town.

A: When are you going back home?
B: I'm leaving today.   oOooO

A: How are you getting to Paris?
B: I'm planning to drive.

A: Do your broken ribs still hurt you?
B: Only when I laugh.

A: What do you think of this photo of Paul?
B: Let me have a look.   OoooO

A: Where do you want this box?
B: Put it on the floor.

A: What did you do with the sugar?
B: I put it in the cupboard.

A: What are you looking for?
B: I'm looking for a pencil.   oOoooOo

A: Do you want anything from the vegetable shop?
B: A kilo of tomatoes.

Box 69   Student handout

1 A: Where's their office? B: On the seventeenth floor.
2 A: Where are you going to hang that picture? B: Over the window.
3 A: What did Francis say when you phoned her?
   B: She didn't answer.
4 A: What did you do with the sugar? B: I put it in the cupboard.
5 A: Do your broken ribs still hurt you? B: Only when I laugh.
6 A: How are you getting to Paris? B: I'm planning to drive.
7 A: What are you looking for? B: I'm looking for a pencil.
8 A: Why are you having a party tonight? B: It's my birthday today.
9 A: What languages do you speak? B: English and Spanish.
10 A: What do you think of this photo of Paul? B: Let me have a look.
11 A: What are you going to eat? B: A plate of pasta.
12 A: Do you want anything from the vegetable shop?
   B: A kilo of tomatoes.
13 A: Where do you want this box? B: Put it on the floor.
14 A: How do you like your coffee? B: With milk and sugar.
15 A: Where did you get your new coat from? B: I bought it in town.
16 A: Where does Becky always sit? B: At the back of the class.
17 A: When did you learn to ski? B: When I was younger.
18 A: When are you going back home? B: I'm leaving today.

© Cambridge University Press 2004

Answer key
The B parts with the same stress patterns are: 1, 8, 16; 3, 11, 14; 2, 9, 17; 6, 15, 18; 5, 10, 13; 4, 7, 12.

4.20 Stress shift in nationality words

Focus	Identifying stress shift in nationality words
Level	Intermediate
Time	25 minutes
Preparation	Copy the material in Box 70 onto a handout or an OHT. Write a nationality and an occupation in the space under each face, selected from those in Box 71. Choose any four nationalities from list 1, any four from list 2, and eight of the occupations from list 3.

Procedure

1 Give out the handout (Box 70) or display the OHT. Practise the pronunciation of nationalities and occupations: Q: Where's *a* from? A: He's Chinese. Q: What does he do? A: He's a dentist. Pay particular attention to stress.

2 Demonstrate that when they are used before a word with stress in the first syllable, some nationality words (those in list 1) have a different stress pattern than when they are used at the end of the sentence (or before words that don't have stress in the first syllable). Compare:

> *a*'s <u>Chinese</u> (oO). He's a <u>Chinese dentist</u> (Oo Oo). (with stress shift)
> *b*'s <u>Malaysian</u> (oOo). She's a <u>Malaysian farmer</u>. (oOo Oo) (without stress shift)

Ask students to predict which nationality words have this stress shift and to put * above these. The stress patterns of the words are given in Box 71.

3 Give students a few moments to try to remember the nationalities and jobs, then turn off the OHT or ask them to turn their handouts face down. Ask students to make sentences of the type: *a's Chinese* or *a's a Chinese dentist*. Give one point for remembering and one for getting stress in the right place in the nationality word.

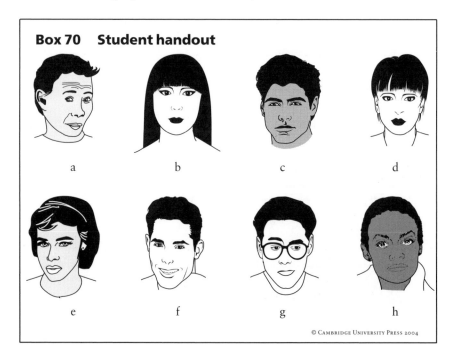

Box 70   Student handout

a   b   c   d

e   f   g   h

© CAMBRIDGE UNIVERSITY PRESS 2004

Box 71	Teacher reference	
List 1 *(Stress shift possible; stress patterns are given for the words without and with stress shift)*	*List 2* *(No stress shift)*	*List 3*
Japanese (ooO/Ooo)	Italian (oOoo)	doctor (Oo)
Chinese (oO/Oo)	Icelandic (oOo)	dentist (Oo)
Taiwanese (ooO/Ooo)	Malaysian (oOo)	farmer (Oo)
Portuguese (ooO/Ooo)	Australian (oOoo)	teacher (Oo)
Singaporean (oooOo/Ooooo)	Peruvian (oOoo)	lecturer (Ooo)
Argentinian (ooOoo/Ooooo)	Nigerian (oOoo)	artist (Oo)
Indonesian (ooOo/Oooo)	Tunisian (oOoo)	author (Oo)
Pakistani (ooOo/Oooo)	Norwegian (oOo)	architect (Ooo)
		sculptor (Oo)
		lawyer (Oo)
		journalist (Ooo)
		footballer (Ooo)
		actor (Oo)

4.21 Stress shift in compounds

Focus	Identifying stress shift in compound words
Level	Advanced
Time	15 minutes
Preparation	Copy the material in Box 72 onto the board, an OHT or a handout. For the Variation, first cut or blank out the words in column B of Box 72 and then copy the material onto the board, an OHT or a handout. If you are going to do the Extension activity, do the same for the material in Box 73.

Procedure

1 Give out or display the material in Box 72. Students repeat the items in column A after you or the recording. Make sure that the main stress is in the second half of the compound, as follows:

broken-down	OoO	semi-detached	OooO
far-reaching	OOo	stress-related	OoOo
long-distance	OOo	three-dimensional	OoOoo

overnight	OoO̱	underground	OoO̱
purpose-built	OoO̱	warm-blooded	OO̱o
second-class	OoO̱		

2 Demonstrate that when these compounds are followed by a word beginning with a stressed syllable, main stress in the compound usually shifts back to the first stressed syllable. For example:

O o O̱	o O̱ o o O
broken-down *but*	a broken-down car

3 Ask students, individually or in pairs, to suggest a word from column B that would naturally follow an item from column A. (Note that there isn't always an exact answer, although possible answers are given in the key.)

4 Students report their answers. Make sure that main stress in the compound shifts back to the first word or first half of the compound.

Variation

Give out or display the blanked copy of the material in Box 72 and follow the procedure for steps 1 and 2. Then students work in pairs to think of suitable nouns to follow the beginnings in column A. These should either have one syllable or, if they have more than one, have stress in the first syllable. This will produce compounds that most regularly have stress shift. Students report their answers. Make sure that main stress in the compound shifts back to the first word or first half of the compound.

Extension

Repeat the activity at a later date using the material in Box 73, which is designed to show that the tendency highlighted in the activity above doesn't always apply. Begin by reminding students that when compound adjectives are combined with nouns the stress may shift back, but not always. The material contains a mixture of compounds that have main stress in the second part, and stress shift when followed by a stressed noun (*first-class, full-time, next door, world-class*); and compounds that always have stress in the first part and no stress shift (*bloodshot, credit card, daylight, rush hour, Stone Age, windscreen*).

Box 72   Student handout

A		B	
broken-down	far-reaching	animal	car
long-distance	overnight	car park	changes
purpose-built	second-class	citizen	factory
semi-detached	stress-related	house	illness
three-dimensional	underground	journey	object
warm-blooded		runner	

Answer key
Possible answers: a semi-detached house, far-reaching changes, a stress-related illness, a long-distance runner, an overnight journey, a purpose-built factory, a three-dimensional object, a second-class citizen, a broken-down car, an underground car park, a warm-blooded animal.

Box 73   Student handout

A		B	
bloodshot	credit card	eyes	footballer
daylight	first-class	fraud	hours
full-time	next door	job	neighbour
rush hour	Stone Age	ticket	traffic
windscreen	world-class	tools	wiper

Answer key
Possible answers: bloodshot eyes, credit card fraud, daylight hours, first-class ticket, full-time job, next door neighbour, rush hour traffic, Stone Age tools, windscreen wiper, world-class footballer.

5 Intonation

Prominence: highlighting words and syllables (5.1–5.3)

5.1 Introducing prominent and non-prominent words: 'James Bond'

Focus	Identifying prominent and non-prominent words in sentences
Level	Elementary+
Time	20 minutes
Preparation	Copy the material in Box 74 onto a handout.

Procedure

1 Begin the activity by reminding or telling students that James Bond often introduces himself in films by saying, 'The name's Bond. James Bond.' Say this a couple of times and write on the board:

> The NAME'S BOND. JAMES bond.

Point out that when *Bond* is said first it is prominent and when it is repeated it is not prominent. (You could use the word *stressed* or *highlighted* instead of *prominent*, or simply demonstrate the difference by gesture.) Both have a falling tone.

2 Introduce yourself in the same way by saying (for example):

> The NAME'S HEWings. MARtin Hewings.

Perhaps shake hands with one of the students to 'dramatise' it.

3 Ask a few students to introduce themselves to you in the same way, and then all students introduce themselves to other students around them. Check that the last name is not prominent and correct where necessary. (If students don't have a name that fits this pattern – perhaps they have only one name or put their family name first – you may have to miss out this step, or adapt as necessary.)

4 Give out the handout (Box 74) to students. First ask them to match the questions and responses. Check the answers by asking the questions and

students respond. Make sure that they use the prominence and intonation pattern practised so far. For example:

What colour's your car?   It's RED. DARK red.

5   Students then work in pairs to ask and answer the questions. Monitor the prominence and intonation in the answers and correct where necessary.

Extension

You could elicit from students, or explain to them, why words are prominent and non-prominent. You could explain this by saying either:

* 'new' information is prominent and 'given' information is non-prominent (this is a simple explanation of prominence/non-prominence), or
* where there is a choice, we make the word which we have chosen prominent, and where there is no choice we make the word non-prominent (this is a more complicated, but perhaps more generalisable, explanation of prominence/non-prominence).

You could demonstrate either of these explanations in the responses to 1 and 2 in Box 74 as follows:

What colour's your car?

It's	RED. blue. green. etc. (= new / a choice is made)	DARK light (= new / a choice is made)	red. (= given / no other word can go here)

Where's Seoul?

It's in	KOREA. Japan. India. etc. (= new / a choice is made)	SOUTH North (= new / a choice is made)	Korea. (= given / no other word can go here)

Box 74   Student handout

1 What colour's your car?	a It's hot. Incredibly hot.
2 Where's Seoul?	b It was boring. Terribly boring.
3 What's the weather like in Malaysia?	c I play football. American football.
4 How was the exam?	d She was delighted. Really delighted.
5 Where shall we have the barbecue?	e It's red. Dark red.
6 Where does Maria live?	f They're in the drawer. The bottom drawer.
7 What did you think of the film?	g It's in Korea. South Korea.
8 Have you seen my car keys?	h In the garden. The front garden.
9 How's your toothache now?	i It's painful. Extremely painful.
10 Do you do any sport?	j He's broken his arm. His left arm.
11 Did Helen like the present?	k In Spain. The north of Spain.
12 What's happened to Jack?	l It was difficult. Very difficult.

© CAMBRIDGE UNIVERSITY PRESS 2004

Answer key

1e   2g   3a   4l   5h   6k
7b   8f   9i   10c   11d   12j

5.2 Hearing and saying prominent words: 'They're on the table'

Focus	Identifying prominent words in sentences
Level	Elementary+
Time	35 minutes
Preparation	Copy the material in Boxes 75–77 onto separate handouts for students (Box 76 could alternatively be put on an OHT).

Procedure

1   Give out *only* Box 75 first. Explain to students that they need to circle the word they hear as prominent in each sentence (you could alternatively talk about 'stressed' or 'highlighted' words). Play the recording or say the utterances as they appear in Box 76. For example: you say, '1A They're ON the TABLE' and students circle *on* and *table*; you say, '1B They're on the TABLE' and students circle *table*; etc. Use the utterances in row 1 as an illustration of what the students need to do and then continue through the remaining rows. Check the answers (students should say which words they have circled) and repeat any utterances that students find problematic.

2 Next give out or show the material in Box 76. Say the utterances in Box 77. First take row 1 and read A, B and C in any order, but keep a note of the order in which you read them. (Note that the questions in Box 77 correspond to the answers in Box 76 – A1 goes with A1, A2 with A2, etc. – so make sure you change the order.) Students listen and choose the most appropriate response in each case. They could write *1*, *2* and *3* next to responses A–C to indicate the order in which they hear them. For example, say 'Row 1, number 1 – I thought I put my book under the table', and students write:

    C

    They're ON the table. 1

3 When you have read the utterances in row 1, check the answers by reading out one of them again. Ask a student to give their answer, replying (for example) 'B: They're on the TABLE.' Check that they get both the letter and the prominence placement correct in their response. Then repeat the procedure for rows 2, 3, etc.

4 Finally, give out the material in Box 77. Students work in pairs. One says the utterances in Box 77, as in step 3, and the other responds with the answers in Box 76. So answer A1 in Box 76 is the correct response to question A1 in Box 77, etc. After a time, they should try to respond *without* looking at Box 76 – from memory with the correct prominence in their response. Monitor and correct when necessary.

Box 75   Student handout

A	B	C
1 They're on the table.	They're on the table.	They're on the table.
2 At ten past eight.	At ten past eight.	At ten past eight.
3 It's a red Ford.	It's a red Ford.	It's a red Ford.
4 She broke her leg.	She broke her leg.	She broke her leg.
5 He's writing a book.	He's writing a book.	He's writing a book.
6 Pizza and salad.	Pizza and salad.	Pizza and salad.
7 The third on the right.	The third on the right.	The third on the right.

Box 76   Student handout

A	B	C
1 They're ON the TABLE.	They're on the TABLE.	They're ON the table.
2 At ten past EIGHT.	At TEN past eight.	At TEN past EIGHT.
3 It's a RED ford.	It's a RED FORD.	It's a red FORD.
4 She broke her LEG.	She BROKE her leg.	She BROKE her LEG.
5 He's WRITING a BOOK.	He's writing a BOOK.	He's WRITING a book.
6 PIZZA and salad.	PIZZA and SALAD.	Pizza and SALAD.
7 The third on the RIGHT.	The THIRD on the right.	The THIRD on the RIGHT.

Box 77   Student handout

A	B	C
1 Where are my books?	Didn't I put my books on the chair?	I thought I put my books under the table.
2 The film starts at ten past nine, doesn't it?	See you at twenty past eight.	What time are we meeting?
3 There's a blue Ford coming.	What car has Vicky got?	Becky's got a red Toyota, hasn't she?
4 Is Jane's broken arm any better?	Did Jane bruise her leg?	How was Jane's skiing holiday?
5 What's David doing these days?	David's writing a play, isn't he?	I've heard David is going to write a book.
6 Did you order pasta and salad?	What would you like to eat?	Is yours the pizza and chips?
7 I take the third turning on the left, don't I?	Your house is the second on the right, isn't it?	Which is your house?

5.3 Prominence contrasts within words: *stalactites* and *stalagmites*

Some of the vocabulary in this activity will be challenging even for advanced students. It may be useful to give students the vocabulary that is going to be used and, as a preparatory exercise (perhaps for homework), ask them to check the meaning of any words they don't know. The words are listed separately in Box 78 to copy as a handout.

Focus Practising contrastive prominence placement in words

Level Advanced

Time 40 minutes

Preparation Copy the material in Box 78 onto a handout and give out in advance. Copy the cartoon in Box 79 onto an OHT. Copy the material in Box 80 onto a handout. (You could add the cartoon in Box 79 to the top of this handout if you don't have access to an OHT.)

Procedure

1 Draw on the board a cave with stalactites and stalagmites, something like this:

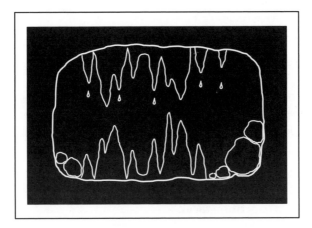

Elicit from students the words *stalactite* and *stalagmite*. Point to a standing column and say, 'It's a STALagmite'. Then point to a hanging column and say 'It's a STALactite'. Write *stalagmite* and *stalactite* on the board and point out that stress is on the first syllable in these words.

2 Show students the cartoon in Box 79 (either on the handout or displayed on the OHT). Discuss with them how the caption would be read aloud,

147

and point out or elicit that *stalagmite* would need to be pronounced *STALagMITE* (rather than the usual *STALagmite*) in this context. You could explain this either by saying that there is a *choice* made on the final syllable (between *-tite* and *-mite*) or that there is a *contrast* made on this syllable (between *stalac<u>tite</u>* and *stalag<u>mite</u>*). The main point to get across is that the normal prominence placement in its citation form (see Introduction, p. 6) is overriden by the prominence placement that is needed in a particular context. Tell students that this is going to be practised in the activity.

3 If you haven't already done so, give out the handout (Box 80).

4 Practise the pronunciation of the words said alone, in Part A of the handout. Prominent syllables are in capital letters. Students repeat after you or the recording.

5 Practise a couple of the dialogues in Part B with the students. Take one from 1–8 (which includes words that have stress on the first syllable in their citation forms, moving to a later syllable in the dialogues) and one from 9–16 (which includes words that have stress in later syllables in their citation forms, moving to the first in the dialogues) to demonstrate what to do. For example:

    1 It's a STALactite, isn't it?
    No, it's a STALagMITE.

    9 Are you trying to reWIND the tape?
    No, it's got tangled. I'm trying to UNwind it.

6 Students work in pairs on the dialogues. Then select a few to perform some of the dialogues for the class. Monitor the contrastive prominence placement and correct where necessary.

Extension

Here are some more pairs of nouns that might be contrasted in the same way. Ask students to work in pairs to write their own dialogues showing the contrast, and then to perform them.

telescope – telephone	relevant – irrelevant
attach – detach	impression – expression
disused – misused	conservatory – observatory
headband – headscarf	accusation – application

Box 78   Student handout

archaeologist – sociologist   cornflour – cornflakes
destructive – constructive   disappeared – reappeared
encouraging – discouraging   geology – biology   harmless – harmful
microscope – microphone   millionaire – billionaire
motorbike – motorboat   rewind – unwind   stalagmite – stalactite
toothbrush – toothpaste   undervalued – overvalued

Box 79   Student handout

*"In a case of this kind, Mrs. Hall, our first concern is
to persuade the patient that he's a stalagmite."*

Box 80   Student handout

Part A

Stress on first syllable   *Stress on later syllables*

STALagmite	reWIND	disaPPEARED
STALactite	unWIND	reaPPEARED
HARMless	geOLogy	millionAIRE
HARMful	biOLogy	billionAIRE
MOtorbike	deSTRUCtive	underVALued
MOtorboat	conSTRUCtive	overVALued
TOOTHbrush	enCOURaging	archaeOLogist
TOOTHpaste	disCOURaging	sociOLogist
MIcroscope		
MIcrophone		
CORNflour		
CORNflakes		

Part B:

1 A: It's a stalactite, isn't it?   B: No, it's a stalagmite.
2 A: Is it harmful?   B: No, it's harmless.
3 A: I hear you travelled by motorboat.   B: No, I went by motorbike.
4 A: Have you forgotten your toothbrush?
   B: No, I've forgotten my toothpaste.
5 A: Did you say microscope?   B: No, I said microphone.
6 A: Do you want me to get cornflakes?   B: No, I want cornflour.
7 A: Has she dyed her eyelashes?   B: No, she's dyed her eyebrows.
8 A: Should I cross the footpath after that?
   B: No, you cross the footbridge.
9 A: Are you trying to rewind the tape?
   B: No, it's got tangled. I'm trying to unwind it.
10 A: I hear you're studying geology.   B: No, I'm studying biology.
11 A: So he suddenly disappeared?
   B: No, I said he suddenly reappeared.
12 A: Disagreements in a relationship can be very destructive.
   B: Yes, but they can be constructive, too.
13 A: I found his comments very encouraging.
   B: Well I thought they were discouraging.
14 A: Do you know he's a millionaire?   B: He's actually a billionaire.
15 A: So you think the company is undervalued?
   B: No, I think it's overvalued.
16 A: Pam's a sociologist, isn't she?   B: No, she's an archaeologist.

Tone units and tonic placement (5.4–5.5)

5.4 Dividing speech into tone units

Focus	Dividing speech into tone units
Level	Intermediate+
Time	25 minutes
Preparation	If you are using the recording, copy the material in Box 81[1] onto a handout. If you are using your own material (see Variation), record a few short pieces of natural speech – four or five seconds for each one will do. Before the class, transcribe the extracts and divide the speech into 'units'. The boundaries of these units may be pauses, or they may come at the end of a fall or rise in intonation. However, don't worry too much about the criteria for deciding on boundaries; if you hear them as units which include sounds that run together without a break, then that is fine. Copy a version of the transcripts (as in Box 81) onto a handout.

Procedure

1 Give out the handout (Box 81). Focus on Part A. Students look at the first extract while you play the recording of this two or three times.

2 Ask individual students to repeat, trying to break up the speech into units in the same way as on the recording. If students have problems, play (or say) single units one at a time until they can say each one fluently. Then ask them to say the whole extract again. Then do the same for the remaining extracts.

3 Focus on Part B. This includes extracts from the recording *without* unit boundaries marked on the written transcript. Ask students to listen to the recording a few times, decide where the natural breaks are and mark these on their handouts. Then follow the procedure in step 2 above. The transcripts with unit boundaries marked are given below Box 81 for your information.

Variation

Rather than using the recording, you could use your own material; for example, recordings accompanying textbooks that you use. Make sure that you don't include commas and full stops, which might give clues to intonation unit boundaries.

---

[1] Source: Brazil, D. (1994 [Part A: 1 from p. 57; 2 from p. 78; 3 from p. 13; 4 from p. 35. Part B: 1 from p. 45; 2 from p. 89; 3 from p. 23 (part); 4 from p. 31]).

Extension

For homework, ask students to record a very short extract from a radio or television news broadcast where the newsreader is talking (this is likely to be the clearest part). They should transcribe this and mark where unit boundaries occur. Encourage them to think about how professional broadcasters divide their speech into units, and discuss one or two of the transcripts in class.

Box 81   Student handout

Part A

1 She's leaving / to take up a post / in Glasgow / we wish her well
2 The door opened and / this person got out / and it was a little old lady / with a shopping bag
3 I hurried across / and turned into an alleyway / and started to walk / it was dark / and drizzling a little
4 At the top of the stairs / was the coffee room / and opposite that / was the photocopying room / just beyond there / was the post room / and Arthur's room / was about three doors along

Part B

1 Well I'm rather busy just at present perhaps you wouldn't mind waiting for a few minutes
2 We need to reduce the numbers of cars on our roads we don't need to increase them
3 The thing to look out for is the playing fields and soon after you've passed them you'll go under an underpass
4 You remember that friend of his though the guy who came from Liverpool he always came on Fridays and nobody quite knew why

© CAMBRIDGE UNIVERSITY PRESS 2004

Transcripts for Part B with unit boundaries marked:
1 Well I'm rather busy / just at present / perhaps you wouldn't mind waiting for a few minutes
2 We need to reduce / the numbers of cars on our roads / we don't need to increase them
3 The thing to look out for / is the playing fields / and soon after you've passed them / you'll go under an underpass
4 You remember that friend of his though / the guy who came from Liverpool / he always came on Fridays / and nobody quite knew why

---

5.5 Tonic word placement: 'At ten to seven, or ten to eight?'

Within each intonation unit (or 'tone unit') there is one word which stands out more than others because it is where the voice begins to fall or rise. This is called the 'tonic word'. (For more information, see Introduction, p. 8.)

Focus Identifying and producing tonic words

Level Intermediate+

Time 20 minutes

Preparation Copy the material in Box 82 onto a handout or an OHT. Alternatively, copy Part A onto an OHT or write it on the board, and copy Part B onto a handout.

Procedure

1 Focus on Part A. Demonstrate the importance of tonic word placement. Say sentences a and b (with a falling tone) for the class so that they understand that the tonic syllable is *ten* in sentence a and *eight* in sentence b. Then ask 'Which comes before a – 1 or 2?' (*a* comes after 2, and *b* after 1.)

2 Focus on Part B. Students repeat all the items in column B (with tonic syllables in capitals) after you or the recording.

3 Students form Student A/B pairs. For the first pair of sentences, Student A says either sentence 1 or 2 and Student B replies with response a or b, as appropriate (Answers: 1 – b, 2 – a). Demonstrate this first.

4 Student A selects randomly from the six pairs of sentences, perhaps repeating items, so that plenty of practice is generated. After a time, Students A and B can exchange roles.

Extensions

1 Give students short sentences such as *I went to Paris last summer* and ask them to suggest the first parts of dialogues to produce the responses:

I went to PARis last summer.
I went to Paris LAST summer.
I went to Paris last SUMMer.

2 In a later lesson, when sufficient time has elapsed so that students have forgotten the details of the exercise, give them the B responses in Box 82, Part B again. Ask them to suggest appropriate A parts to elicit each of the responses.

Box 82   Student handout

Part A

1 See you at ten to seven.   a At TEN to eight.

2 See you at five to eight.   b At ten to EIGHT.

Part B

A	B
① 1 I thought the office was in West Oldtown.	a No, it's in West NEWtown.
2 I thought the office was in East Newtown.	b No, it's in WEST Newtown.
② 1 Isn't Kate a chemist?	a No, my SISter's a doctor.
2 Your brother's a doctor, isn't he?	b No, my sister's a DOCtor.
③ 1 How do you like your coffee?	a With MILK, please.
2 You have your coffee black, don't you?	b WITH milk, please.
④ 1 I can't find the car keys in your handbag.	a They're in my black HANDbag.
2 Where did you put the car keys?	b They're in my BLACK handbag.
⑤ 1 When do you think Jill will get here?	a She's coming AFTer lunch.
2 What do you think Jill will want for lunch?	b She's coming after LUNCH.
⑥ 1 Do you think leaving school at 16 was a mistake?	a It was a big misTAKE.
2 Why did the police arrest Tom?	b It was a BIG mistake.

Answer key

1 1a, 2b   **2** 1b, 2a   **3** 1a, 2b   **4** 1b, 2a   **5** 1b, 2a   **6** 1b, 2a

Tones (5.6–5.9)

5.6 Choosing tones: fall or rise?

This activity can be used to introduce the four most frequent tones in British English – fall, fall-rise, rise, level – or to remind students of them before an activity such as Activities 5.7 or 5.8 below.

Focus Identifying tones: fall, fall-rise, rise, level

Level Elementary+

Time 10 minutes

Procedure

1 Draw on the board the following tones (fall, fall-rise, rise, level) and number them *1* to *4*.

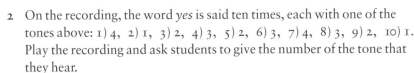

2 On the recording, the word *yes* is said ten times, each with one of the tones above: 1) 4, 2) 1, 3) 2, 4) 3, 5) 2, 6) 3, 7) 4, 8) 3, 9) 2, 10) 1. Play the recording and ask students to give the number of the tone that they hear.

3 Repeat with words that have more than one syllable. The recording gives ten versions of the following words:
question – 1) 2, 2) 3, 3) 4, 4) 2, 5) 3, 6) 1, 7) 2, 8) 4, 9) 1, 10) 2
pronunciation – 1) 3, 2) 3, 3) 1, 4) 4, 5) 2, 6) 2, 7) 3, 8) 1, 9) 1, 10) 4
Alternatively, you could say the words with different tones yourself.

4 Ask a student to take the role of teacher, saying a word that you give them using different tones, while other students answer with the appropriate tone number.

5.7 Tone choice in questions

Many textbooks teach that *wh*-questions end with a falling tone, and *yes/no* questions end with a rising tone. While this is often true, students will sometimes hear questions in natural speech which break this rule. This activity begins by reminding students of the 'textbook rule', and then goes beyond this to give students a more general understanding of the relationship between questions and intonation. When we ask a question we might be trying to *find out* information that we don't already know. Alternatively, we might ask a question in order to *make sure* that information we think we know is correct. *Finding out* questions usually end with a falling tone, and *making sure* questions usually end with an 'end-rising' tone (that is, falling-rising tone or rising tone). As *wh*-questions are often used to find out, they often have falling tone, and as *yes/no* questions are often used to make sure, they often have falling-rising or rising tone. However, *wh*-questions can also be used to make sure, and so have falling-rising or rising tone, and *yes/no* question can also be used to find out, and so have falling tone.

Focus	Identifying tones in *wh-* and *yes/no* questions; distinguishing between tones in 'finding out' and 'making sure' questions
Level	Upper-intermediate+
Time	35 minutes
Preparation	Copy the material in Box 83 onto a handout or an OHT, or write the sentences on the board. Copy the material in Box 84 onto a handout.

Procedure

1 Give out or show the material in Box 83. Play the recording of the questions. Alternatively, say the questions yourself with the intonation at the end of the questions as given below. This is also the intonation used on the recording. (Note that for the sake of simplicity, falling-rising tones are used on the recording rather than rising tones. However, you could use a rising tone instead of the falling-rising, with a similar meaning.)

    1 How's Tom getting to PARis?

    2 Do you want a lift to the STATion?

    3 Why's ALice coming this evening?

    4 Are you going to the PARTy tonight?

    5 Do you like OYSTers?

    6 What do you want for your BIRTHday?

    7 When are you going back HOME?

    8 Did you get back this MORNing?

    9 Was SUSan at the meeting?

    10 Who's the man in the blue SUIT?

Ask students to listen in particular to the end of the question, starting with the syllable in capital letters, and decide whether they hear a falling or a falling-rising tone. Try to elicit from students a relationship between the type of question and the intonation in these sentences: that is, *wh-* questions end with a falling tone, and *yes/no* questions end with a falling-rising tone.

2 Explain to students the distinction between *finding out* and *making sure*, and the connection with *wh-* and *yes/no* questions (see above).

3 Give out the handout (Box 84). Focus on Part A. Students repeat the questions after you with the intonation shown. Then take the B parts in the dialogues and students ask you questions. *I told you* is inserted in the answers in 6–10 to emphasise that this is information A should already know. Finally, students work in pairs to ask and answer the questions as A and B. Monitor the intonation in the questions and correct if necessary.

4 Focus on Part B. Say that *wh*-questions can also be used for *making sure* – to check information that you have already been told (but may have forgotten) – and these questions often have a fall-rise starting on the *wh*-word. Play the recording of the first five questions, or say them with the intonation shown, and follow the procedure as in step 3.

5 Then explain that *yes/no* questions can also be used for *finding out*, and these questions often have a falling tone. Play the recording of the next five questions, or say them with the intonation shown, and follow the procedure as in step 3. The difference between these questions and those in Part A is that in Part A (with falling-rising tone) the questions are checking (we think we know the answer) and in Part B (with falling tone) they are finding out information we don't know.

6 Focus on Part C. Explain that students should ask the questions again with an intonation appropriate to the purpose (find out / make sure) given on the left. The B responses should be taken from those given in Parts A and B and should be appropriate to the intonation used. Give a few examples to illustrate and then students work in pairs.

Extension

After you have used a recorded dialogue in class, go back and focus on the intonation at the end of any questions in it. Ask students to identify whether there is a falling or end-rising tone (rising or falling-rising). In most cases, the *finding out* or *making sure* distinction will help explain intonation choice. For more advanced students, you could go on to consider whether the alternative intonation choice might also be appropriate in the context and if not, why not.

Box 83   Student handout

1 How's Tom getting to PARis?
2 Do you want a lift to the STATion?
3 Why's ALice coming this evening?
4 Are you going to the PARTy tonight?
5 Do you like OYSTers?
6 What do you want for your BIRTHday?
7 When are you going back HOME?
8 Did you get back this MORNing?
9 Was SUSan at the meeting?
10 Who's the man in the blue SUIT?

Box 84   Student handout

Part A

finding out	1 A: How's Tom getting to PARis?	B: By train.
finding out	2 A: Why's ALice coming this evening?	B: To borrow some CDs.
finding out	3 A: What do you want for your BIRTHday?	B: A new jumper.
finding out	4 A: When are you going back HOME?	B: Tomorrow.
finding out	5 A: Who's the man in the blue SUIT?	B: The marketing manager.
making sure	6 A: Do you want a lift to the STATion?	B: No, I told you, I'll walk.
making sure	7 A: Are you going to the PARTy tonight?	B: No, I told you, it's been cancelled.
making sure	8 A: Do you like OYSTers?	B: Yes, I told you, I love them.
making sure	9 A: Did you get back this MORNing?	B: No, I told you, last night.
making sure	10 A: Was SUSan at the meeting?	B: Yes, I told you, she was there.

Part B

making sure	1 A: HOW'S Tom getting to Paris?	B: I told you, by train.
making sure	2 A: WHY'S Alice coming this evening?	B: I told you, to borrow some CDs.

Box 84 continued

making sure	3 A: WHAT do you want for your birthday?	B: I told you, a new jumper.
making sure	4 A: WHEN are you going back home?	B: I told you, tomorrow.
making sure	5 A: WHO'S the man in the blue suit?	B: I told you, the marketing manager.
finding out	6 A: Do you want a lift to the STATion?	B: No, I'll walk.
finding out	7 A: Are you going to the PARTy tonight?	B: No, it's been cancelled.
finding out	8 A: Do you like OYSTers?	B: Yes, I love them.
finding out	9 A: Did you get back this MORNing?	B: No, last night.
finding out	10 A: Was SUSan at the meeting?	B: Yes, she was there.

Part C

find out	1 A: How's Tom getting to Paris?
make sure	2 A: Why's Alice coming this evening?
make sure	3 A: What do you want for your birthday?
find out	4 A: When are you going back home?
find out	5 A: Who's the man in the blue suit?
make sure	6 A: Do you want a lift to the station?
find out	7 A: Are you going to the party tonight?
make sure	8 A: Do you like oysters?
make sure	9 A: Did you get back this morning?
find out	10 A: Was Susan at the meeting?

© CAMBRIDGE UNIVERSITY PRESS 2004

Answer key

Part C

1 A: How's Tom getting to PARis?	B: By train.
2 A: WHY'S Alice coming this evening?	B: I told you, to borrow some CDs.
3 A: WHAT do you want for your birthday?	B: I told you, a new jumper.
4 A: When are you going back HOME?	B: Tomorrow.
5 A: Who's the man in the blue SUIT?	B: The marketing manager.
6 A: Do you want a lift to the STATion?	B: No, I told you, I'll walk.
7 A: Are you going to the PARTy tonight?	B: No, it's been cancelled.
8 A: Do you like OYSTers?	B: Yes, I told you, I love them.
9 A: Did you get back this MORNing?	B: No, I told you, last night.
10 A: Was SUSan at the meeting?	B: Yes, she was there.

5.8 Falling and falling-rising tones: reservation

Focus	Practising falling tone for definite *yes/no* answers and fall-rise tone for answers with some reservation
Level	Elementary+
Time	15 minutes
Preparation	Write each of the following questions (or think of other *yes/no* questions relevant to your own situation) on a small piece of paper:

Have you ever been to Paris? Were you hard working at school?

Do you enjoy teaching us? Are you going to give us any

Can you speak German? homework today?

Are you a good swimmer? Do you play any musical

Do you watch TV a lot? instruments?

Write the following on the board:

Yes↘ Yes↗. No↘ No.↗

Procedure

1 Distribute the pieces of paper with questions on to a number of students, but don't explain what they are for. Then prompt students to ask you the questions they have on their pieces of paper. Answer using all four responses on the board, showing that a falling tone is used for definite *yes/no* answers, and that a fall-rise tone indicates some reservation or limitation which you can go on to give. For example:

Have you ever been to Paris? No↘

Do you enjoy teaching us? Yes↗, most of the time,

Can you speak German? No↗, but I'd like to learn.

Are you a good swimmer? Yes↘

Do you watch TV a lot? No↗, no more than average.

Were you hard working at school? Yes↗, in the last couple of years.

Are you going to give us any
homework today? Yes↘

Do you play any musical instruments? No↘

2 Give students time to think of and write down one or two additional *yes/no* questions each, or brainstorm ideas for questions on the board.

One student asks a question to a selected member of the class, who should respond with one of the *yes* or *no* patterns on the board. Continue with other students. To encourage a range of answers, you may need to point to one of the patterns and ask the responding student to begin their answer in this way. (Of course, not all questions will permit all four responses.)

5.9 'News' and 'not news': correcting

	If possible, begin this activity as you are returning students' exercise books or homework and start at step 1a below. If this is not possible, start at step 1b.
Focus	Practising the falling tone for telling something new and the rising/falling-rising tone for something already known
Level	Intermediate+
Time	20 minutes
Preparation	Copy the material in Box 85 onto a handout.

Procedure

1a Return the students' work, but give the exercise books or papers to the wrong people. Give back the first book/paper, and when the student objects, elicit from them the following:

   But this is (FaRIDah's) book/work, not MINE.

Alternatively, students can use a rising tone instead of a fall-rise:

   But this is (FaRIDah's) book/work, not MINE.

Make sure the first student uses one of the two intonation patterns shown, with the syllables in capitals indicating the place where the falling and falling-rising (or rising) tones begin (i.e. the tonic syllables). Repeat this with other students. (Note that some of your students may have names in which more than one syllable, or even all syllables, are stressed. This activity should still work, using a falling tone on the last stressed syllable of the name.)

 b As an alternative, 'borrow' a few of the students' belongings (pens, books, rulers, etc.), mix them up and return them to the wrong people. Then follow the procedure in step 1a.

 2 When students are familiar with the intonation pattern, explain that we use a falling tone when we tell something new, and a rising or

falling-rising tone (it doesn't matter which) for something that is 'already known' or 'assumed'. The labels *News* (signalled with a falling tone) and *Not news* (signalled with a rising or falling-rising tone) might be helpful.

3   Give out the handout (Box 85). Explain to students that they are going to practise the same 'news' and 'not news' pattern in correcting what people say. Take the part of A in the first dialogue and ask a number of students in turn to take the B part. Monitor and correct the intonation pattern where necessary. Do the same with the remaining dialogues. The activity gets progressively more difficult: 1–3 have intonation and tonic syllables marked; 4–6 have only tonic syllables marked; and the rest have neither marked. The most likely intonation patterns and choice of tonic syllables are shown below, and these are given on the recording.

1   A: Have a great time in Norway.

    B: I'm going to SWEDen, not to NORway.

2   A: Mary's house is the one with a green door.

    B: Her house has got a BLUE door, not a GREEN one.

3   A: I'd hate to be a painter like John. I don't like going up ladders.

    B: He's an ARTist, not a DECorator.

4   A: I hear Sue's going to India this summer.

    B: She's going there PERManently, not just for the SUMMer.

5   A: Tom's trying to get fit. He's on a diet.

    B: He'll have to do more EXercise, not just EAT less.

6   A: It's cheaper to go to Barcelona by plane than train.

    B: It's EASier, not only CHEAPer.

7   A: I'll get the number sixty-two into town.

    B: You catch the sixty-ONE, not the sixty-TWO.

8   A: It'll be really hot in Greece in July.

    B: We're going in OcTOBer, not in JuLY.

9   A: You should easily beat Emma at tennis.

    B: I'm playing SuZANNE, not EMMa.

10 A: I want to learn to drive. I've read lots of books about it.

B: You'll need to PRACTise, not just read BOOKS about it.

11 A: The new farming policy is good for Germany.

B: It's good for EUrope, not only GERMany.

12 A: We're not allowed to smoke in the offices, are we?

B: Smoking's banned in the whole BUILDing, not only in the OFFices.

Note that in British English at least, a falling-rising tone is often used in correcting (as in 1 . . . *not to Norway*; 2 . . . *not a green one*, etc.). The effect of this tone is to make the correction less confrontational and so appear more polite; the correction is a reminder of something they may have forgotten. Although a falling tone could replace a falling-rising tone in the examples above, it might be heard as less polite; telling A that they have got their facts wrong.

4   Finally, students work in pairs on the dialogues. Monitor and correct intonation where necessary.

Extension

Ask students to reverse the order of the information in the B parts (e.g. 1 *I'm not going to Norway, I'm going to Sweden*; 2 *Her house hasn't got a green door, it's got a blue one*; 3 *He's a decorator, not an artist*; 4 *She's not just going there for the summer, she's going permanently*; 5 *He won't just have to eat less, he'll have to do more exercise*; etc.). Then they should work in pairs on the new dialogues. In the B parts the fall-rise (or rise) should come first (for the information which is 'not news') and the fall should come second (for the information which is 'news'). For example:

A: Have a great time in Norway.

B: I'm not going to NORway, I'm going to SWEDen.

Box 85   Student handout

1 A: Have a great time in Norway.

   B: I'm going to SWEDen, not to NORway.

2 A: Mary's house is the one with a green door.

   B: Her house has got a BLUE door, not a GREEN one.

3 A: I'd hate to be a painter like John. I don't like going up ladders.

   B: He's an ARTist, not a DECorator.

4 A: I hear Sue's going to India this summer.
   B: She's going there PERManently, not just for the SUMMer.

5 A: Tom's trying to get fit. He's on a diet.
   B: He'll have to do more EXercise, not just EAT less.

6 A: It's cheaper to go to Barcelona by plane than train.
   B: It's easier, not only cheaper.

7 A: I'll get the number sixty-two into town.
   B: You catch the sixty-one, not the sixty-two.

8 A: It'll be really hot in Greece in July.
   B: We're going in October, not in July.

9 A: You should easily beat Emma at tennis.
   B: I'm playing Suzanne, not Emma.

10 A: I want to learn to drive. I've read lots of books about it.
    B: You'll need to practise, not just read books about it.

11 A: The new farming policy is good for Germany.
    B: It's good for Europe, not only Germany.

12 A: We're not allowed to smoke in the offices, are we?
    B: Smoking's banned in the whole building, not only in the offices.

6 Pronunciation and other parts of language: spelling, grammar and vocabulary

Pronunciation and spelling (6.1–6.6)

6.1 Grouping English alphabet letters

This could be done as a revision activity after the pronunciation of the letters of the alphabet has been introduced.

Focus Classifying the letters of the alphabet according to their vowel sounds

Level Elementary

Time 15 minutes

Procedure

1 Divide the board into seven columns and write the following at the top of each:

1 A	2 B	3 I	4 O	5 U	6 R	7 F

Students copy this into their notebooks and then they repeat the letters along the top after you (/eɪ/, /biː/, /aɪ/, etc.). Tell students that all the letters of the alphabet include a vowel sound like the ones in the letters on the board. Their task is to put the letters of the alphabet into the seven groups. Give a couple of examples: C goes in column 2 under B (/siː/, /biː/), L goes in column 7 under F (/el/, /ef/). Then ask students to work in pairs to do the other letters. Their tables should eventually look like this:

1 A	2 B	3 I	4 O	5 U	6 R	7 F
H J K	C D E G P T V	Y	–	Q W	–	L M N S X Z

Note that: *W* is pronounced like *U* in its second part; in North American English *Z* is pronounced /ziː/, like *B*.

2   Students report back their answers. Ask: 'What other letters go in column 1?' etc. Make sure that all the letters in each group are said with the same vowel sound, correcting where necessary. Then ask individual students to say all the letters in a particular column: 'What letters go in column 5?' etc. Monitor letter pronunciation and correct where necessary.

Extension

In a later class, write the seven columns on the board again, as in step 1. Nominate a student (or ask the class in general for an answer) and say: 'Tell me a letter in column 2' etc. If correct, write the letter in the appropriate column on the board, and continue until all the letters have been given.

6.2 Pronouncing single vowel letters (1)[1]

Focus	Pronouncing simple vowels in one-syllable words
Level	Elementary
Time	20 minutes
Preparation	Copy the material in Box 86 onto a handout. Write the following abbreviations on the board: *USA, EU, PTO, IOU, UN, UK, UAE, i.e.*

Procedure

1   Focus attention on the pronunciation of the vowel letters *a, e, i, o* and *u* by asking students how the abbreviations on the board are said. Check that they are saying the vowels with their 'alphabet names' (a = /eɪ/, e = /iː/, etc.) and introduce this term. Go on to ask students if they know what the abbreviations stand for (*USA* = United States of America; *EU* = European Union; *PTO* = Please turn over; *IOU* = I owe you; *UN* = United Nations; *UK* = United Kingdom; *UAE* = United Arab Emirates; *i.e.* = *id est* [Latin] – that is).

2   Give out the handout (Box 86) and focus on Part A. Students repeat the words chorally and individually after you or the recording.

3   Ask students to underline all the words that contain a vowel with its alphabet name.

---

[1] Based on Hewings, M. (1993, pp. 91–92).

4   Focus on Part B. Explain that *C* stands for consonant letter and *V* for vowel letter. *(C)CVCe* means a word beginning with one (or two) consonant letters, followed by a vowel letter, a consonant letter and then the letter *e*. *(C)CVC(C)* means a word beginning with one (or two) consonant letters, followed by a vowel letter, and then one (or two) consonant letters. Students write the words from Part A into the table in Part B. Give a couple of examples to check that they understand: *cake* goes in the first row of column 2; *fact* goes in the first row of column 3; etc. Then they should complete the rule at the bottom of Part B.

5   Finally, ask students to find five or six (or more) examples of words with the same pattern of consonants and vowels. (They could search for these in their coursebooks.) They should check which of the words follow the rule and which (if any) don't. If they are not sure of the pronunciation of words they have found, they should ask you.

Box 86   Student handout

Part A

cake	fact	game	life	tap	cup
test	home	these	left	bit	tune
spell	bag	drop	plane	mine	tube
soft	nose	kill	dust		

Part B

Pronunciation in words written . . .

Vowel letter	(C)CVCe	(C)CVC(C)
a		
e		
i		
o		
u		

Rule
When a one-syllable word ends with ...., the vowel letter is pronounced with its alphabet name.

> **Answer key**
>
> Part A: The following words have a vowel with its alphabet name: cake, game, life, home, these, tune, plane, mine, tube, nose.
>
> Part B:
>
> | Vowel letter | (C)CVCe | (C)CVC(C) |
> |---|---|---|
> | a | cake, game, plane | fact, tap, bag |
> | e | these | test, left, spell |
> | i | life, mine | bit, kill |
> | o | home, nose | drop, soft |
> | u | tune, tube | cup, dust |
>
> When a one-syllable word ends with *e*, the vowel letter is pronounced with its alphabet name. Note that some exceptions to this rule, which students will have come across, are: *give, have, live* (verb) and *come*.

6.3 Pronouncing single vowel letters (2)

Focus	Identifying and practising different pronunciations of single vowel letters in words
Level	Intermediate+
Time	30 minutes
Preparation	Copy the material in Box 87 onto a handout or an OHT, or write the words on the board. For the second part of this activity (from step 4 onwards) you will need a dice.

Procedure

1 Give out or show the material in Box 87. Check that the students know all the words.

2 Students work in pairs to decide how many ways the underlined letters *A, E, I, O, U* and *Y* are pronounced and to count how many examples of each pronunciation there are. (This procedure can be the starting point of a number of similar activities focusing on spelling–sound correspondence. See, for example, Activity 6.7.) You could point out that you are only looking at these letters:

   • as single vowels (not part of a pair of vowels such as in *OUT*)

- when they do not come before the letter *R* (because combinations such as *AR*, *ER*, etc. may have other pronunciations)
- in a stressed syllable or a word with one syllable.

Possible single vowel letter to sound correspondence is given in Box 88.

3 Check the answers. Ask for the number of sounds for each letter and all the words with a particular vowel letter sound. Students repeat the words chorally and individually. Correct vowel pronunciations where necessary.

4 Divide the board into six columns and write the following at the top of each column:

> A   E   I   O   U   Y

Divide the class into teams (any number of teams can play, but more than about five or six might slow the activity down too much). Throw the dice and call out the number for the first team. For example, if the dice shows 4, one of the team has to say a word which includes the letter O, but is not one of those used in Box 87. Explain (as in step 2) that the letter: must be a single vowel (not part of a pair of vowels such as in <u>OU</u>T); must not come before the letter *R*; must be in a stressed syllable or a word with one syllable. If the answer is correct, write the word in the O column. Move on to the second team and repeat the procedure. Try to keep the pace fairly fast, and don't allow each team too much thinking/discussion time. You could penalise wrong answers (i.e. if words break any of the three rules) by awarding no points and moving on to the next team. If a team is able to say a word with a sound–letter correspondence that hasn't been used before, they get two points. For a word including a sound–letter correspondence that is repeated, they get one point. For example, under *A* you might have: *cat* (two points; /æ/), *bad* (one point; also /æ/), *rather* (two points; /ɑː/), *trap* (one point; also /æ/), *ask* (one point; /ɑː/ or /æ/ – both pronunciations are acceptable). Appoint a student to keep score on another part of the board. Repeat a few times and then add up the scores to find the winning team.

Box 87   Student handout

h<u>a</u>nd   c<u>u</u>t   pol<u>i</u>ce   s<u>y</u>mbol   <u>e</u>mpty   th<u>e</u>se   <u>E</u>ngland   r<u>u</u>de
m<u>a</u>ke   cr<u>y</u>   w<u>o</u>lf   fr<u>o</u>g   c<u>a</u>ll   m<u>y</u>stery   t<u>i</u>me   r<u>i</u>ght   f<u>a</u>ther
s<u>u</u>gar   b<u>e</u>   l<u>u</u>ck   m<u>a</u>ny   mach<u>i</u>ne   m<u>o</u>ve   tr<u>u</u>th   b<u>e</u>d   s<u>o</u>n
cr<u>y</u>stal   pr<u>e</u>tty   f<u>u</u>ll   w<u>i</u>th   h<u>o</u>t   t<u>y</u>pe   s<u>i</u>t   s<u>o</u>   b<u>y</u>   w<u>a</u>s

---

Box 88   Teacher reference

Letter	Number of sounds	Sounds and example word
A	6	/æ/ h<u>a</u>nd; /ɑ:/ f<u>a</u>ther; /ɒ/ w<u>a</u>s; /ɔ:/ c<u>a</u>ll; /eɪ/ m<u>a</u>ke; /e/ m<u>a</u>ny
E	3	/i:/ th<u>e</u>se, b<u>e</u>; /ɪ/ pr<u>e</u>tty, <u>E</u>ngland; /e/ b<u>e</u>d, <u>e</u>mpty
I	3	/ɪ/ s<u>i</u>t, w<u>i</u>th; /aɪ/ t<u>i</u>me, r<u>i</u>ght; /i:/ pol<u>i</u>ce, mach<u>i</u>ne
O	5	/ɒ/ fr<u>o</u>g, h<u>o</u>t; /əʊ/ s<u>o</u>; /ʌ/ s<u>o</u>n; /ʊ/ w<u>o</u>lf; /u:/ m<u>o</u>ve
U	3	/ʊ/ f<u>u</u>ll, s<u>u</u>gar; /ʌ/ c<u>u</u>t, l<u>u</u>ck; /u:/ r<u>u</u>de, tr<u>u</u>th
Y	2	/ɪ/ s<u>y</u>mbol, cr<u>y</u>stal, m<u>y</u>stery; /aɪ/ b<u>y</u>, t<u>y</u>pe, cr<u>y</u>

6.4 Pronouncing pairs of vowel letters: *OU, OA, OE, OI, OO*

The aim of this activity is to learn about some of the different pronunciations of pairs of vowel letters. Many of these can be pronounced in a variety of ways, but this activity focuses on the most common pronunciations of vowel letter pairs beginning O.

Focus Identifying and practising different pronunciations of vowel letter pairs beginning O

Level Elementary+

Time 10 minutes

Preparation Find small pictures that show words having one of the vowel pairs *OU, OA, OE, OI* or *OO* in their spelling. Catalogues from shops that sell a wide variety of goods are useful for this, or you could download pictures from the Internet. The pictures should illustrate words with a number of different pronunciations of these vowel pairs. Put the pictures in random order on a page and include about the same number of pictures that include different vowel pairs (these are 'distractors'). An example is given in Box 89, which you could photocopy and use.

Procedure

1 Write the vowel letter pairs *OU, OA, OE, OI* and *OO* on the board. Students should look at the pictures and find the words that contain each of these pairs (not all of them do) and decide how many different pronunciations of each there are. Teach new words and their meanings as necessary.

2   Ask students to report their answers. Check these, then say the words and students repeat after you.

Box 89   Student handout

Tomato

TEA BAGS
80 bags

ORANGE
ORANGE

Homework
pages 27–32

© CAMBRIDGE UNIVERSITY PRESS 2004

Vowel letter pair	Common pronunciations			Notes
Answer key				

Vowel letter pair	Common pronunciations			Notes
OU	house /aʊ/	soup /u:/	shoulder /əʊ/	Exclude *OUR* and *OUGH* words as these can be pronounced in other ways.
OA	coat /əʊ/	blackboard /ɔ:/		*OAR* is included as it has only one pronunciation, /ɔ:/.
OE	toes /əʊ/	shoes /u:/		
OI	coin /ɔɪ/			
OO	spoon /u:/	book /ʊ/		Exclude *OOR* words as these are pronounced in other ways.

Vowel letter pairs	Pronunciations and example nouns
AI	Usual pronunciation: /eɪ/ brain, chain, drain, tail, nail, rain Occasional pronunciation: /ɪ/ captain, mountain
AU	Usual pronunciation: /ɔ:/ astronaut, author, autograph, autumn, exhaust pipe, laundry, saucepan, saucer Occasional pronunciation: /ɒ/ cauliflower, sausage
EA	Usual pronunciations: /i:/ tea, beach, beans, eagle, east; /e/ bread, dead, head, feather Occasional pronunciation: /eɪ/ steak, break
IE	Usual pronunciations: /aɪ/ tie, pie, flies; /i:/ briefcase, priest, shield; /ɪ/ babies, batteries, berries, cookies
UE	Usual pronunciations: /u:/ glue, tissue; /ju:/ barbecue, statue
UI	Usual pronunciation: /u:/ fruit, suit, juice, bruise Occasional pronunciation: /ɪ/ biscuit, building, guitar

Extension

The table at the bottom of p. 172 gives information about the pronunciations of some common vowel letter pairs beginning with *A*, *E*, *I* and *U*, together with some nouns including these pairs. You could devise a similar activity to the one above focusing on some of these. To make the task of finding relevant pictures easier, ask students (for homework) to find small pictures for words that include one or more of the vowel pairs you want to focus on. Stick these (and some distractors) on a handout to be used at a later date. For simplicity, vowel letter pairs followed by *R* (e.g. *EIR*, *OUR*) and by *GH* (e.g. *AUGH*, *EIGH*) have been excluded as these can have different pronunciations from those shown in the table. With more advanced students, you could also use words including these combinations and highlight their pronunciations.

6.5 Pronouncing consonant letters: *C* and *G*

Focus	Identifying and practising different pronunciations of consonants *C* and *G*
Level	Elementary+
Time	15 minutes
Preparation	Copy Box 90 onto a handout or an OHT.

Procedure

1 Give out the handout (Box 90) and focus on Part A. Students repeat the sentences after you. It can be difficult to repeat long stretches of speech like this, so to make the process easier and help build up fluency, ask them to repeat short sections from the end of the sentence to the beginning (a process sometimes called 'backchaining'). For example, you could divide sentence 1 into the following sections:

/a week/ (repeat); /twice a week/ (repeat); /the gym/ (repeat); /to the gym/ (repeat); I go (repeat); /I go to the gym/ (repeat); /I go to the gym twice a week/ (repeat)

Check that students understand the meaning of the sentences.

2 Explain that you are focusing on the pronunciation of the letters *C* and *G*. Students work in pairs. Ask them to circle all the *C* and *G* letters in the sentences and to decide how many different pronunciations of *C* and *G* there are.

3 Write the four pronunciations of *C* and *G* used in this activity on the board as phonetic symbols, with an example word for each:

/k/ cat   /s/ ice   /g/ give   /dʒ/ age

Focus on Part B of the handout. Ask students to complete the rules using the information they have in the sentences in Part A. Check the answers.

Extension

Like most 'rules' that relate to spelling and pronunciation, the ones above have exceptions. For homework, ask students to find words in which the rules do not apply. You might even ask them to work out other rules for the exceptions. For example, they might find:

1 The letter *C* is pronounced /ʃ/ (as in *shop*) at the end of a stressed syllable before *I* and another vowel (e.g. *special*, *musician*). But notice that when there is another /ʃ/ sound in the word, *C* is pronounced /s/ (e.g. *pronunciation*).

2 The letter *G* is sometimes pronounced /ʒ/. This happens in a few words, mainly with French origins (e.g. *prestige*, *genre*), and in some people's pronunciation of the second *G* of *garage*.

Box 90   Student handout

Part A

1 I go to the gym twice a week.
2 In an emergency give me a call.
3 The girls went together to the city centre.
4 Gary crossed the dangerous road to the cinema.
5 A cyclist from Egypt won the competition in Germany.
6 Mrs Giles took the register at the beginning of the class.

Part B

Rules

Before the letters *E*, *I* and *Y*, the letter *C* is usually pronounced ....
Everywhere else it is pronounced ....
Before the letters *E*, *I* and *Y*, the letter *G* is sometimes pronounced ....
and sometimes .... Everywhere else it is pronounced ....

Answer key

Part A:

Two pronunciations of *C*: /k/ (e.g. *call*) and /s/ (e.g. *twice*)

Two pronunciations of *G*: /g/ (e.g. *go*) and /dʒ/ (e.g. *gym*)

Part B:

Before the letters *E*, *I* and *Y*, the letter *C* is usually pronounced /s/. Everywhere else it is pronounced /k/.

Before the letters *E*, *I* and *Y*, the letter *G* is sometimes pronounced /g/ and sometimes /dʒ/. Everywhere else it is pronounced /g/.

6.6 Pronouncing consonant pairs: *PH, CH, SH, TH* and *GH*

Focus	Identifying and practising different pronunciations of consonant pairs: *PH, CH, SH, TH* and *GH*
Level	Intermediate
Time	25 minutes
Preparation	Copy the material in Box 91 onto a handout or an OHT, or write the words on the board.

Procedure

1 Give out the handout or display the material. Focus on Part A. Students repeat the words after you or the recording. Then check that students understand the meaning of the words.

2 Students work in pairs to find how many ways there are of pronouncing the letter pairs *PH, CH, SH, TH* and *GH* in the words in Part A, and how many examples of each pronunciation there are in these words.

3 When students have finished, give them an opportunity to check their answers. Say the words or play them on the recording.

4 Focus on Part B to review the pronunciation of the consonant letter pairs. Students work in pairs to find three words from Part A for each of the categories listed in Part B. When they report back their answers, monitor the pronunciation of the letter pairs *PH, CH, SH, TH* and *GH* and correct where necessary.

Box 91   Student handout

Part A
cheese   rough   shampoo   author   Philip   tights   champagne
toothpaste   Thomas   stomach   ship   geography   chef
Ghanaian   chemistry   cherries   smooth   headache   shoes
Stephen   pharmacist   coach   shower   Chinese   Thai   yacht
shorts   cough   throat   physics   chest   shiver   light

Part B
1 three things you can eat or drink ....
2 three things you find in the bathroom ....
3 three things you might do or have when you are ill ....
4 three nationalities ....
5 three male names ....
6 three means of transport ....
7 three words describing how things feel ....
8 three jobs ....
9 three school subjects ....
10 three parts of the body ....
11 three items of clothing ....

Answer key
Part A:

Letter pair	Number of sounds	Sounds and example word
CH	4	/tʃ/ cheese, cherries, Chinese, coach, chest; /ʃ/ champagne, chef; /k/ headache, chemistry, stomach; *'silent'* yacht
GH	3	/g/ Ghanaian; /f/ cough, rough; *'silent'* tights, light
PH	2	/f/ Philip, pharmacist, geography, physics; /v/ Stephen
SH	1	/ʃ/ shoes, shorts, shampoo, shower, shiver, ship
TH	3	/θ/ author, throat, toothpaste; /ð/ smooth; /t/ Thai, Thomas

Part B:
1 cheese, champagne, cherries
2 toothpaste, shampoo, shower
3 cough, headache, shiver
4 Chinese, Ghanaian, Thai
5 Stephen, Philip, Thomas
6 yacht, coach, ship
7 rough, smooth, light
8 chef, pharmacist, author
9 chemistry, physics, geography
10 throat, stomach, chest
11 tights, shorts, shoes

6.7 Homographs: a row about rowing?

Focus Homographs: words with different meanings and sounds, which are
spelt the same
Level Advanced
Time 25 minutes
Preparation Copy the material in Box 92 onto a handout or an OHT.

Procedure

1 Give an example of a homograph. Write the word *row* on the board and
ask students how many meanings it has. (Pronounced /rəʊ/ it means
either a line of things or people, or to move a boat through water using
oars; pronounced /raʊ/ it means a noisy argument.)
2 Give out or display the material in Box 92. Students work in pairs. Ask
them to identify the homographs in each sentence, and to decide how the
two forms of the word are pronounced. (Perhaps go through item 1 to
illustrate this.) If your students have dictionaries showing pronunciation,
they could use them to find out or check pronunciation and meaning.
3 Check answers by asking students to read out the sentences. Ask a
number of students to say each sentence to give plenty of practice.
Monitor the pronunciation of the homographs and correct where
necessary.

Box 92 Student handout

1 The refuse collectors refuse to work on Sunday.
2 Her invalid parking permit is invalid.
3 This furniture polish is Polish.
4 The guide threatened to desert us in the desert.
5 We'd like to present you with this leaving present.
6 I'll project the results of the project on the screen.
7 I lead a busy life buying and selling lead and other metals.
8 There was a tear in her eye when she saw the tear in her dress.
9 As the winning archer put down his bow he gave a bow to the crowd.
10 It's getting close to the time for the museum to close.
11 Come and look at this minute insect when you've got a minute.
12 'Don't you like the new vase?' 'No! I object to having that ugly object in my house.'

Answer key

1 refuse /ˈrefjuːs/ – /rɪˈfjuːz/
2 invalid /ˈɪnvəlɪd/ (or /ˈɪnvəliːd/) – /ɪnˈvælɪd/
3 polish/Polish /ˈpɒlɪʃ/ – /ˈpəʊlɪʃ/
4 desert /dɪˈzɜːt/ – /ˈdezət/
5 present /prɪˈzent/ – /ˈprezənt/
6 project /prəˈdʒekt/ – /ˈprɒdʒekt/
7 lead /liːd/ – /led/
8 tear /tɪə/ – /teə/
9 bow /bəʊ/ – /baʊ/
10 close /kləʊs/ – /kləʊz/
11 minute /maɪˈnjuːt/ – /ˈmɪnɪt/
12 object /əbˈdʒekt/ – /ˈɒbdʒekt/

Pronunciation and grammar (6.8 and 6.9)

6.8 Pronouncing -s in plurals, verbs and possessives

Focus Identifying and practising different pronunciations of -s endings in plurals, verbs and possessives
Level Elementary+
Time 25 minutes
Preparation Copy the material in Box 93 onto a handout or an OHT.

Procedure

1 Write the following words on the board:

begins	Sue's	bags
keeps	Frank's	cats
dances	George's	classes

Remind students that -s endings are important in English in the third person present simple (*begins, keeps, dances*), in possessives (*Sue's*, etc.) and in plurals (*bags*, etc.). Ask students what different pronunciations -s endings have in these words. (Answer: /z/: *begins, Sue's, bags*; /s/ *keeps*, etc.; /ɪz/ *dances*, etc.) Then say the words and students repeat.

2 Give out the handout (Box 93) and focus on Part A. Check that students know the meaning of the words. Students work in pairs and identify the odd one out in each list of words: four of the words have the same -s pronunciation and one (the odd one out) is different.

3 Allow students to check their answers by saying each list (or play the recording) with the odd one out at the end. Explain this to students first. For example, read list 1 as 'jokes, grapes, boats, coughs, addresses'. Then say each list again and students repeat.

4 Explain that the pronunciation of -s in words like this depends on the previous sound. Ask students to complete Part B using the words they have practised in Part A. If students know phonetic symbols, they could use these; otherwise they can write letters. The only real complication here is the two pronunciations of *th*; /θ/ is followed by /s/ and /ð/ is followed by /z/. The full answers are given below Box 93.

5 Finally, ask students if they can see any patterns relating the -s pronunciation to the previous sound. It is not necessary to be too technical about this: /ɪz/ follows sounds that 'hiss'; /s/ follows other voiceless sounds (where you can't feel a vibration on your throat when

the sound is made); and /z/ follows voiced consonants and vowels (where you can feel a vibration).

If the /z/ vs /s/ distinction is difficult for your students, see 'Correcting particular consonants' for ideas (pp. 63–65).

Box 93   Student handout

Part A

1 jokes   grapes   boats   addresses   coughs
2 loves   clothes   sizes   ribs   Tom's
3 Thomas's   animals   crashes   teaches   villages
4 things   cooks   Robert's   cliffs   paths
5 birds   legs   Alison's   menus   stops
6 brushes   catches   baths   freezes   cages

Part B

Pronunciation of -*s* ending	/s/	/z/	/ɪz/
Previous sound			

© Cambridge University Press 2004

Answer key

Part A:

The odd ones out are:

1 addresses (/ɪz/, the others are /s/)   4 things (/z/, the others are /s/)
2 sizes (/ɪz/, the others are /z/)   5 stops (/s/, the others are /z/)
3 animals (/z/, the others are /ɪz/)   6 baths (/s/, the others are /ɪz/)

Part B:

Pronunciation of -s ending	/s/	/z/	/ɪz/
Previous sound	Letters: f, th, p, t, k Phonetic symbols: /f/, /θ/, /p/, /t/, /k/	Letters: v, th, b, d, g, m, n, ng, l and vowels Phonetic symbols: /v/, /ð/, /b/, /d/, /g/, /m/, /n/, /ŋ/, /l/ and vowels	Letters: s, z, sh, ch, g Phonetic symbols: /s/, /z/, /ʃ/, /tʃ/, /dʒ/, /ʒ/
Examples (These include words from Box 93 and extra examples of /z/ endings for information.)	/f/ coughs, cliffs /θ/ paths, baths /p/ stops, grapes /t/ boats, Robert's /k/ cooks, jokes	/v/ loves, moves /ð/ breathes, clothes /b/ ribs, verbs /d/ birds, weeds /g/ legs, bags /m/ Tom's, storms /n/ begins, Alison's /ŋ/ rings, things /l/ animals, wheels vowel answers: menus, Sue's	/s/ addresses, Thomas's /z/ sizes, freezes /ʃ/ crashes, brushes /tʃ/ catches, teaches /dʒ/ cages, villages

6.9 Pronouncing -ed in past tense verbs

Focus Identifying and practising different pronunciations of -ed endings in past tense verbs

Level Intermediate+

Time 40 minutes

Preparation Copy the material in Box 94 onto a handout.

Procedure

1 Give out the handout (Box 94) and focus on Part A. Explain that the -ed endings of verb past tenses have one of three pronunciations: /t/, /d/ and /ɪd/. Say the verbs in Part A (or play the recording), and students write the verbs down in the appropriate column in Part B.

2   Then say the words in each column aloud (see the key below). Students check their answers and repeat after you. Monitor the pronunciation of the *-ed* endings, and correct if necessary. Teach or elicit the meanings of words as you go.

3   Put the verbs (they are all 'speaking' words) into context. Students work in pairs and use the verbs to complete the story dialogue in Part C. In most cases a number of verbs are possible in each gap, but students should try to use all the verbs, and use each once only.

4   Pairs of students read their story dialogues aloud. (You could organise this in various ways: one student could expressively read out the quoted speech, and the other adds 'she asked', 'he admitted', etc.; or they could simply read out alternate lines.) As they do this, ask others to suggest any alternative reporting verbs. Monitor the pronunciation of *-ed* endings and correct where necessary.

5   Go on to ask for suggestions on who the people are, where they are, and what is the situation. Encourage different interpretations.

6   Finally, ask students if they can see any patterns in how *-ed* endings are pronounced. Focus attention on the sounds before *-ed* if necessary. The rules are that before /d/ or /t/ the pronunciation is /ɪd/; before other voiced sounds the pronunciation is /d/; before other unvoiced sounds the pronunciation is /t/.

Answer key

Part B:

/t/: asked, chorused, confessed, promised, shrieked, laughed

/d/: apologised, called, complained, explained, offered, replied, whispered

/ɪd/: added, admitted, demanded, insisted, objected, repeated

Part C:

Example answers:

1 asked, 2 admitted, 3 demanded, 4 complained, 5 insisted, 6 repeated, 7 shrieked, 8 promised, 9 apologised, 10 confessed, 11 offered, 12 laughed, 13 objected, 14 whispered, 15 called, 16 replied, 17 chorused, 18 explained, 19 added.

Box 94   Student handout

Part A

promised   complained   called   repeated   asked   added   objected
explained   whispered   laughed   apologised   confessed   admitted
insisted   offered   replied   chorused   demanded   shrieked

Part B

Pronunciation of *-ed* ending	/t/	/d/	/ɪd/
Verbs			

Part C

'Where's Tom?' she ....[1].
'No idea,' he ....[2].
'Well, look for him,' she ....[3].
'But I'm tired,' he ....[4].
'But you *must* find him,' she ....[5].
'But I'm tired,' he ....[6].
'GO NOW!' she ....[7].
'Okay, I'll find him,' he ....[8].
'I'm sorry I shouted,' she ....[9].
'That's okay. I'm worried about him, too,' he ....[10].
'I suppose I could go,' she ....[11].
'You! Ha!' he ....[12].
'There's nothing funny about that,' she ....[13].
'Sh! What's that noise? Listen,' he ....[14].
'Tom! Is that you?' she ....[15].
'Yes, it's me,' Tom ....[16].
'Where have you been?' they ....[17].
'Sorry, I forgot what time we were meeting,' he ....[18].
'And then I got lost,' he ....[19].

Pronunciation and vocabulary (6.10–6.12)

Encourage students to learn the meaning of words and their pronunciation at the same time. Activities 6.10, 6.11 and 6.12 are short, simple activities that you can use regularly to help students to improve pronunciation while learning or revising vocabulary.

6.10 Classifying words

Focus	Classifying new words according to their pronunciation
Level	Elementary+
Time	10 minutes

Procedure

1   Ask students to find five (or more) words they have learned this week (or whatever period is relevant in your teaching situation) that:
 • include a particular vowel sound (either a simple vowel such as /ɪ/ or /e/ or a diphthong such as /aɪ/ or /əʊ/)
 • include a particular consonant sound
 • have stress on a particular syllable (the first, second, third, etc.)
 • have a particular number of syllables with a given stress pattern (for example, ask them to find words with three syllables with the stress pattern Ooo).
2   When they report back their words, correct pronunciation where necessary.

6.11 Odd one out

Focus	Identifying words with a different pronunciation
Level	Elementary+
Time	10 minutes

Procedure

1   Ask students to write one line in an 'odd one out' exercise using vocabulary they have learned this week, i.e. four out of five words share the same feature of pronunciation, but the fifth is different (e.g. four words contain a particular vowel sound, and one doesn't).
2   Collect the lists of words on a handout or an OHT, use them as a quiz, and get students to repeat them, correcting where necessary.

6.12 Problem pronunciations

Focus	Practising words with a difficult pronunciation
Level	Elementary+
Time	10 minutes

Procedure

During the week collect new words that cause your students pronunciation difficulties. Write these on an OHT or a poster and regularly display them, getting students to repeat the words after you. Keep the list of words close by, adding to it during the week, and end up with a 'problem pronunciations of (e.g.) week beginning 15th July'. Build up a collection of these and bring them out occasionally for revision and practice.

7 Testing pronunciation

The first activity in this chapter (7.1) provides an evaluation of a student's overall pronunciation competence. It could be used either as part of a test of language ability more generally, or to give feedback to students on how much they have achieved. The second activity (7.2) diagnoses particular pronunciation difficulties, focusing on vowels and consonants. The rest of the activities (7.3–7.7) can be used in two ways. First, they can be used to test students' ability to hear and distinguish certain features of English pronunciation (vowels, consonants, weak and contracted forms, etc.), i.e. to test their *receptive* skills. Tests of receptive skills are given in Version 1 in each activity. These tests can be done as a class activity. Second, the activities can be used to test students' ability to say different features of pronunciation, i.e. to test their *productive* skills. Tests of productive skills are given in Version 2 in each activity. These tests should be done with individual students either saying their answers directly to the teacher, who marks them immediately, or (preferably) recording their answers onto a cassette for the teacher to mark later. See Introduction, pp. 17–19 for a fuller discussion of receptive and productive skills in pronunciation, and also of the advantages and disadvantages of using text read aloud and spontaneous speech in testing pronunciation.

7.1 General evaluation of pronunciation

Focus	Evaluating pronunciation using a grading scale
Level	Elementary+
Preparation	Make a copy of the material in Box 95 for each student.

Procedure

The evaluation scale in Box 95 can be used to give a broad class of pronunciation ability (in column 1) and a finer grade (in column 2). Simply circle one of the grades (1 is highest and 12 lowest) to give an overall evaluation. If you are using the scale in order to provide feedback, regular evaluation can be done. Using the scale rather than the broad classes makes it easier to encourage students, by making sure they move up the grade scale if they have worked hard on their pronunciation.

You could either make a very informal evaluation, basing your judgement on what you have heard of the student's pronunciation in their regular classroom speech, or you could make it more formal by getting students to read a text aloud (see Activity 7.2) or, for example, to tell a story from a sequence of pictures (see Activity 7.2, Extension for more ideas).

Box 95   Student handout

Your pronunciation is . . .	*Grade*
always easy to understand (You rarely have pronunciation problems.)	1 2 3
usually easy to understand (You occasionally have pronunciation problems.)	4 5 6
sometimes difficult to understand (You quite often have pronunciation problems.)	7 8 9
often difficult to understand (You frequently have pronunciation problems.)	10 11 12

7.2 Diagnosing particular problems

This activity could be used as an initial diagnostic assessment of pronunciation in order to help prioritise teaching goals. The text[1] for reading aloud includes examples of most English vowel and consonant sounds and these are the focus of a systematic diagnosis. A number of contracted forms (see pp. 87–93), links (see pp. 79–87) and weak forms (see pp. 7, 94–99) are included, so problems in these areas can also be diagnosed.

Focus   Diagnosing pronunciation problems
Level   Intermediate+/Elementary
Time   30 minutes per student

---

[1]   This was written jointly with Janet Jones of the Learning Centre, University of Sydney.

Preparation	Copy the material in Box 96 onto a handout. If you are going to use the checklist, make copies of the material in Box 98, one for each student. You will also need a cassette recorder, microphone and blank cassette for this activity. For the Variation, copy the material in Box 97 and Box 99.

Procedure

1 Give out the handout (Box 96) and let students spend some time familiarising themselves with the context (this is in bold, not to be read aloud) and the text. It is not essential for students to understand all the vocabulary.
2 Individual students read the text aloud as you record it.
3 Listen to each recording and on another copy of the text circle the sounds that students have difficulties with. You may also want to transfer details onto the checklist in Box 98. A space is provided for comments, which could either be notes to yourself or to the student, clarifying what kind of problem is involved. In this way you can build up a picture of the pronunciation priorities for individual students or a group of students as a whole.

Note
The 'target' single consonants in the checklist are those which either have a vowel on either side (e.g. *nee<u>d</u>ed*) or come before a punctuation mark and so are likely to be preceded by a pause, i.e. they do not form part of a consonant cluster. 'Target' vowels are in stressed syllables of words and so are likely to be pronounced more clearly than vowels in unstressed syllables.

Variation
For elementary students, short sentences and utterances can be used in the same way as the material in Box 96. Example material is given in Boxes 97 and 99.

Extension
Other texts intended for pronunciation diagnosis can be found in:

• Celce-Murcia, M., Brinton, D.M. and Goodwin, J.M. (1996, pp. 398–399)
• Swan, M. and Smith, B. (2001, p. 360).

A text read aloud could be supplemented with a sample of more spontaneous speech from students; for example, talking about their family, home town or hobbies, or telling a story from a series of pictures. From this sample, further information can be gathered about problem sounds, consonant clusters and word stress. (See Introduction, pp. 18–19.)

Box 96 Student handout

Imagine that you have just moved into a new house and are describing some of the things that you have had to buy. You start by describing what you have bought for the kitchen.

In here, the dearest things were the electrical appliances – things like a dishwasher, a fridge and a stove. There was no cutlery, so I bought some knives, forks and spoons. I'd been given some bowls, but no cups and saucers, so I bought six of each. I needed furniture, too, and curtains for some of the rooms. I had to make some difficult choices. I bought purple curtains for the dining room. That wasn't my idea, but they should look really good in there. They'll help keep out the noise. And I got a nice old wooden table and some chairs. They cost about a thousand dollars. I've painted the walls pale orange and hung a large poster near the window. And I've put an oil painting on the opposite wall with an unusual pair of lamps. Yesterday I bought blue carpet for the stairs. And I had to get a barbecue for the yard. Another job is to paint the outside of the house and the garage. I'll enjoy doing that.

Box 97 Student handout

1   See you later.
2   Are you thirsty?
3   I have to go now.
4   What's that noise?
5   By tomorrow evening.
6   It's about five o'clock.
7   I sent a cheque to Roy.
8   It's on television today.
9   She's upstairs in the bath.
10 Peter works in a shoe shop.
11 Do you really want a drink?
12 I'll go to see Sarah before July.
13 'Thanks a lot.' 'It's a pleasure.'
14 I forgot to pay Mark for the toys.
15 Your jacket is on the chair outside.
16 'Shall I do the washing?' 'Good idea.'
17 We're usually home before the children.
18 There's a zoo near Hull. It's not far.
19 We bought an amazing orange and purple car. It's in the garage.
20 Can you just put the books over there by the door?

Box 98   Teacher reference (or Student handout)

Consonants	Words in text	Comment
p	kee**p**, o**pp**osite, car**p**et, **p**aint	
b	**b**ought, **b**ut, a**b**out, **b**ar**b**ecue, jo**b**	
t	**t**oo, cur**t**ains, go**t**, abou**t**, pu**t**, ge**t**, tha**t**	
d	**d**earest, **d**ishwasher, nee**d**ed, **d**ining,	
	i**d**ea, goo**d**, yester**d**ay, outsi**d**e, **d**oing	
k	li**k**e, **c**utlery, **c**ups, diffi**c**ult, **c**ost, **c**arpet	
g	**g**ood, **g**ot, **g**et, **g**arage	
tʃ	ea**ch**, furni**t**ure	
dʒ	fri**dge**, **j**ob	
f	**f**orks, di**ff**icult, **f**or	
v	sto**v**e, (six) o**f** (each)	
θ	**th**ings, **th**ousand	
ð	**th**e, **th**ere, **th**at, **th**ey, wi**th**, ano**th**er	
s	**s**o, **s**au**c**ers, (for) **s**ome (of), choi**c**es,	
	ni**c**e, hou**s**e	
z	applian**c**e**s**, saucer**s**, choice**s**, noi**s**e, chair**s**,	
	thou**s**and, dollar**s**, oppo**s**ite, stair**s**	
ʃ	dishwa**sh**er, **sh**ould	
ʒ	unu**s**ual, gara**g**e	
h	**h**ad, **h**ouse	
m	(for) so**m**e (of), **m**ake, roo**m**	
n	**n**eeded, fur**n**iture, **n**oise, **n**ice, **n**ear, a**n**,	
	a**n**other	
ŋ	painti**ng**	
l	e**l**ectrica**l**, rea**ll**y, do**ll**ars, pa**l**e, **l**arge, I'**ll**	
r	dea**r**est, cutle**r**y, **r**ooms, o**r**ange, pai**r** (of)	
j	**y**esterday, **y**ard	
w	**w**as, **w**alls, **w**indow	

© Cambridge University Press 2004

Box 98 continued

Vowels	Words in text	Comment
ɪ	in, things, dishwasher, fridge, given, six, difficult, window	
e	electrical, help, yesterday, get	
æ	had, lamps, garage, that	
ɒ	wasn't, cost, dollars, orange, opposite, job	
ʌ	cutlery, cups, hung, another	
ʊ	look, good, wooden, put	
iː	each, needed, really, keep	
eɪ	table, painted, pale, painting, paint	
aɪ	appliances, knives, dining, nice	
ɔɪ	choices, noise, oil, enjoy	
uː	spoons, too, rooms, unusual, blue	
əʊ	stove, bowls, old, poster	
aʊ	about, thousand, outside, house	
ɪə	here, dearest, idea, near	
eə	there, chairs, pair, stairs	
ɑː	large, carpet, barbecue, yard	
ɔː	bought, forks, saucers, walls, wall	
ɜː	furniture, curtains, purple	

Contracted forms	Comment
I'd, wasn't, they'll, I've	

Links	Comment
electrical appliances, like a, and a, so I, forks and, cups and, six of, some of, good in, keep out, and I, got a, nice old, cost about, about a, pale orange, hung a, and I've, put an, the opposite, with an, an unusual, pair of, get a, job is, the outside, I'll enjoy	

Weak forms	Comment
the, were, and, there, was, some, but, of, for, to	

Box 99   Teacher reference (or Student handout)

Consonants	Words in text	Comment
p	Peter, shop, pay, put	
b	by, about, bath, before, bought, books	
t	later, tomorrow, Peter, lot, toys, bought	
d	today, do, outside, good, idea, door	
k	clock, jacket, can	
g	go, forgot, good, garage	
tʃ	cheque, chair, children	
dʒ	July, jacket, just	
f	before, forgot, far	
v	evening, five, television, over	
θ	thirsty, bath, thanks	
ð	the, there's, there	
s	see, sent, Sarah	
z	noise, upstairs, toys, zoo, amazing	
ʃ	she's, shoe, shop, shall, washing	
ʒ	television, pleasure, usually, garage (or /dʒ/)	
h	have, home, Hull	
m	tomorrow, Mark, amazing	
n	now, evening, near	
ŋ	evening, washing, amazing	
l	later, television, really, July, lot, Shall, usually, Hull	
r	tomorrow, Roy, really, Sarah, orange, garage	
j	you, your, usually	
w	what's, works, want, washing, we	

Vowels	Words in text	Comment
ɪ	in, drink, it's, children, orange	
e	sent, cheque, television, pleasure	
æ	have, that, thanks, jacket, garage	
ɒ	tomorrow, clock, shop, want, lot, forgot, on, washing, not, orange	
ʌ	upstairs, Hull, just	
ʊ	good, books, put	
iː	see, evening, Peter	

Box 99   continued

Vowels	Words in text	Comment
eɪ	l**a**ter, tod**ay**, p**ay**, am**a**zing	
aɪ	b**y**, f**i**ve, Jul**y**, outs**i**de	
ɔɪ	n**oi**se, R**oy**, t**oys**	
uː	sh**oe**, **u**sually, z**oo**	
əʊ	g**o**, h**o**me, **o**ver	
aʊ	n**ow**, ab**ou**t, **ou**tside	
ɪə	r**ea**lly, id**ea**, n**ear**	
eə	upst**airs**, S**a**rah, ch**air**, th**ere**	
ɑː	M**ar**k, f**ar**, c**ar**	
ɔː	bef**ore**, b**ough**t, d**oor**	
ɜː	th**ir**sty, w**or**ks, p**ur**ple	

Contracted forms	Comment
what's, it's, she's, I'll, we're, there's	

Links	Comment
tomorrow evening, It's about, five o', sent a, It's on, She's upstairs, upstairs in, works in, want a, Thanks a, It's a, jacket is, chair outside, Shall I, Good idea, There's a, bought an, amazing orange, orange and, It's in, books over	

Weak forms	Comment
you, are, to, a, the, do, for, your, and, can	

7.3 Testing vowels and consonants

Focus	Testing reception and production of vowels and consonants
Level	Elementary+
Time	15 minutes (Version 1); 30 minutes per student (Version 2)
Preparation	Version 2: copy the material in Box 101 and Box 102 onto separate handouts. These use the words in Box 100. You will need a cassette recorder, microphone and a blank cassette for this activity.

Procedure

Version 1: Testing receptive skills

1 Students write the numbers 1 to 20 in their notebooks. Give them the following instructions: 'You will hear a key word repeated three times. Listen to the first vowel. Then you will hear four different words. How many of these four have the same first vowel as that in the key word?'

2 Give the following as an example: 'top, top, top; comb, want, clock, goat'. Check the answer with them (two – *want* and *clock* have the same vowel as *top*).

3 In the same way, read the words in the first two columns of Box 100 (say '1 tin, tin, tin; spill, same, lift, pick. 2 sand', etc.) or play the recording. Mark the test out of 20, giving one mark for the correct number of words.

4 Follow the same procedure to test recognition of consonants using the material in Box 103.

Version 2: Testing productive skills

1 Give out the first handout (Box 101) and give students time to read through the words. As it is not a test of vocabulary, you do not have to explain any unknown words to students, although you might want to do this.

2 Individual students read the lists of words aloud and record these. Notice that in each list there are four different 'target' vowel sounds (underlined in Box 100), with four examples of each target vowel sound in total. The words are divided into sets of four to make it easier for students to process them, breaking up what would otherwise be a long list of 80 words.

3 Later, listen to the students' recordings. For each student, tick the words (in Box 101) in which the target vowels are produced correctly and cross those which are not. Then transfer this information to a feedback sheet for each student (Box 102). On the feedback sheet, all the words with the same target vowel sound are on the same line. This gives a clearer picture of which sounds are produced correctly and which not, than if the words were listed as in Box 101. Give one mark for a correctly produced target vowel, no marks for an incorrectly produced vowel, and write the mark (out of 4) for each vowel sound in the right-hand column. You can then give a total score out of 80. From this you will not only get an overall evaluation of ability to produce English vowels, but an indication of which vowels are particularly problematic for individual students.

Note

If you do not have access to a cassette recorder, listen to individual students reading the word lists and, as they do this, make a judgement of correctness, ticking and crossing the words on a version of Box 101. Then transfer this to the feedback sheet as above.

Variation

Follow the same procedure to test reception and production of consonants, using the material in Boxes 103–105. The 'target' consonants are at the beginning of each word. Note that the consonants /ʒ/ and /ŋ/ are not included because they do not occur at the beginning of English words, and that the total mark you give will be out of 88.

Box 100	**Teacher reference**	
Key word and first vowel	*Words (the underlined vowels are the same as in the key word)*	*First vowels (and number)*
1 tin /ɪ/	spill, same, lift, pick	/ɪ/ (3); /eɪ/ (1)
2 sand /æ/	first, crash, hang, lamp	/æ/ (3); /ɜː/ (1)
3 wide /aɪ/	coat, here, night, full	/aɪ/ (1); /əʊ/ (1), /ɪə/ (1), /ʊ/ (1)
4 lend /e/	slept, desk, bad, tent	/e/ (3); /æ/ (1)
5 saw /ɔː/	got, call, taught, shock	/ɔː/ (2); /ɒ/ (2)
6 fool /uː/	too, blue, more, caught	/uː/ (2); /ɔː/ (2)
7 cheap /iː/	sheep, least, green, leave	/iː/ (4)
8 cow /aʊ/	lied, pet, kind, down	/aʊ/ (1); /aɪ/ (2), /e/ (1)
9 play /eɪ/	they, nurse, proud, mouth	/eɪ/ (1); /aʊ/ (2), /ɜː/ (1)
10 wrote /əʊ/	show, turn, stone, home	/əʊ/ (3); /ɜː/ (1)
11 come /ʌ/	but, son, luck, new	/ʌ/ (3); /uː/ (1)
12 top /ɒ/	box, want, car, father	/ɒ/ (2); /ɑː/ (2)
13 stood /ʊ/	look, dear, would, who	/ʊ/ (2); /ɪə/ (1), /uː/ (1)
14 boy /ɔɪ/	join, noise, voice, oil	/ɔɪ/ (4)
15 arm /ɑː/	hard, fair, ship, hair	/ɑː/ (1); /eə/ (2), /ɪ/ (1)
16 bird /ɜː/	rub, burn, ripe, poor	/ɜː/ (1); /ʌ/ (1), /aɪ/ (1), /ʊə/ (1)
17 near /ɪə/	real, say, shape, beard	/ɪə/ (2); /eɪ/ (2)
18 where /eə/	how, care, bear, heart	/eə/ (2); /aʊ/ (1), /ɑː/ (1)
19 sure /ʊə/	fewer, cure, pure, cook	/ʊə/ (3); /ʊ/ (1)
20 ago /ə/	agree, alive, amount, annoy	/ə/ (4)

Box 101   Student handout

1	coat	call	agree	car
2	bear	cook	ripe	how
3	box	green	lamp	real
4	turn	new	luck	pick
5	but	spill	too	first
6	would	kind	mouth	care
7	say	voice	tent	cure
8	hard	stone	more	amount
9	fewer	noise	they	desk
10	down	fair	night	full
11	dear	hang	least	shock
12	blue	nurse	lift	son
13	show	alive	father	taught
14	caught	home	heart	annoy
15	slept	same	poor	join
16	leave	want	beard	bad
17	got	crash	here	sheep
18	proud	look	hair	lied
19	pure	oil	shape	pet
20	rub	ship	burn	who

Box 102   Student handout

Feedback sheet

1	/ɪ/	spill	lift	pick	ship	/4
2	/æ/	crash	hang	lamp	bad	/4
3	/aɪ/	night	lied	kind	ripe	/4
4	/e/	slept	desk	tent	pet	/4
5	/ɔː/	call	taught	more	caught	/4
6	/uː/	too	blue	new	who	/4
7	/iː/	sheep	least	green	leave	/4
8	/aʊ/	down	proud	mouth	how	/4
9	/eɪ/	same	they	say	shape	/4
10	/əʊ/	coat	show	stone	home	/4
11	/ʌ/	but	son	luck	rub	/4
12	/ɒ/	got	shock	box	want	/4
13	/ʊ/	full	look	would	cook	/4

Box 102   continued

14	/ɔɪ/	join	noise	voice	oil	/4
15	/ɑ:/	car	father	hard	heart	/4
16	/ɜ:/	first	nurse	turn	burn	/4
17	/ɪə/	here	dear	real	beard	/4
18	/eə/	fair	hair	care	bear	/4
19	/ʊə/	poor	fewer	cure	pure	/4
20	/ə/	agree	alive	amount	annoy	/4

Box 103   Teacher reference

Key word and first consonant	Words (the underlined consonants are the same as in the key word)	First consonants (and number)
1 bed /b/	day, bear, den, bet	/b/ (2); /d/ (2)
2 do /d/	just, dare, zoo, those	/d/ (1); /dʒ/ (1), /z/ (1), /ð/ (1)
3 fill /f/	view, fast, ferry, pace	/f/ (2); /v/ (1), /p/ (1)
4 good /g/	goat, cap, card, game	/g/ (2); /k/ (2)
5 you /j/	yet, yard, jewel, yoke	/j/ (3); /dʒ/ (1)
6 cat /k/	could, guard, gap, coat	/k/ (2); /g/ (2)
7 look /l/	lake, lay, lent, rate	/l/ (3); /r/ (1)
8 man /m/	met, knee, mine, mile	/m/ (3); /n/ (1)
9 no /n/	me, net, Nile, nine	/n/ (3); /m/ (1)
10 put /p/	push, pond, ban, pest	/p/ (3); /b/ (1)
11 run /r/	wake, late, rent, ray	/r/ (2); /w/ (1), /l/ (1)
12 soon /s/	thin, sip, she, zeal	/s/ (1); /θ/ (1), /ʃ/ (1), /z/ (1)
13 top /t/	test, tick, tie, taste	/t/ (4)
14 vote /v/	very, fat, boat, than	/v/ (1); /f/ (1), /b/ (1), /ð/ (1)
15 win /w/	rake, way, went, wait	/w/ (3); /r/ (1)
16 zero /z/	sat, then, Joan, zip	/z/ (1); /s/ (1), /ð/ (1), /dʒ/ (1)
17 ship /ʃ/	thank, shy, zone, see	/ʃ/ (1); /θ/ (1), /z/ (1), /s/ (1)
18 choose /tʃ/	chalk, chip, share, cheap	/tʃ/ (3); /ʃ/ (1)
19 thick /θ/	sing, thigh, thumb, first	/θ/ (2); /s/ (1), /f/ (1)
20 than /ð/	they, vat, van, doze	/ð/ (1); /v/ (2), /d/ (1)
21 June /dʒ/	joke, shin, yes, cherry	/dʒ/ (1); /ʃ/ (1), /j/ (1), /tʃ/ (1)
22 hat /h/	hurt, harm, hate, heat	/h/ (4)

Box 104   Student handout

1	rate	hate	shy	could
2	pond	just	gap	wake
3	first	those	van	Nile
4	met	den	tie	thigh
5	card	sat	bet	shin
6	lent	cheap	test	dare
7	mile	fast	very	thin
8	then	good	went	knee
9	rent	zeal	yoke	hurt
10	heat	she	coat	rake
11	yet	jewel	pest	zip
12	way	nine	goat	than
13	thumb	doze	mine	taste
14	ban	see	lake	chalk
15	sip	share	bear	cap
16	chip	boat	lay	sing
17	vat	they	fat	net
18	yes	ray	harm	zone
19	Joan	zoo	yard	pace
20	wait	push	guard	joke
21	tick	cherry	late	day
22	me	view	thank	ferry

Box 105   Student handout

Feedback sheet

1	/b/	bear	bet	ban	boat	/4
2	/d/	dare	day	den	doze	/4
3	/f/	fast	ferry	fat	first	/4
4	/g/	goat	good	guard	gap	/4
5	/j/	yet	yard	yoke	yes	/4
6	/k/	could	coat	cap	card	/4
7	/l/	lake	lay	lent	late	/4
8	/m/	met	mine	mile	me	/4
9	/n/	net	Nile	nine	knee	/4
10	/p/	push	pond	pest	pace	/4
11	/r/	rent	ray	rate	rake	/4
12	/s/	sip	sat	see	sing	/4
13	/t/	test	tick	tie	taste	/4

Box 105   continued

14	/v/	very	view	vat	van	/4
15	/w/	way	went	wait	wake	/4
16	/z/	zip	zoo	zeal	zone	/4
17	/ʃ/	shy	she	share	shin	/4
18	/tʃ/	chalk	chip	cheap	cherry	/4
19	/θ/	thigh	thumb	thin	thank	/4
20	/ð/	they	those	than	then	/4
21	/dʒ/	joke	just	jewel	Joan	/4
22	/h/	hurt	harm	hate	heat	/4

7.4 Testing weak and contracted forms

Focus Testing reception and production of weak and contracted forms
Level Elementary+
Time 10–20 minutes (Version 1); 30–40 minutes per student (Version 2)
Preparation Version 1: copy the material in Box 106 onto a handout. For more advanced students include the material in Box 107 and Box 108 (see below for details). Version 2: copy the material in Box 112 onto a handout. Use the material in Boxes 113 and 114 as well or instead for more advanced students. You will need a cassette recorder, microphone and a blank cassette for this activity.

Procedure

Version 1: Testing receptive skills

1 Give students a copy of the handout. Explain that they will hear a number of sentences read aloud and they should complete the gaps with what they hear. Say that in some of the sentences they will hear contracted forms. Where these occur they should write the contracted form in the gap and then expand this form after the sentence. Give some examples: if they hear *it's*, they should write this in the gap and then expand it to *it is* after the sentence; if they hear *will've*, they should write this in the gap and then expand it to *will have* after the sentence. Getting both answers will allow you to check both that they hear the contracted form and also know what it means.
2 Read aloud the sentences in Box 109 or play the recording. The weak forms of grammar words and contracted forms are left out in Box 106.

If you have included the material in Box 107 and/or Box 108, read aloud the sentences in Box 110 and Box 111, or play the recording.

3 Collect in the handouts. To mark the test, give one mark for each correctly completed gap. You may want to give a half mark where a student has completed the gap partially correctly or has expanded a contracted form incorrectly.

Note that the test items in Box 106 are relatively easy, with only one weak form or one contracted form in each gap. Boxes 107 and 108 include more difficult items, with two weak or contracted forms missing from some gaps in Box 107, and more than two in some gaps in Box 108.

Box 106   Student handout

1 .... taller .... me. ....
2 .... Ken come .... London? ....
3 .... a card .... Ron. ....
4 Where .... I put .... books? ....
5 I .... see .... now. ....
6 Did .... go shopping .... lunchtime? ....
7 .... go .... have .... drink. ....
8 .... like .... meet .... some time. ....
9 .... got .... hat .... not .... coat. ....
10 .... like .... more .... that one .... well. ....

© Cambridge University Press 2004

Box 107   Student handout

1 When .... finish work? ....
2 I met .... university. ....
3 I .... see .... about five minutes. ....
4 He .... give .... back. ....
5 .... two presents .... Thomas. ....
6 .... want .... go. ....
7 .... those .... ones .... ordered? ....
8 .... better .... brother .... tennis. ....
9 .... want .... give .... call? ....
10 .... my friends .... there. ....

© Cambridge University Press 2004

Box 108   Student handout

1 .... ask .... party.   ....
2 .... friends .... be round later.   ....
3 .... something wrong with .... car.   ....
4 .... invited, ... want to go.   ....
5 I .... taken .... interview.   ....
6 .... here earlier .... accident in town.   ....
7 .... photographs here .... seen before.   ....
8 .... recognised Tony, if .... pointed .... out. ....

Box 109   Teacher reference

1 She's taller than me.
2 Does Ken come from London?
3 It's a card for Ron.
4 Where shall I put your books?
5 I can't see him now.
6 Did you go shopping at lunchtime?
7 Let's go and have a drink.
8 We'd like to meet her some time.
9 I've got your hat but not your coat.
10 I'd like some more of that one as well.

Box 110   Teacher reference

1 When does she finish work?
2 I met him at university.
3 I can see them for about five minutes.
4 He won't give us them back.
5 There were two presents from Thomas.
6 She doesn't want you to go.
7 Are those the ones that he ordered?
8 He's better than his brother at tennis.
9 Do you want me to give her a call?
10 Some of my friends should've been there.

Box 111   Teacher reference

1 I'll ask <u>them to the</u> party.
2 <u>Some of her</u> friends<u>'ll</u> be round later.
3 <u>There must've been</u> something wrong with <u>his</u> car.
4 <u>He was</u> invited, <u>but he doesn't</u> want to go.
5 I <u>could've</u> taken <u>her to her</u> interview.
6 <u>We'd've been</u> here earlier <u>but there was an</u> accident in town.
7 <u>There're some</u> photographs here <u>that you'll've</u> seen before.
8 <u>I wouldn't have</u> recognised Tony, if <u>you hadn't</u> pointed <u>him</u> out.

Version 2: Testing productive skills

1 Give out the handout (Box 112) and allow students some time to read through the sentences. Explain that they should try to say the sentences as if they were parts of a conversation. Say that sometimes students might choose to use contracted forms of parts of the sentences. Illustrate with item 1 from Box 112. Say that this is likely to be said as 'She's taller than me' rather than the expanded form 'She is . . .'.

2 Individual students read the sentences aloud and record these. Encourage students to spend a few moments before each sentence saying them in their head before saying them aloud. This will give them some time to think about how the sentences might be said fluently.

3 Later, listen to the students' recordings and mark the test, giving one mark for each correctly produced weak or contracted form. You may want to give a half mark for a good attempt. The marking of the contracted forms will be to some extent subjective. You may want to give marks (or part marks) for fluent-sounding uncontracted or partly contracted (e.g. Box 114, 7 . . . *that you'll have* . . .) forms. Put the marks and a total mark on the students' answer handout, to be given back to students as feedback.

Extension

In the test, students are required to produce weak and contracted forms in text read aloud. It would be more natural to test this feature of pronunciation in spontaneous speech, but it can be difficult to assess this in an efficient and systematic way. However, you might want to supplement the formal test given here by asking students to talk briefly about a topic relevant to them and record this on the cassette. For example, they could talk about

Box 112   Student handout

1 She is taller than me.
2 Does Ken come from London?
3 It is a card for Ron.
4 Where shall I put your books?
5 I can not see him now.
6 Did you go shopping at lunchtime?
7 Let us go and have a drink.
8 We would like to meet her some time.
9 I have got your hat but not your coat.
10 I would like some more of that one as well.

Box 113   Student handout

1 When does she finish work?
2 I met him at university.
3 I can see them for about five minutes.
4 He will not give us them back.
5 There were two presents from Thomas.
6 She does not want you to go.
7 Are those the ones that he ordered?
8 He is better than his brother at tennis.
9 Do you want me to give her a call?
10 Some of my friends should have been there.

Box 114   Student handout

1 I will ask them to the party.
2 Some of her friends will be round later.
3 There must have been something wrong with his car.
4 He was invited, but he does not want to go.
5 I could have taken her to her interview.
6 We would have been here earlier but there was an accident in town.
7 There are some photographs here that you will have seen before.
8 I would not have recognised Tony, if you had not pointed him out.

their families or their interests. You could evaluate this either by giving an impressionistic mark for how well they produce weak and contracted forms or, if you have more time, work through the recording noting weak and contracted forms produced appropriately, or not produced when they perhaps should have been. If necessary, work out a marking scheme that includes both the formal and more spontaneous components of the test.

7.5 Testing word stress

Focus	Testing reception and production of word stress
Level	Elementary+
Time	15 minutes (Version 1); 25 minutes per student (Version 2)
Preparation	Version 2: prepare a handout containing a list of words that you want to test. Alternatively, put these words into context. For example, the first set of words in Version 1 are put into short contexts in Box 115. You will need a cassette recorder, microphone and a blank cassette for this activity.

Procedure

Version 1: Testing receptive skills

1   Students write down the numbers *1* to *20* on a piece of paper.
2   Write the following on the board:
        1 = Oo (e.g. open) 2 = oO (e.g. alone) 3 = Ooo (e.g. yesterday)
        4 = oOo (e.g. tomorrow) 5 = ooO (e.g. afternoon)
    Explain to students that they will hear 20 words and they have to decide which of the stress patterns written on the board the words have. For example, *open* has two syllables with stress on the first syllable, etc. Their answers should be a number from 1 to 5.
3   Read aloud the following words, saying each word twice, or play the recording:
        1 beautiful (Answer: 3), 2 before (2), 3 tomato (4), 4 furniture (3),
        5 flower (1), 6 unemployed (5), 7 relax (2), 8 banana (4), 9 understand
        (5), 10 arrive (2), 11 winter (1), 12 timetable (3), 13 engineer (5),
        14 chemistry (3), 15 trousers (1), 16 control (2), 17 daughter (1),
        18 detective (4), 19 Japanese (5), 20 September (4)
4   Collect in the papers and mark them, or ask students to mark each other's work. Give one mark for each correct answer. For convenience, the words are categorised as follows:

1 (Oo) daughter, flower, trousers, winter
2 (oO) arrive, before, control, relax
3 (Ooo) beautiful, chemistry, furniture, timetable
4 (oOo) banana, detective, September, tomato
5 (ooO) understand, engineer, Japanese, unemployed

As a test for upper-intermediate to advanced students, write the following on the board

1 = Ooo (e.g. dinosaur) 2 = oOo (e.g. expected)
3 = ooO (e.g. magazine) 4 = Oooo (e.g. communism)
5 = oOoo (e.g. removable) 6 = ooOo (e.g. competition)

Then read aloud the following words or play the recording:

1 furthermore (3), 2 American (5), 3 economics (6), 4 computer (2), 5 positive (1), 6 helicopter (4), 7 understand (3), 8 vandalism (4), 9 pedestrian (5), 10 preposition (6), 11 newspaper (1), 12 important (2), 13 television (4), 14 incorrect (3), 15 romantic (2),16 reservation (6), 17 apology (5), 18 badminton (1)

For convenience, the words are categorised as follows:

1 (Ooo) badminton, newspaper, positive
2 (oOo) computer, romantic, important
3 (ooO) furthermore, incorrect, clarinet
4 (Oooo) helicopter, television, vandalism
5 (oOoo) American, apology, pedestrian
6 (ooOo) economics, preposition, reservation

You could, of course, devise a similar test with vocabulary that your students have learnt during their course.

Version 2: Testing productive skills

1 Give out the handout (your own material or Box 115) and allow students some time to read through the words or sentences.
2 Individual students read the words or sentences aloud and record these.
3 Later, listen to the students' recordings and give one mark for each of the 'target' words correctly stressed. Put the total mark on the students' answer handout, to be given back as feedback.

Note

If you do not have access to a cassette recorder, listen to individual students reading the words or the words in context. As they do so, make a judgement of the correctness of stress in 'target' words, ticking or crossing the words on a version of the students' handout.

Box 115   Student handout

1 It was a beautiful day.	11 I hate winter.
2 I'd seen her before.	12 I've got a new timetable.
3 Can you get some tomatoes?	13 She's an engineer.
4 We've got some new furniture.	14 I'm doing chemistry.
5 I gave him some flowers.	15 I bought some trousers.
6 She's unemployed.	16 It's out of control.
7 Just relax.	17 My daughter.
8 Do you want a banana?	18 He wants to be a detective.
9 I don't understand.	19 It's Japanese.
10 When do they arrive?	20 In September.

© CAMBRIDGE UNIVERSITY PRESS 2004

7.6 Testing prominence

Focus Testing reception and production of tonic prominence
Level Elementary+
Time 15 minutes (Version 1); 25 minutes per student (Version 2)
Preparation Version 1: copy the material in Box 116 onto a handout or an OHT.
Version 2: copy the material in Box 117 onto a handout. If you choose to record the students' answers (see below), you will need a cassette recorder, microphone and a blank cassette for this activity.

Procedure

Version 1: Testing receptive skills

1   Give out or show the material in Box 116. Explain to students that they will hear ten sentences. They have to decide which of the pair of sentences, a or b, is more likely to come *before* each sentence they hear. Give the example at the top of Box 116. Say the following twice or play the recording:

I went to London YESterday. (with tonic prominence, i.e. the 'main stress', on *yes-*)

Ask students which of the two questions given in the example is more likely to come before this sentence (Answer a: *What time are you going to London today?*). Then say the following twice or play the recording:

I went to LONdon yesterday. (with tonic prominence, i.e. the main stress, on *Lon-*)

Explain that this is more likely to come before question b (*How was your trip to Paris yesterday?*)

2 Say the following sentences twice, or play the recording, and students choose a or b in each case.

1 At TEN past two.	6 Gail's got a blue FORD.
2 It's on top of the WARDrobe.	7 She lives OUTside New York.
3 WITH milk, please.	8 He was very ANGry.
4 I thought you liked RED.	9 He was born in 156(SIXty)4.
5 He plays EVery week.	10 I've GOT a good job.

Box 116   Student handout

Example
   a What time are you going to London today?
   b How was your trip to Paris yesterday?

1a What time are we meeting?
 b I'll see you at five past two.
2a Where did you put my old handbag?
 b I thought I put my old handbag in the wardrobe.
3a You have your coffee without milk, don't you?
 b How do you like your coffee?
4a I don't like that coat, it's red.
 b What a nice coat. Blue's my favourite colour.
5a David plays badminton every other week.
 b How often does David play badminton?
6a Is that Gail in the red Ford?
 b Is that Gail in the blue Toyota?
7a Where does Ann live?
 b Ann lives in New York, doesn't she?
8a How did your father react?
 b I suppose your father was angry about it.
9a Shakespeare was born in 1554.
 b Shakespeare died in 1564.
10a Why don't you want to move away from London?
  b Now you've finished your course, I suppose you're looking for a good job.

Answer key
1b 2a 3a 4b 5a 6b 7b 8a 9a 10b

Version 2: Testing productive skills

1   Give out the handout (Box 117). Explain the test to students (either to the class as a whole or to individual students, as appropriate). Say that on the handout is a series of answers to questions that can be said in different ways. Focus on the example with the answer *I went to London yesterday*. If the question they hear is *What time are you going to London today?*, then they should say the answer with prominence (you could use the word *stress* or *emphasis*) on *yesterday*. If the question they hear is *How was your trip to Paris yesterday?*, then they should say the answer with prominence on *London*. The example questions and answers are on the recording.

2   Test students individually. Say one of the a or b sentences from each pair in Box 118. The correct responses to these sentences are given on the right. You could either mark the test as you are doing it, giving one mark for each correct response or, preferably, record the test and mark it later. Note that a possible set of test questions for the sentences in Box 118 is on the recording, with the following answers: 1b, 2a, 3b, 4b, 5a, 6b, 7b, 8a, 9a, 10b.

Box 117   Student handout

Example

If the question is:	What time are you going to London today?
You answer:	I went to London YESterday.
If the question is:	How was your trip to Paris yesterday?
You answer:	I went to LONdon yesterday.

  1   At ten past two.
  2   It's on top of the wardrobe.
  3   With milk, please.
  4   I thought you liked red.
  5   He plays every week.
  6   Gail's got a blue Ford.
  7   She lives outside New York.
  8   He was very angry.
  9   He was born in 1564.
 10   I've got a good job.

Box 118   Teacher reference

1a What time are we meeting?	1a At ten past TWO.
b I'll see you at five past two.	b At TEN past two.
2a Where did you put my old handbag?	2a It's on top of the WARDrobe.
b I thought I put my old handbag in the wardrobe.	b It's on TOP of the wardrobe.
3a You have your coffee without milk, don't you?	3a WITH milk, please.
b How do you like your coffee?	b With MILK, please.
4a I don't like that coat, it's red.	4a I thought you LIKED red.
b What a nice coat. Blue's my favourite colour.	b I thought you liked RED.
5a David plays badminton every other week.	5a He plays EVery week.
b How often does David play badminton?	b He plays every WEEK.
6a Is that Gail in the red Ford?	6a Gail's got a BLUE Ford.
b Is that Gail in the blue Toyota?	b Gail's got a blue FORD.
7a Where does Ann live?	7a She lives outside New YORK.
b Ann lives in New York, doesn't she?	b She lives OUTside New York.
8a How did your father react?	8a He was very ANGry.
b I suppose your father was angry about it.	b He was VERy angry.
9a Shakespeare was born in 1554.	9a He was born in 156(SIXty)4.
b Shakespeare died in 1564.	b He was BORN in 1564.
10a Why don't you want to move away from London?	10a I've got a good JOB.
b Now you've finished your course, I suppose you're looking for a good job.	b I've GOT a good job.

7.7 Testing tone

Focus Testing reception and production of falling and end-rising tones
Level Advanced
Time 15 minutes (Version 1); 20 minutes per student (Version 2)
Preparation Version 1: copy the material in Box 119 onto a handout or an OHT. Version 2: copy the material in Box 120 onto a handout. You will need a cassette recorder, microphone and a blank cassette for this activity.

Procedure

Version 1: Testing receptive skills

1 Give out the handout (Box 119). Explain to students that they will hear six sentences and they have to decide which of the pair of sentences, a or b, is more likely to come *after* each sentence they hear. Focus on the example at the top of the handout (Box 119). Say the following twice or play the recording:

I hoped you would have FINished by now.

As the implication is that 'you' have not finished, response a is more likely. If the sentence was said (say this or play the recording):

I HOPED you would have finished by now.

the implication would be that 'you' have finished, so response b would be more likely.

2 Say the following sentences twice, or play the recording, and students choose a or b in each case.

1 She's always wanted to be a DOCtor.

2 I THOUGHT you'd be pleased.

3 My sister wasn't at the party because she wasn't inVITed.

4 It's about time he rePAID you.

5 You TOLD me it would be difficult to get tickets.

6 He didn't take the exam because of his poor HEALTH.

Box 119   Student handout

Example

I hoped you would have finished by now.
a Just give me five minutes more.
b Yes, I got it done by lunchtime.

1 She's always wanted to be a doctor.
   a So I was surprised when she said she wanted to study engineering.
   b So she must be really pleased now that she's got into medical school.
2 I thought you'd be pleased.
   a Well you were wrong!
   b Yes, it's excellent news.
3 My sister wasn't at the party because she wasn't invited.
   a I only asked friends.
   b She was out of the country.
4 It's about time he repaid you.
   a Well, he says he never has any money.
   b Well, he did apologise for the delay when he gave me the money.
5 You told me it would be difficult to get tickets.
   a And you were right.
   b But I didn't have any problems at all.
6 He didn't take the exam because of his poor health.
   a So he'll take it next year instead.
   b He just decided that he hadn't revised enough.

Version 2: Testing productive skills
This is based on Version 1, but uses slightly different material.

1 Give out the handout (Box 120). Explain to students that they need to say each sentence in the right-hand column twice; first as an appropriate response to sentence a, and then as an appropriate response to sentence b. Illustrate with the example. In response to sentence a, the sentence in the right-hand column is likely to be said:

   I hoped you would have FINished by now.

with a falling tone beginning on *fin-*. In response to sentence b, the sentence is likely to be said either with a falling-rising tone beginning on *hoped*:

   I HOPED you would have finished by now.

or with a rising tone beginning on *fin-* (perhaps after a fall beginning on *hoped*):

   I HOPED you would have FINished by now.

Say that students should decide whether falling or falling-rising (or rising) tone is more likely to be used in each response. (Note: You may have introduced the term 'end-rising' as a general term for both rising and falling-rising tones [see pp. 7–9]. If so, use this term here.)

2 Test individual students. Say each of the sentences in the left-hand column and the student answers. Record both parts onto a cassette. It is a good idea to allow students a few seconds before each item to give them time to 'say in their heads' how they think the responses should be said.

3 Later, listen to the recording and mark the test, giving one mark for a correct falling tone and one for a correct end-rising tone (it doesn't matter whether a rising or falling-rising tone is used). Note that there may be some variation in where the tone starts. There is no need to take this into account unless it is clearly wrong. Likely answers are given in Box 121.

Box 120   Student handout

Example
  a I just need a few more minutes to get it done.
  b I got it all done before lunchtime today.

I hoped you would have finished by now.

1a That's wonderful news.
  b That's terrible news.

I thought you'd be pleased.

2a You said it would be easy getting tickets.
  b I had real problems getting tickets.

I told you it would be difficult.

3a Shouldn't we wait for Tom before we go?
  b Tom didn't get home until after midnight.

He said he'd be late.

4a Jack just gave me back the £50 he owed me.
  b Jack's owed me £50 for over a year now.

It's about time he repaid you.

5a You must have been surprised when Kate said she wanted to study engineering.
  b You must have been pleased when Kate got into medical school.

Yes, she's always wanted to be a doctor.

6a It's a pity Ann was ill and couldn't come to the party.
  b I wonder why Ann wasn't at the party.

She didn't come because she was ill.

Box 121   Teacher reference

1a I thought you'd be pleased.

1b I thought you'd be pleased.

2a I told you it would be difficult.

2b I told you it would be difficult.

3a He said he'd be late.

3b He said he'd be late.

4a It's about time he repaid you.

4b It's about time he repaid you.

5a Yes, she's always wanted to be a doctor.

5b Yes, she's always wanted to be a doctor.

6a She didn't come because she was ill.

6b She didn't come because she was ill.

8 Resources for pronunciation teaching

Using a dictionary (8.1–8.2)

To do the activities in this section, students should have access to either monolingual or bilingual dictionaries which include a representation of the pronunciation of words (perhaps using phonetic symbols), including stress.

8.1 Finding out about word stress

Focus	Using a dictionary to find out about word stress
Level	Elementary+
Time	25 minutes
Preparation	Choose a number of words with two syllables, some with stress on the first and some with stress on the second. Do the same with words with three syllables, having a variety of different stress patterns. Examples are given in Box 122. These should be words that students are *unlikely* to know, otherwise they can do this activity without using dictionaries. You could, of course, extend the activity to include words with four or more syllables. Copy the material you use onto the board, a handout or an OHT.

Procedure

1 If you are using the material in Box 122, ask students first to predict the stress pattern of the words in Part A and write them under the headings shown in Part B. Alternatively, use the words and stress patterns you have selected for your students.

2 Students then use their dictionaries to find out what the words mean and to check their answers.

3 Students repeat the words after you or the recording. Talk about any differences between predicted and correct answers.

Note

Many dictionaries use the symbol ' before the main stressed syllable in a word and the symbol ˌ before a secondary stressed syllable. It can be useful for students to understand these even if they don't understand other phonetic symbols. There is an extract from the *Cambridge Advanced Learner's Dictionary* on the following page to illustrate.

outcast

outcast /'aʊt.kɑːst/ ⑩ /-kæst/ *noun* [C] a person who has no place in their society or in a particular group, because the society or group refuses to accept them: *She has spent her life trying to help gypsies, beggars and other social outcasts.* ○ *She was a political outcast after the Party expelled her in 1982.*

> This word has two syllables, the first stressed and the second unstressed

outclass /ˌaʊt'klɑːs/ ⑩ /-'klæs/ *verb* [T] to be much better than someone or something: *The latest 500 cc road bike easily outclasses all the competition.*

> This word has two syllables. Primary stress is on the second syllable and secondary stress on the first.

> This word has three syllables. Primary stress is on the second syllable, with secondary stress on the first. The third syllable is unstressed.

outdated /ˌaʊt'deɪ.tɪd/ ⑩ /-tɪd/ *adj* old-fashioned and therefore not as good or as fashionable as something modern: *outdated weapons/ideas* ○ *Nowadays this technique is rather outdated.* ⊃See also out-of-date.

outdoor /'aʊt.dɔː/ ⑩ /-dɔːr/ *adj* [before n] 1 existing, happening or done outside, rather than inside a building: *an outdoor swimming pool/festival* ○ *outdoor clothes* 2 liking or relating to outdoor activities, such as walking and climbing: *Sara's not really the outdoor type.*

outdoors /ˌaʊt'dɔːz/ ⑩ /-'dɔːrz/ *adv, noun* outside: *If the weather's good, we'll eat outdoors* (= not in a building). ○ *Every year he takes a month off work to go trekking in the great outdoors* (= in the countryside, far away from towns). ⊃See also out of doors at door.

> This word has two syllables. As an adjective, it has primary stress on the first syllable and secondary stress on the second. As an adverb, with an added 's', it has primary stress on the second syllable and secondary stress on the first.

(Note that in the *Cambridge Advanced Learner's Dictionary* the symbol . comes before each new syllable.)

Extension

If each student has access to the same dictionary, and this dictionary marks word stress in some way, just choose a double page at random. If not, copy a double page for each student from a dictionary that marks stress. Give out the handout, or ask students to open their dictionaries at a particular double page, and explain how stress is shown in the dictionary. Students have to classify all the words on those pages according to stress pattern. They write O, Oo, oO, etc. in a table and put words underneath. Check whether they all agree and discuss any difficulties. As a variation, write a stress pattern on the board (e.g. oOo, Oooo), and the first person/group to correctly call out a word on the page with that pattern wins a point. (But check first that there is at least one!)

Answer key

Oo: fruitful, bullet, downpour, cookie
oO: distinct, assent, convene, incur
Ooo: obstinate, surgery, synonym, increment
oOo: meander, excursion, effusive, prospectus

Box 122   Student handout

Part A

convene   prospectus   downpour   fruitful   surgery   meander
distinct   increment   assent   cookie   synonym   excursion
effusive   obstinate   incur   bullet

Part B

Oo	oO	Ooo	oOo

8.2 Finding out about secondary stress: shifting stress

For this activity, students need access to a dictionary which shows primary and secondary stress in words, such as the *Cambridge Advanced Learner's Dictionary*, or to a pronunciation dictionary (e.g. *Cambridge English Pronouncing Dictionary*, 2003) which shows possible stress shift. Before doing the activity, students should have been introduced to the idea of stress shift. For example, they could have done either Activity 4.20 or 4.21.

Focus Using a dictionary to find out about stress shift

Level Advanced

Time 35 minutes

Preparation Write the words in Part A of Box 123 on the board. Copy the material in Box 123 onto a handout or an OHT.

Procedure

1 Remind students that some words can have stress on different syllables, depending on context. Write the following on the board, with the likely stress patterns marked:

   1 INcoRRECT.

   2 The ANSwer was incoRRECT.

   3 It was an INcorrect ANSwer.

   4 It was an INcorrect deCISion. *or* It was an incoRRECT deCISion.

Explain that some words such as *incorrect* have two stresses. The main stress is on the last stressed syllable (as in 1 and 2) unless it is 'pushed back' to earlier in the word (as in 3). In 4, main stress might go on either of the two possible syllables as the main stress in the following word is not stressed. Explain that some dictionaries show which two syllables can be stressed in words like *incorrect*. Here is an extract from the *Cambridge Advanced Learner's Dictionary*:

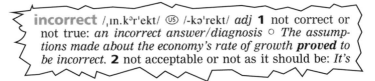

incorrect /ˌɪn.kəˈrekt/ ⑤ /-kəˈrekt/ *adj* **1** not correct or not true: *an incorrect answer/diagnosis* ○ *The assumptions made about the economy's rate of growth* **proved** *to be incorrect.* **2** not acceptable or not as it should be: *It's*

2 Ask students to use their dictionaries to find out which of the words in Part A of Box 123 can have stress shift.
3 Give out the handout or display the OHT (Box 123). The sentences in Part B include words from Part A that *do* allow stress shift. Students should underline the *likely* stressed syllable in these words in the sentences. In one of the sentences in the pair an early syllable in the word is likely to be stressed, and in the other a later syllable in the word is likely to be stressed.
4 Check the answers by asking students to read aloud the sentences with stress in these words as they have marked it.

Answer key
Part A:
The following words do allow stress shift: *controversial, democratic, idiotic, outside, scientific, unfinished*
The following words don't allow stress shift: *demanding, humiliating, invisible, original, successful*

Part B:
1 a sci<u>en</u>tific, b scientific; 2 a idi<u>ot</u>ic, b id<u>iot</u>ic; 3 a <u>dem</u>ocratic, b demo<u>crat</u>ic; 4 a out<u>side</u>, b <u>out</u>side; 5 a <u>con</u>troversial, b contro<u>ver</u>sial; 6 a un<u>fin</u>ished, b <u>Un</u>finished.

Box 123   Student handout

Part A

controversial   demanding   democratic   humiliating   idiotic
invisible   original   outside   scientific   successful   unfinished

Part B

1 a The research was published in a scientific journal.
   b This scientific discovery will affect us all.
2 a Her suggestion was completely idiotic.
   b I asked him a serious question, but he gave some idiotic answer.
3 a The country had its first democratic government in 1948.
   b The decision was democratic.
4 a The car's parked outside.
   b The house has got an outside toilet.
5 a He made a controversial speech.
   b Their decision was controversial.
6 a She left her answer unfinished.
   b It's called his Unfinished Symphony.

Using phonetic symbols (8.3–8.5)

If students use a dictionary in which pronunciation is represented by phonetic symbols, then they may need some help in learning these symbols before they can make full use of their dictionary as a pronunciation resource. The symbol for most consonant sounds is the same as the letter, so students will generally have few problems understanding /b/, /d, /f/, /g/, /h/, /k/, /l/, /m/, /n/, /p/, /r/, /s/, /t/, /v/, /w/ and /z/. The remaining consonant symbols – /j/, /ʃ/, /ʒ/, /ŋ/, /tʃ/, /θ/, /ð/ and /dʒ/ – are more problematic, as are all of the vowel symbols. Obviously, you will need to decide whether teaching phonetic symbols is an effective use of time in your particular teaching context. Activities 8.3, 8.4 and 8.5 aim to help students learn phonetic symbols. For a list of phonetic symbols used in this book, see Appendix 1. (Adrian Underhill gives many ideas for using a chart of phonetic symbols in his book *Sound Foundations*, 1994.)

8.3 Finding out about sounds

Focus Using phonetic symbols to help pronounce words
Level Elementary+

Procedure

Keep a chart showing phonetic symbols, together with a word or words which include each sound, on the wall of your classroom. Students can refer to it when they are looking up pronunciation of words in their dictionaries. Alternatively, when students ask how a word is pronounced, point to the sounds it consists of on the poster: for example, if the word is *chaos*, point to /k/ then /eɪ/ then /ɒ/ and then /s/. In addition, students could photocopy a key to phonetic symbols (such as the one in Appendix 1) and keep it with them for reference.

8.4 Relating sounds and symbols

Focus Relating sounds in words to phonetic symbols
Level Elementary+
Time 5 minutes

Procedure

Highlight two or three problem symbols on a phonetics chart or write these on the board. Number them 1, 2, 3 (etc.). Say words which include one of the sounds, and students say the number of the sound the word contains. For example, focus on /ʃ/ (number this 1), /tʃ/ (number this 2), /θ/ (number this 3), /ð/(number this 4) and give examples of these sounds in words (or use example words on the phonetics chart). Then say words at random from the following list: *shelf, fashion, crash* (1); *choose, teacher, watch* (2); *thanks, bath, mouth* (3); *these, father, breathe* (4).

8.5 Transcribing words

Focus Transcribing words using phonetic symbols
Level Intermediate+
Time 10 minutes

Procedure

Although only some students will find it valuable to be able to write a phonetic transcription of words, it can be useful to produce transcriptions of words in order to learn to read phonetic symbols. You could do a series of simple transcription exercises that focus on contrast between particular vowels or particular consonants. For example, to help students learn the symbols /ɑː/, /ɔː/ and /ɒ/, first highlight the target sounds on a phonetics chart. Then say some of the following words (in random order) for students to transcribe: *heart*, *half*, *hard*, *laugh*, *start* (all with /ɑː/); *talk*, *hall*, *bought*, *taught*, *raw* (all with /ɔː/); *rod*, *dog*, *hop*, *stop*, *not*, *loft* (all with /ɒ/). In all these words only the vowel symbol is problematic; the consonant symbols are the same as their letters. Do similar exercises with other groups of vowels and problem consonant symbols.

Using authentic material (8.6–8.10)

8.6 'Knock, knock' jokes

	Many jokes are based on features of pronunciation. The following activity, which uses 'Knock, knock' jokes, highlights this.
Focus	Understanding jokes based on features of pronunciation
Level	Intermediate+
Time	25 minutes
Preparation	Copy the material in Box 124 onto a handout.

Procedure

1 If students aren't familiar with 'Knock, knock' jokes, introduce them with a couple of simple examples such as:

Knock, knock.	Knock, knock.
Who's there?	*Who's there?*
Ann.	Police.
Ann who?	*Police who?*
Ann apple hit me on the head.	Police open the door.

In the first example, *Ann* (a name) sounds the same as *an* (*An apple hit me*). In the second, *police* sounds similar to *please* (*Please open the door*). Write the first example on the board to show the dialogue pattern, and perform it (you should take the 'Knock, knock' part) with a student. Then do the second without writing it on the board.

2 Organise students into pairs and give a copy of the handout (Box 124)[1] to one of the students in each pair, who should take the 'Knock, knock' part. Their partner shouldn't see the handout.

3 Students work through the jokes. Encourage them to repeat each one until they understand all of the jokes.

4 Finally, working as a whole class, perform the jokes again with a number of students, alternating between you and the students taking the 'Knock, knock' parts. With more advanced students, you could discuss the features of connected speech that each joke depends on. These are summarised in Box 125.

Box 124   Student handout

1	2	3
Knock, knock.	Knock, knock.	Knock, knock.
Who's there?	*Who's there?*	*Who's there?*
Scott.	Freeze.	Adam.
Scott who?	*Freeze who?*	*Adam who?*
Scott nothing to do with you.	Freeze a jolly good fellow.	Adam up and tell me the total.

4	5	6
Knock, knock.	Knock, knock.	Knock, knock.
Who's there?	*Who's there?*	*Who's there?*
Dozen.	Felix.	Bingo.
Dozen who?	*Felix who?*	*Bingo who?*
Dozen anyone want to let me in?	Felix my ice cream, I'll lick his.	Bingo in to come and see you for ages.

7	8	9
Knock, knock.	Knock, knock.	Knock, knock.
Who's there?	*Who's there?*	*Who's there?*
Michelle.	Juno.	Wooden shoe.
Michelle who?	*Juno who?*	*Wooden shoe who?*
Michelle had a big crab inside it.	Juno what time it is?	Wooden shoe like to know.

© CAMBRIDGE UNIVERSITY PRESS 2004

---

[1] Jokes 1, 2, 9 are from *The Funniest Joke Book in the World Ever!* (2000) Random House Children's Books (1 p. 46; 9 p. 47; 2 p. 43).

Box 125   Teacher reference

Features of connected speech in the jokes

1 *It's got* /ɪts gɒt/ changes to *(t)sgot* /tsgɒt/ (which sounds like *Scott*) in fast speech.

2 *For he's* /fə hi:z/ changes to *f'r'e's* /fri:z/ (which sounds like *Freeze*) in fast speech.

3 *Add them* /æd ðəm/ changes to *Add 'em* /ædəm/ (which sounds like *Adam*) in fast speech.

4 *Doesn't* /dʌznt/ changes to *Doesn* /dʌzn/ (which sounds like *Dozen*) in fast speech.

5 *If he licks* /ɪf hi: lɪks/ changes to *fe licks* /fi:lɪks/ (which sounds like *Felix*) in fast speech.

6 *I've been going* /aɪv bi:n gəʊɪŋ/ changes to *been goin'* /bɪn gəʊɪn/ (which sounds like *Bingo in*) in fast speech.

7 *My shell* /maɪ ʃel/ changes to *Mi shell* /mi ʃel/ (which sounds like *Michelle*) in fast speech.

8 *Do you know* /du: ju: nəʊ/ changes to *D'you know* /dʒə nəʊ / (which sounds like *Juno*) in fast speech.

9 *Wouldn't you* /wʊdnt ju:/ changes to *Wouldn'choo* /wʊdntʃu:/ (which sounds like *Wooden shoe*) in fast speech.

8.7 Tongue twisters

In the tongue twisters in Box 126 the problem is saying words that contain similar sounds; for example, the sounds /r/ and /l/ or the consonant clusters /fr/ and /fl/. The aim, as with all tongue twisters, is to say them as quickly as possible. Only included here are tongue twisters with vocabulary that is relatively easy to understand.

Focus Saying words with similar sounds

Level Intermediate+

Time 5 minutes+

Preparation Copy each of the tongue twisters in Box 126 onto a large card or an OHT. You can then use them repeatedly when you want to briefly practise a sound or set of sounds.

Procedure

Display a tongue twister. Students repeat after you. Then choose individuals to try to say it.

Variations

1   Use the *She sells sea shells . . .* tongue twister. Divide the class into two groups. One group should say all of the words that begin /ʃ/, the other half all of the words that begin /s/ and you say the rest. So the first line begins:
     She (group 1) – sells (group 2) – sea (2) – shells (1) – by the (you) – sea (2) – shore (1)

2   Use a short, repeated tongue twister (e.g. *Truly rural . . .*; *Red lorry, yellow lorry . . .*; *Please pay promptly . . .*; *Chop shops stock chops . . .*). Choose two students to say the tongue twister in turn. For example:
     Truly rural (student 1) – Truly rural (student 2) – Truly rural (1) – Truly rural (2) . . . Red lorry (1) – yellow lorry (2) – Red lorry (1) – yellow lorry (2) . . .

The students continue until one of them makes a mistake (you should be the judge) and this student is eliminated. Choose another student (or ask for a volunteer) to take the place of the eliminated student to 'challenge' the winner.

Box 126   Student handout

Tongue twister

To practise single consonants

/r/ and /l/	Truly rural. Truly rural. Truly rural. (etc.)
/r/ and /l/	Red lorry, yellow lorry, red lorry, yellow lorry. (etc.)
/s/ and /ʃ/	Mrs Smith's Fish Sauce Shop.
/s/ and /ʃ/	She sells sea shells by the sea shore.
	The shells she sells are surely seashells.
	So if she sells shells on the seashore,
	I'm sure she sells seashore shells.
/p/ and /f/	Give papa a cup of proper coffee in a copper coffee cup.

To practise consonants and consonant clusters

/s/ and /sl/	Sly Sam slurps Sally's soup.
/b/, /br/ and /bl/	Betty and Bob brought back blue balloons from the big bazaar.
/p/, /pr/ and /pl/	Please pay promptly. Please pay promptly. (etc.)
/s/, /sl/ and /sn/	Six slippery snails, slid slowly seaward.
/fr/ and /fl/	Freshly fried fresh flesh. Freshly fried fresh flesh. (etc.)
/f/, /fr/ and /fl/	Friendly Frank flips fine flapjacks.

Box 126   continued

/θr/ and /fr/	Three free throws. Three free throws. (etc.)
/t/, /tw/, /tr/ and /θr/ (also good for practising a variety of vowels)	The two-twenty-two train tore through the tunnel.
/tʃ/, /ʃ/ and a variety of consonant clusters	Chop shops stock chops. Chop shops stock chops. (etc.)
/ʃr/, /sw/ and /tʃ/	Shredded Swiss cheese. Shredded Swiss cheese. (etc.)
A variety of clusters	A box of biscuits, a batch of mixed biscuits.

Vowels

The vowel /ɔɪ/, alternating with other vowels	What noise annoys a noisy oyster? A noisy noise annoys a noisy oyster.
A variety of vowels	Swan swam over the sea, Swim, swan, swim! Swan swam back again Well swum, swan!
A variety of vowels and also /w/	While we were walking, we were watching window washers wash Washington's windows with warm washing water.
A variety of vowels, particularly /ʌ/ (and perhaps /ɒ/) and /uː/. Note that in British English *one* is pronounced either /wʌn/ or /wɒn/.	One-One was a racehorse. Two-Two was one, too. When One-One won one race, Two-Two won one, too.

8.8 Limericks

Limericks provide a way of practising a number of features of pronunciation in a very controlled way. They are best recited with a steady rhythm, and this requires lengthening and shortening sounds, using weak forms, and putting stress in appropriate places. In addition, words at the ends of lines 1, 2 and 5, and those at the ends of lines 3 and 4, need to rhyme, so the vowel sounds in these words need to be produced consistently.

Focus	Using limericks to practise features of pronunciation
Level	Intermediate+
Time	20 minutes
Preparation	Copy one of the limericks from Box 127 (or another one that you are familiar with) onto the board or an OHT. Copy the material in Box 127 onto a handout. For the Variation, make one copy of the limericks (minus the limerick written on the board) and cut up the limericks so that you have one line on each piece of paper.

Procedure

1 Write one limerick on the board or an OHT. Read through the limerick and point out its form: the number of lines (5), the rhyming scheme (AABBA) and the number of stressed syllables in each line (3, 3, 2, 2, 3).
2 Give out the handout (Box 127).[2] Simply ask students to repeat limericks after you a line at a time, and then select individuals to say them aloud. Encourage students to say them with a steady rhythm, and appropriate stress, weak forms, line-end vowel sounds, etc.

Variation

Follow the procedure for step 1, then give one line of the cut-up limericks to each student (or more than one, or students share one, depending on numbers). Ask students whether they think they have the first line of a limerick. If they think they have, they should read it aloud. Ask who has the next line. The student reads this line out. Continue until the limerick is finished. Then all five students read the limerick out, a line at a time. Ask for another first line, and continue in this way until all the limericks have been reassembled and read aloud. Then give out a copy of all the limericks for students to take away.

Extension

Encourage students to find other limericks or other poems that are very rhythmical or have a fixed rhyming scheme. When they bring these into class, read them out. Students chorally and individually repeat after you, and then individuals can read the poems aloud. The Internet is a good source of material. For example, some of Ogden Nash's short, rhythmical poems are at: http://www.westegg.com/nash/baby.cgi

---

[2] Limericks 1 and 4 are from *The Usborne Book of Funny Poems* (1990): 1, p. 15 (Anon); 4, p. 24 (Anon); Limericks 2, 3, 5, 6 are from *The Biggest Kids' Joke Book Ever!* Brandreth, G. (2002) Andre Deutsch: 2, p. 281; 3, p. 279; 5, p. 280; 6, p. 279 (adapted slightly).

Box 127   Student handout

1
There was a young lady of Riga,
Who rode with a smile on a tiger;
They returned from the ride
With the lady inside,
And the smile on the face of the tiger.

2
A fellow named Malcolm MacHairs
Kept a number of grizzly bears.
He ran out of money
For they ate so much honey,
And then they ate Malcolm – who cares?

3
There was an old woman from China
Who once went to sea on a liner.
She fell off the deck
And twisted her neck
And now she can see right behind her.

4
There once was a man of Bengal
Who was asked to a fancy dress ball;
He murmured: 'I'll risk it
and go as a biscuit . . .'
But a dog ate him up in the hall.

5
There was an old person of Dover
Who rushed through a field of blue clover;
But some very large bees
Stung his nose and his knees,
So he very soon went back to Dover.

6
There was a young lady whose eyes
Were unique as to colour and size;
When she opened them wide,
People all turned aside,
And hurried away in surprise.

8.9 Poems with features of connected speech

Some poetry is not only best said with a steady rhythm, but also includes features of connected speech. In the poem used here there are contracted forms (*We're*, *I'm*, etc.), reduced forms (*'em*, *gonna*), and prominence for contrast or particular emphasis (*I'm smiling . . .*, *. . . not all bad*).

Focus Practising different features of connected speech

Level Intermediate+

Time 25 minutes

Preparation Copy the poem in Box 128[3] onto a handout so that you have one for each student. Also, cut up some copies (the number will depend on the number of students in your class) with one verse on each piece of paper.

Procedure

1 Explain that you are going to look at a poem about parents' evening at school. Talk to students about their experience of such events. In a multinational group, ask whether parents' evenings are held in the different countries represented and what form these typically take. Ask students for their experiences and memories of parents' evenings as students, and perhaps also parents or teachers.

2 Divide the class into groups of four. Give one verse to each member of the group so that between them each group has the whole poem. Explain that the poem has four verses, the first from the viewpoint of a boy, the second his mother, the third his father, and the fourth his teacher.

3 Students silently read their own verses and ask you to explain any problem language. Then the groups should read the poems aloud. Go around the class at this stage, encouraging a steady rhythm in the reading, and checking that contracted and other reduced forms are used.

4 At this stage, you could get one or two groups to perform their readings or select readers from four different groups. Alternatively, if the class is reasonably small, you could get all groups to perform and then ask the class to vote for the 'best son', 'best mother', etc. The four 'best readers' can then perform the poem.

5 Finally, ask students to compare the experiences of the characters in the poem with their own experiences of parents' evenings. Give students a copy of the full poem to take home.

[3] Ahlberg A. (1991) *Heard it in the Playground*. Published Puffin edition 1991. Copyright Allan Ahlberg 1989 (pp. 36 and 37).

Box 128   Student handout

Parents' Evening

We're waiting in the corridor,
My dad, my mum and me.
They're sitting there and talking;
I'm nervous as can be.
I wonder what she'll tell 'em.
I'll say I've got a pain!
I wish I'd got my spellings right.
I wish I had a brain.

We're waiting in the corridor.
My husband, son and me.
My son just stands there smiling;
I'm smiling, nervously.
I wonder what she'll tell us.
I hope it's not *all* bad.
He's such a good boy, really;
But dozy – like his dad.

We're waiting in the corridor,
My wife, my boy and me.
My wife's as cool as cucumber;
I'm nervous as can be.
I hate these parents' evenings.
The waiting makes me sick.
I feel just like a kid again
Who's gonna get the stick.

I'm waiting in the classroom.
It's nearly time to start.
I wish there was a way to stop
The pounding in my heart.
The parents in the corridor
Are chatting cheerfully;
And now I've got to face them,
And I'm nervous as can be.

8.10 Short texts showing features of pronunciation

Focus	Practising different features of pronunciation
Level	Elementary +

Procedure

Encourage students to look for and note (or if possible, cut out and bring to class) short texts that in some way represent or exploit pronunciation. This is commonly done in advertisements, newspaper headlines and the captions for cartoons, for example. Some newspapers and magazines also include misprints and mistakes that have been found in other publications. Some of these depend on features of pronunciation for their humour. When you or your students find them, briefly talk to students about the pronunciation feature involved and build up a collection on a display board if possible, with the general aim of developing students' awareness of the role of pronunciation in communication. Here are some examples with a brief commentary on each:

From advertisements

Everything you want from a store
... and a little bit <u>more</u>.[1]

They taste so good because they are so good[2]

BE AWAKE.
BE VERY AWAKE.[3]

Commentary

To make sense of these, they need to be read in a particular way with prominence and falling tone as follows:

... and a little bit MORE

... because they ARE so good

... be VERY awake.

Notice that only in the first example is this suggested by underlining.

Push 'n' go[4]
Mix 'n' match[5]
Fish 'n' chips[6]

The weak form of *and* (/ən/) is often represented in informal writing by *'n'*.

The examples are from advertisements for: [1] a supermarket, [2] biscuits, [3] breakfast cereal, [4] a child's toy, [5] children's clothing, [6] a shop sign.

SPORTS BAG OFFER	Noun compounds are often used in advertisements. Prominence placement can sometimes be difficult in these compounds. In these examples prominence would normally be as follows if the compounds were read aloud: SPORTS bag offer TAKE-away food
TAKE-AWAY FOOD	

From newspaper headlines
SERVING TIME IN SUNLESS
CELLS AND SICK AT HEART

Commentary
The headline repeats /s/ sounds in order to attract the reader. The article was about prisoners in the famous Dartmoor prison in the south west of England. (*serving time* = spending time in prison; *sick at heart* = very sad)

From pop songs
'I don't *wanna* say that I've been unhappy with you'
'All you've *gotta* do is call'
"Cos I'm happy just to dance with you'
'I'm *gonna getcha* . . . I'm *gonna meetcha*'
'You *gotta teach 'em 'bout* freedom'

Commentary
The words of pop songs include features of connected speech.
wanna = want to
gotta = got to
'Cos = because
gonna getcha = going to get you
gonna meetcha = going to meet you
You *gotta teach 'em 'bout* = You've got to teach them about . . .

Misprints and mistakes

'Twelve year old Roger Catchpole was granted a shotgun licence this summer and learnt the safe use of a gun from his grandmother, Joan Catchpole, who frequently shoots herself.'

(The Sudbury Mercury: September 1992)

Commentary

The last part of this could be read in two ways. The way it was intended would be '. . . who frequently SHOOTS herSELF' (i.e. Joan Catchpole herself shoots). However, it could also be read '. . . who frequently SHOOTS herself' (i.e. she tries to kill herself!) which is, of course, ridiculous.

Commentary

What George Bush said was:

'No NEW TAXes'

But what he claims he said was:

'No NEWT axes'.

Web-based resources

A number of websites have useful pronunciation and other relevant material that is freely available. Here is a list of some, together with a brief description of what you will find there. For an up-to-date report, see http://artsweb.bham.ac.uk/MHewings/pronunciationresources.html

http://www.phon.ucl.ac.uk/home/johnm/eptotd/tiphome.htm
The 'Pronunciation Tip of the Day' from John Maidment's website. Quizzes and answers on many topics including stress in compounds, the pronunciation of difficult words and the pronunciation of word-final endings (e.g. *-se, -et, -ac*).

http://www.marlodge.supanet.com/wordlist/index.html
http://www.marlodge.supanet.com/wordlist/homophon.html
The first is lists of minimal pairs and the second a list of homophones, both compiled by John Higgins.

http://www.unique.cc/ron/english.htm
Fun material on pronunciation, including tongue twisters and poems.

http://www.btinternet.com/~ted.power/phono.html
Includes lists of common English pronunciation problems according to the first language of learners with suggested practice material from a variety of published sources.

Appendix 1

Key to phonetic symbols

Vowels			Consonants	
Symbol	*Examples*		*Symbol*	*Examples*
/ɪ/	pit, it		/b/	bee, about
/e/	wet, end		/d/	do, side
/æ/	cat, apple		/f/	fat, safe
/ʌ/	run, up		/g/	go, big
/ɒ/	hot, opposite		/h/	hat, behind
/ʊ/	put, would		/j/	yet, you
/ə/	ago, doctor		/k/	key, week
/iː/	see, eat		/l/	led, allow
/ɑː/	part, arm		/m/	map, lamp
/ɔː/	saw, always		/n/	nose, any
/uː/	too, you		/p/	pen, stop
/ɜː/	her, early		/r/	red, around
/eɪ/	day, eight		/s/	soon, us
/aɪ/	my, eyes		/t/	ten, last
/ɔɪ/	boy, join		/v/	vat, live
/əʊ/	low, open		/w/	wet, swim
/aʊ/	how, out		/z/	zip, loves
/ɪə/	near, here		/dʒ/	general, age
/eə/	hair, where		/ŋ/	hang, hoping
/ʊə/	poor, sure		/ð/	that, other
/i/	cosy, happy		/θ/	thin, bath
/u/	influence, annual		/ʃ/	ship, push
			/ʒ/	measure, usual
			/tʃ/	chin, catch

Other symbols used in this book:

ˈ primary stress (before a syllable that is said with relatively more force, or heard as being more emphatic than others, as in *about* /əˈbaʊt/)

ˌ secondary stress (before a syllable that has an intermediate level of force or emphasis between primary stressed and unstressed syllables, as in *lemonade* /ˌleməˈneɪd/)

/ʔ/ a glottal stop (a sound like the beginning of a short cough, made when the vocal folds are pressed together)

Appendix 2

Common pronunciation problems

Some common English pronunciation problems for speakers of a number of major languages are shown below. Examples such as /ɪ/ vs /e/ (pin:pen) indicate that words with these sounds are often confused; for example, *pin* is said or heard as *pen*, and *pen* is said or heard as *pin*. Examples such as /v/ vs /f/ (vast→fast) indicate that the second sound is often used instead of the first; for example, *vast* is said or heard as *fast*. When sounds are included on their own (e.g. /tʃ/), this means that students often have difficulty with this sound, but there is not a particular frequent replacement. The main sources of information used in compiling this list are *Learner English* (Swan and Smith, 2001) and *Teaching English Pronunciation* (Kenworthy, 1987).

Arabic

Vowels
/ɪ/ vs /e/ (pin:pen), /ɒ/ vs /ɔ:/ (shot:short), /eɪ/ vs /e/ (late:let), /əʊ/ vs /ɒ/ (note:not).

Consonants
/g/ vs /k/ (gap:cap), /p/ vs /b/ (pie:buy), /v/ vs /f/ (vast→fast), /dʒ/ vs /g/ (John→gone), /θ/ vs /t/ (thin→tin), /ð/ vs /d/ (then→den), /tʃ/, /h/, /r/, /ŋ/.

Consonant clusters
Tendency to insert a short vowel between consonants in a cluster at the beginning and at the end of words (play→/pəleɪ/); and before initial consonant clusters (start→/ɪstɑ:t/).

Chinese

Vowels
/ɪ/ vs /i:/ (rid:read), /ʊ/ vs /u:/ (pull:pool), /eɪ/ vs /e/ (late→let), /æ/, /ɒ/, /ʌ/, /əʊ/.

Pronunciation Practice Activities

Consonants

In word-final position /p/ vs /b/ (cap→cab), /t/ vs /d/ (hat→had), /k/ vs /g/ (back→bag), /s/ vs /z/ (price→prize); /l/ vs /r/ especially in word-final position (wall→war); /n/ vs /l/ (net→let), /v/, /θ/, /ð/, /h/, /dʒ/, /ʃ/.

Word-final consonants tend to be 'clipped' (back→/bæʔ/), or a vowel added after them (/bækə/).

Consonant clusters

Tendency to insert a short vowel between consonants in a cluster at the beginning and the end of words (play→/pəleɪ/, proved→/pruːvɪd/).

Others

Tendency to produce strong forms where weak forms should be used, and to make words prominent where they should be non-prominent.

French

Vowels

/ɪ/ vs /iː/ (rid:read), /ʌ/ vs /ɜː/ (bud→bird), /ʊ/ vs /uː/ (pull:pool), /ɔː/ vs /əʊ/ (call:coal), /ɒ/ vs /ʌ/ (rob→rub), /æ/, /eɪ/. Tendency to produce vowels in unstressed syllables as they are written, where /ə/ is normally used (/æləʊn/ for /ələʊn/ [alone]).

Consonants

/tʃ/ vs /ʃ/ (cheap→sheep), /dʒ/ vs /ʒ/ (page→/peɪʒ/), /θ/, /ð/, /h/, /ŋ/.

Others

Tendency to produce strong forms where weak forms should be used, and to place word stress on later syllables where they should be placed on the first syllable (Over→oVER).

German

Vowels

/e/ vs /æ/ (bed:bad), /ɔː/ vs /əʊ/ (call:coal), /ɒ/, /ʌ/, /eɪ/.

Consonants

/v/ vs /w/ (vest:west), /ʒ/ vs /ʃ/ (pleasure→/pleʃə/), /dʒ/ vs /tʃ/ (joke→choke), /θ/ vs /s/ (thing→sing), /ð/ vs /z/ (then→/zen/), and the sounds /z/, /v/, /b/, /d/ and /g/ tend to be pronounced /s/, /f/, /p/, /t/ and /k/ respectively at the end of words (e.g. prize→price, save→safe).

Greek

Vowels
/ɔ:/ vs /ʌ/ vs /ʊ/ (port:putt:put), /ɪ/ vs /i:/ (did→deed), /æ/ vs /e/ (had→head), /ʌ/ vs /æ/ (but→bat), /ɜ:/ vs /e/ (bird→bed), /ə/.

Consonants
/p/ vs /b/ (pear→bear), /t/ vs /d/ (tie→die), /k/ vs /g/ (cave→gave), /ʃ/ vs /s/ (shave→save), /ʒ/ vs /z/ (pleasure→/plezə/), /tʃ/ vs /ʃ/ (cheap→sheep), /dʒ/ vs /ʒ/ (page→/peɪʒ/), /h/.

Consonant clusters
In the clusters /mp/, /nt/ and /nk/, tendency to produce /mb/, /nd/ and /ng/ (e.g. lamp→/læmb/).

Others
Tendency to add a short vowel after words ending in /b/, /d/ or /g/ (e.g. rob→/rɒbə/).

Italian

Vowels
/ʌ/ vs /æ/ (but:bat), /ɪ/ vs /i:/ (did→deed), /æ/ vs /e/ (had→head). Tendency to produce vowels in unstressed syllables as they are written, where /ə/ is normally used (/æbaʊt/ for /əbaʊt/ [about]).

Consonants
/θ/ vs /t/ (thin→tin), /ð/ vs /d/ (then→den), /s/ vs /z/ (snow→/znəʊ/), /ʒ/, /ŋ/. Tendency to omit /h/, or to include it before word-initial vowels.

Others
Tendency to add a short vowel after words ending in /p/, /t/, /k/, /b/, /d/ and /g/ (e.g. drop→/drɒpə/).

Japanese

Vowels
/ɔ:/ vs /əʊ/ (call:coal), /ʌ/ vs /æ/ (but:bar), /ɜ:/ vs /ɑ:/ (fur→far), /u:/. Tendency to produce vowels in unstressed syllables as they are written, where /ə/ is normally used (/æbaʊt/ for /əbaʊt/ [about]).

Consonants

/r/ vs /l/ (rock:lock), /v/ vs /b/ (vest→best), /h/, /f/, /θ/, /ð/. Tendency to produce /g/ as /ŋg/ between vowels (ago→/əŋgəʊ/). Tendency to produce /t/, /d/, /s/ and /z/ as /tʃ/, /dʒ/, /ʃ/ and /dʒ/ respectively before /ɪ/ and /iː/ (e.g. tip→chip, dear→jeer). Tendency to produce /t/ and /d/ as /ts/, /dʒ/ respectively before /ʊ/ and /uː/ (e.g. two→/tsuː/, do→/dʒuː/). Tendency to add a short vowel after a word-final consonant (e.g. stop→/stɒpə/).

Consonant clusters

Tendency to insert a short vowel between consonants in a cluster at the beginning of words (e.g. play→/pəleɪ/).

Korean

Vowels

/ɪ/ vs /iː/ (rid:read), /ʌ/ vs /ɑː/ (come→calm), /æ/ vs /e/ (had→head), /ɔː/, /əʊ/, /ɜː/. Tendency to produce vowels in unstressed syllables as they are written, where /ə/ is normally used (/æbaʊt/ for /əbaʊt/ [about]).

Consonants

/p/ vs /b/ (pie:buy), /t/ vs /d/ (ten:den), /k/ vs /g/ (cap:gap), /r/ vs /l/ (rock:lock), /b/ vs /v/ (bet→vet), /f/ vs /p/ (foot→put), /z/ vs /dʒ/ (zone→Joan), /θ/ vs /s/ (thing→sing), /ð/ vs /d/ (then→den).

Others

Tendency to add a short vowel after words ending in /tʃ/, /ʃ/, /dʒ/, /z/ and /t/ (e.g. each→/iːtʃi/). Tendency to produce strong forms where weak forms should be used.

Malay/Indonesian

Vowels

/ɪ/ vs /iː/ (rid:read), /ʊ/ vs /uː/ (pull:pool), /ɒ/ vs /ɔː/ (shot:short), /æ/ vs /e/ (had→head).

Consonants

/p/ vs /b/ (pear→bear), /t/ vs /d/ (tie→die), /k/ vs /g/ (cave→gave), /θ/ vs /t/ (thin→tin), /f/ vs /p/ (prefer→/prɪpɜː/), /tʃ/ vs /ʃ/ (cheap→sheep), /dʒ/ vs /ʒ/ (page→/peɪʒ/), /v/. Tendency to 'clip' or omit word final /b/, /d/, /g/, /v/, /z/, /ʃ/, /tʃ/ and /dʒ/ (e.g. rob→/rɒʔ/).

Consonant clusters
Tendency to insert a short vowel between consonants in a cluster at the beginning and at the end of words, and tendency to omit last consonant in word-final consonants (play→/pəleɪ/, hand→/hæn/).

Polish

Vowels
/e/ vs /æ/ (bed:bad), /ɪ/ vs /iː/ (rid:read), /æ/ vs /ɑː/ (had:hard), /ɔː/ vs /əʊ/ (saw→so). Tendency to produce vowels in unstressed syllables as they are written, where /ə/ is normally used (/æbaʊt/ for /əbaʊt/ [about]).

Consonants
In word-final position, /t/ vs /d/ (sat→sad), /s/ vs /z/ (ice→eyes), /k/ vs /g/ (back→bag). Also /θ/, /ð/, /ʃ/, /ʒ/, /tʃ/, /dʒ/, /h/.

Others
Tendency to produce strong forms where weak forms should be used.

Russian

Vowels
/ɪ/ vs /iː/ (rid:read), /æ/ vs /e/ (had→head), /ɔː/ vs /əʊ/ (saw→so), /ɜː/, /ɑː/.

Consonants
In word-initial position /p/ vs /b/ (pear→bear), /t/ vs /d/ (tie→die), /k/ vs /g/ (cave→gave). In word-final position /b/ vs /p/ (rib→rip), /d/ vs /t/ (had→hat), /g/ vs /k/ (bag→back). Also /θ/ vs /s/ (thing→sing), /ð/ vs /z/ (then→/zen/), /ŋ/ vs /g/ (sing→sin or /sɪg/), /h/, /dʒ/.

Consonant clusters
Tendency to insert a short vowel between consonants in a cluster at the beginning of words (play→/pəleɪ/).

Spanish

Vowels
/ɪ/ vs /iː/ (rid:read), /æ/ vs /ɑː/ vs /ʌ/ (hat:heart:hut), /ɒ/ vs /ɔː/ (shot:short), /ʊ/ vs /uː/ (pull:pool), /ɜː/. Tendency to produce vowels in unstressed syllables as they are written, where /ə/ is normally used (/æbaʊt/ for /əbaʊt/ [about]).

Consonants

In word-initial position /p/ vs /b/ (pear→bear), /t/ vs /d/ (tie→die), /k/ vs /g/ (cave→gave). In word-final position /b/ vs /p/ (rib→rip), /d/ vs /t/ (had→hat), /g/ vs /k/ (bag→back). Also /b/ vs /v/ (best:vest), /z/ vs /s/ (prize→price), /j/ vs /dʒ/ (yet→jet), /m/ vs /n/ or /ŋ/ in word-final position (cream→/kriːn/ or /kriːŋ/), /ʃ/, /ʒ/, /dʒ/, /h/.

Consonant clusters

Tendency to omit first or last consonants from clusters (instead→/ɪsted/, hand→/hæn/).

Turkish

Vowels

/ɔː/ vs /əʊ/ (call:coal), /iː/ vs /ɪ/ (seat→sit), /æ/ vs /e/ (bad→bed), /uː/ vs /ʊ/ (pool→pull), /eə/ vs /eɪ/ (hair→hay). Tendency for /ɪ/ or /ə/ to be omitted between *s* and a consonant (supply→/splaɪ/).

Consonants

In word-final position /b/ vs /p/ (rib→rip), /d/ vs /t/ (had→hat), /g/ vs /k/ (bag→back), and /dʒ/ vs /tʃ/ (edge→etch); between vowels /p/ vs /b/ (supper→/sʌbə/), /t/ vs /d/ (eaten→Eden), /k/ vs /g/ (maker→/meɪgə/), and /tʃ/ vs /dʒ/ (catches→cadges); /v/ vs /w/ (vest:west), /θ/ vs /t/ (thin:tin), /ð/ vs /d/ (then:den).

Consonant clusters

Tendency to insert a short vowel between consonants in a cluster or before a cluster at the beginning of words (play→/pəleɪ/, start→/ɪstɑːt/).

Appendix 3

Initial consonant clusters in English

1 Consonant + consonant

	p	t	k	b	d	g	m	n	f	v	θ	h
l	play	✗	class	black	✗	glass	✗	✗	fly	✗	✗	✗
r	pray	trip	crime	brown	drop	grow	✗	✗	fry	✗	three	✗
w	✗	twins	queen	✗	dwell	✗	✗	✗	✗	✗	✗	✗
j	pure	tube	queue	beauty	due	✗	music	news	few	view	✗	huge

In addition, /s/ can be followed by:
/l/: slow, /w/: swim, /p/: spot, /t/: star, /k/: sky, /m/: smile, /n/: snow, /f/: sphere

2 Consonant + consonant + consonant

	sp	st	sk
l	splash	✗	✗
r	spray	straw	scream
w	✗	✗	squeak
j	✗	stew	skewer

In a few cases combinations marked ✗ are possible in English, but are very rare or used in words unlikely to be heard or used by most learners. These are /gw/ (e.g. the name *Gwen*, or *Gwent* in Wales), /θw/ (*thwart* and *thwack*), /spj/ (*spew*), /skl/ (e.g. *sclerosis*).

Appendix 4

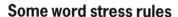

Some word stress rules

The rules below indicate the relationship between certain suffixes and word stress. Only simple relationships are included (there are many other suffixes with more complicated effects on word stress), which are usually true. However, you will find some exceptions to most of the rules given here.

1 Some suffixes don't usually change the stress pattern of the root word:
   -able (e.g. underSTAND/underSTANDable)
   -age (e.g. perCENT/perCENTage)
   -ance (e.g. atTEND/atTENDance)
   -ancy (e.g. conSULT/conSULTancy)
   -ant (forming nouns e.g. conSULTant)
   -cy (e.g. PRESident/PRESidency)
   -ful (e.g. BEAUty/BEAUtiful)
   -hood (e.g. NEIGHbour/NEIGHbourhood)
   -ist (e.g. geOLogy/geOLogist)
   -ise/-ize (e.g. SYMpathy/SYMpathise)
   -less (e.g. deFENCE/deFENCEless)
   -ly (e.g. CAREful/CAREfully)
   -ment (e.g. enCOURage/enCOURagement)
   -ness (e.g. HAPPy/HAPPiness)
   -or/-er (e.g. DECorate/DECorator)
   -ous (e.g. HUmour/HUmorous)
2 Some suffixes are themselves stressed:
   -ade (e.g. LEMon/lemonADE)
   -aire (e.g. MILLion/millioNAIRE)
   -cratic (e.g. DEMocrat/demoCRATic)
   -ee (e.g. ABsent/absenTEE)
   -ivity (e.g. SUBject/subjecTIVity)
3 With some suffixes, the stress is usually on the syllable immediately before the suffix:
   -cracy (e.g. DEMocrat/deMOCracy)
   -ety (e.g. SOCial/soCIety)

-ial (e.g. conSPIRacy/conspiraTORial)
-ian (e.g. HIStory/hisTORian)
-ic (e.g. SCIence/scienTIFic)
-ical (e.g. biOLogy/bioLOGical)
-ify (e.g. PERson/perSONify)
-ion (e.g. CELebrate/celeBRAtion)
-ious (e.g. VICtory/vicTORious)
-ive (e.g. PRODuct/proDUCTive)
-ity (e.g. eLECtric/elecTRICity)

Bibliography

Reference and methodology

Celce-Murcia, M., Brinton, D. M. and Goodwin, J. M. (1996) *Teaching Pronunciation: A Reference for Teachers of English to Speakers of Other Languages.* Cambridge: Cambridge University Press.

Cruttenden, A. (1994) *Gimson's Pronunciation of English*, 5th edn. London: Edward Arnold.

Crystal, D. (1987) *The Cambridge Encyclopedia of Language.* Cambridge: Cambridge University Press.

Dalton, C. and Seidlhofer, B. (1994) *Pronunciation.* Oxford: Oxford University Press.

Jenkins, J. (2000) *The Phonology of English as an International Language: New models, New Norms, New Goals.* Oxford: Oxford University Press.

Jones, D. (2003) *English Pronouncing Dictionary*, 15th edn. Edited by P. Roach and J. Hartman. Cambridge: Cambridge University Press.

Kelly, G. (2000) *How to Teach Pronunciation.* Harlow: Pearson.

Kenworthy, J. (1987) *Teaching English Pronunciation.* Harlow: Longman.

Pennington, M. (1996) *Phonology in English Language Teaching.* Harlow: Pearson.

Roach, P. (2000) *English Phonetics and Phonology: A practical course*, 3rd edn. Cambridge: Cambridge University Press.

Swan, M. and Smith, B. (eds.) (2001) *Learner English: A Teacher's Guide to Interference and Other Problems*, 2nd edn. Cambridge: Cambridge University Press.

Underhill, A. (1994) *Sound Foundations.* Oxford: Heinemann.

Wells, J. (1990) *Longman Pronunciation Dictionary.* Harlow: Longman.

Teaching materials

Bowen, T. and Marks, J. (1992) *The Pronunciation Book: Student-Centred Activities for Pronunciation Work.* Harlow: Longman.

Bowler, B. and Cunningham, S. (1991) *Headway Upper-Intermediate Pronunciation.* Oxford: Oxford University Press. (And other *Headway Pronunciation* books.)

Bradford, B. (1998) *Intonation in Context: Intonation Practice for Upper-Intermediate and Advanced Learners of English*. Cambridge: Cambridge University Press.

Brazil, D. (1994) *Pronunciation for Advanced Learners of English*. Cambridge: Cambridge University Press.

Cauldwell, R. (2002) *Streaming Speech: Listening and Pronunciation for Advanced Learners of English* (CD-ROM). Birmingham: Speechinaction.

Gilbert, J. B. (2001) *Clear Speech From the Start*. Cambridge: Cambridge University Press.

Hancock, M. (1995) *Pronunciation Games*. Cambridge: Cambridge University Press.

Hancock, M. (2003) *English Pronunciation In Use*. Cambridge: Cambridge University Press.

Hewings, M. (1993) *English Pronunciation Tasks: A Course for Pre-Intermediate Learners*. Cambridge: Cambridge University Press.

Hewings, M. and Goldstein, S. (1998) *Pronunciation Plus: Practice through Interaction*. Cambridge: Cambridge University Press.

Vaughan-Rees, M. (2002) *Test Your Pronunciation*. Harlow: Pearson.

Index